The CHOCTAWS

The CHOCTAWS

Cultural Evolution of a Native American Tribe

by Jesse O. McKee and Jon A. Schlenker

UNIVERSITY PRESS OF MISSISSIPPI • *Jackson*

Copyright © 1980 by the University Press of Mississippi
Manufactured in the United States of America
All Rights Reserved
Book Design by Larry E. Hirst
Print-on-Demand Edition

Library of Congress Cataloging in Publication Data
McKee, Jesse O.
    The Choctaws.

    Bibliography: p.
    Includes index.
    1. Choctaw Indians—History.   2. Acculturation—Mississippi—Case studies.   3. Acculturation—Oklahoma—Case studies.   I. Schlenker, Jon A., joint author.   II. Title.
E99.C8M23   970".004"97   79-17034
ISBN 0-87805-107-4

The emblem of the Mississippi Band of Choctaw Indians is an arrowhead with a circle contained within it, together with a stickball (towa), stickball sticks (kabucha), drum, and drumsticks. These items are symbolic of the tribe's traditional culture (emblem designed by Leonard Jimmie).

The great seal of the Choctaw Nation was adopted by an act of the Choctaw General Council, Doaksville, Indian Territory, October 16, 1860.

"Description: The symbol of the ancient seal of the Choctaw Nation, namely: with the words The Great Seal of The Choctaw Nation around the edge, and a design of an unstrung bow, with three arrows and a pipe hatchet blended together, engraven in the center, which shall be the proper seal of this Nation, until altered by the General Council, with the concurrence thereof."

In the Oklahoma state seal, the "upper left hand ray shall contain the symbol of the ancient seal of the Choctaw Nation: namely, A tomahawk, and three crossed arrows, that symbolize a united people and one arrow for each great Chief in history, Apuckshunnubee, Pushamataha and Mosholatubbee."

Contents

Preface and Acknowledgments   xiii

Introduction   xv

1. Indigenous Period, ?–1698   3
2. European-American Period, 1699–1800   32
3. Choctaw Land Cessions and Acquisitions, 1801–1830   50
4. Tribal Separation and Divergence, 1831–1917   75
5. Twentieth-Century Developments in Mississippi and Oklahoma   148

    Epilogue   193

Appendices   195

Bibliography   209

Index   223

LIST OF FIGURES

1.	Location of Native Americans in the Southeast	xx
2.	Core of the Choctaw Homeland	4
3.	Early Mississippi Tribal Organization	41
4.	The Old Choctaw Country, Mississippi	42
5.	Land Cessions and Acquisitions	52
6.	Indian Territory, 1803–1830	52
7.	Major Choctaw Removal Routes	79
8.	Physiography of Removal Areas	80
9.	Indian Territory, 1830–1855	85
10.	Settled Area to 1845	86
11.	Choctaw Districts	87
12.	Indian Territory, 1855–1866	88
13.	Five Civilized Tribes in Indian Territory, Circa 1855	89
14.	Five Civilized Tribes in Indian Territory, Circa 1867	92
15.	Five Civilized Tribes in Indian Territory, Circa 1890	94
16.	Choctaw Nation: Important Places	100
17.	Choctaw Nation: Political Divisions	109
18.	Oklahoma Counties, 1907	113
19.	Indian Territory, 1889	123
20.	Missions in Oklahoma	128
21.	Oklahoma Academies	129
22.	Mississippi Tribal Government Structure, 1971	159
23.	Oklahoma Choctaw Political Organization	164
24.	Occupational Classifications of Oklahoma and Mississippi Choctaw	173
25.	Choctaw Income v. Overall Income for Oklahoma Counties in Choctaw Nation	173
26.	Educational Attainment of Oklahoma and Mississippi Choctaw	180

27.	Choctaw Educational Attainment by Age Categories and Mean/Median Grade Completed	180
28.	Choctaw Population, 1974	185
29.	The Choctaw Nation, 1975	186
30.	Age and Sex Structure of Choctaw Population	188

LIST OF TABLES

1.	Choctaw Contact History	xvii
2.	Choctaw Citizen Census of 1867	91
3.	Choctaw Citizen Census of 1885	93
4.	Choctaw Population, 1906	95
5.	Church Membership, 1890	130
6.	Skill Attainment of Persons in Labor Force, 1974 (Mississippi)	166
7.	Occupational Classification of All Persons in the Labor Force, 1974 (Mississippi)	167
8.	Average Hourly Wages by Occupational Classification, 1974 (Mississippi)	168
9.	Family Income, 1970 (Mississippi)	168
10.	Land Owned by the Mississippi Choctaw Indians	169
11.	Existing Land Use, 1974 (Mississippi)	169
12.	Choctaw Land Status in Acres in Oklahoma	170
13.	Distribution of Employed Ten-County Civilian Labor Force, 16 Years of Age and Older by Industry, 1970 (Oklahoma)	171
14.	Occupational Classification of Employed Choctaws, 1975 (Oklahoma)	175
15.	Choctaw Income, 1975 (Oklahoma)	176
16.	Educational Attainment of Persons 16 Years of Age and Older, and Median Grade Completed, 1974 (Mississippi)	178

17.	Educational Attainment of Persons 16 Years of Age and Older and Mean Grade Completed, 1975 (Oklahoma)	179
18.	Mississippi Choctaw Population Change, 1968–1974	184
19.	Reservation and Choctaw Agency Service Area Population Forecasts (Mississippi)	184
20.	Oklahoma Choctaw Population Change, 1950–1975	186
21.	Mississippi and Oklahoma Choctaw Population by Age and Sex	188
22.	Population of Western Tennessee Community by Age and Sex, 1974	189
23.	Language Spoken Most Often in Household by Community, 1974 (Mississippi)	191

LIST OF PLATES

1.	Choctaw—Chickasaw Separation	9
2.	Nanih Waiya Today	13
3.	Lithograph of Push-ma-ta-ha, a Choctaw Warrior	55
4.	Greenwood Le Flore	60
5.	Moshulatubbee (He-who-puts-out-and-kills)	62
6.	Treaty of Dancing Rabbit Creek Site in Noxubee County, Mississippi	81
7.	A Characteristic River Scene during Indian Removal	82
8.	Remains of the Choctaw "Trail of Tears" at Washington, Arkansas	82
9.	Cypress Swamp in Arkansas	83
10.	Cypress Swamp in Arkansas Today	83
11.	First Choctaw Chief's House in Oklahoma Territory	101

12.	Red River	101
13.	Giant Cypress Tree, a Favorite Council Place	102
14.	Eagletown, an early Choctaw Town	103
15.	Eagletown Today	103
16.	Doaksville, Capital of the Old Choctaw Nation in Indian Territory 1851-1860	104
17	Remains of Downtown Doaksville	104
18.	Remains of Fort Towson	105
19.	Marker of Early Choctaw Town	105
20.	Skullyville Cemetery	106
21.	Temporary Council House at Nanih Waiya	115
22.	Remains of Council House at Nanih Waiya	116
23.	Choctaw Capitol Building Historical Marker	116
24.	Sign at Entrance to Choctaw Capitol	117
25.	Choctaw Capitol Building now a Museum	117
26.	Old Town—Tuskahoma Cemetery	118
27.	Tuskahoma Post Office	118
28.	Choctaw Light Horsemen	119
29.	Last Choctaw Tribal Council, 1905	120
30.	Peter P. Pitchlynn, Member of 1853 Delegation	121
31.	Landscape near Atoka, Oklahoma	125
32.	Kiamichi Landscape	126
33.	Holy Rosary Indian Mission at Tucker, Mississippi	133
34.	Wheelock Historical Marker	133
35.	Remains of Wheelock Academy	134
36.	Wheelock Church	134
37.	Armstrong Academy at Bokchito	135
38.	Remains of Armstrong Academy	135
39.	Choctaw Female Seminary, Tuskahoma, Oklahoma	136
40.	Tullock-Chisk-Ko, Champion Choctaw Ball Player	137
41.	Choctaw Ball Play Dance at Skullyville	138

42.	Choctaw Indian Ballgame	146–147
43.	Harry J. W. Belvin, Principal Chief of the Oklahoma Choctaw Nation, 1948-1975	155
44.	Hollis Roberts, Principal Chief of the Oklahoma Choctaw Nation, 1978	156
45.	Phillip Martin Tribal Chief of the Mississippi Band of Choctaws, 1979	160
46.	Mrs. Susan Denson, Mississippi Choctaw	161
47.	Choctaw Stick-ball Players in Mississippi	162
48.	Choctaw Health Center Pearl River Community, Mississippi	182

Preface and Acknowledgments

The most widely read book on the Choctaws, and one regarded as a classic in the field, is Angie Debo's *The Rise and Fall of the Choctaw Republic*, originally published in 1934. Other important early writings by John R. Swanton, H. B. Cushman, and H. S. Halbert, to mention a few, have aided in understanding Choctaw history prior to the twentieth century. In this century, contributions to the literature by Arthur DeRosier, Jr., John R. Peterson, Jr., and David Baird have been of particular significance. But, since one of the last books to treat the Choctaws in a comprehensive manner was Debo's, which examined Choctaw history until the resolvement of their nation in 1906, we decided that a need existed for one that would stress the overall development of the Choctaws from early times to the present. Implicit in this need is the desire to combine Choctaw history and development in Mississippi and Oklahoma into one book. The methodological framework utilized to accomplish this task is the theme of cultural change.

To improve upon the work of Debo is difficult and is not our purpose. However, much new information has been written concerning the Choctaws since dissolution. If we can update their development since 1906 and analyze, synthesize, and incorporate the recent research into our book, then one of our major goals will be accomplished.

This book has been made possible primarily because of the kindness, interest, and cooperation of many persons. Since 1975, when we began the book, several persons have become directly or indirectly involved in our research effort. Not everyone can be mentioned here, but some deserve special recognition.

Gratitude is extended to Glenn Jordan, Western History Collection, University of Oklahoma Library; June Witt, University of Oklahoma Library; Martha Blaine, Indian Archives, Oklahoma City; Angie Debo, Marshall, Oklahoma; Paul Parker, tribe planner, Kiamichi Economic Development District, Wilburton, Oklahoma; G. F. Parsons, extension agent, Indian Program, Idabel, Oklahoma; Mike Walls, planner, Mississippi Band of Choctaw Indians, Philadelphia, Mississippi; Jan Warren, editor, *Choctaw Community News;* Jo Ann Bomar, Mississippi Department of Archives and History; John Peterson, Jr., Mississippi State University; Robert Norris, Oklahoma State University; Daniel Jacobson, Michigan State University; and John Morris, professor emeritus, University of Oklahoma. Special appreciation goes to Harry ("Jimmy") Belvin.

A word of thanks is expressed to James Latham for his cartographic assistance and to Tim Hudson for assistance in gathering field data. Appreciation is also extended to Debbie Marchman and Brenda Boro for typing and proofreading the original manuscript and to administrative officials at the University of Southern Mississippi and the University of Maine, at Augusta, for their fine cooperation.

Finally, we acknowledge our families, for without their patience, understanding, and cooperation the preparation of this book would have been a more difficult task.

Jesse O. McKee
Jon A. Schlenker

Introduction

The Choctaws, together with the Chickasaws, Creeks, Cherokees, and Seminoles, were known as the "Five Civilized Tribes." Originally they were all located in the southeastern portion of the United States (Fig. 1), but during the 1830s many were "removed" to Oklahoma. Prior to removal the Choctaws, members of the Muskogean linguistic group, resided predominantly in present-day Mississippi near their sacred mound Nanih Waiya.

While in Mississippi the Choctaws developed a sedentary lifestyle based primarily on agriculture supplemented by hunting and fishing. The explorer Hernando De Soto and his expedition were the first whites to encounter the Choctaws. As time passed, the Choctaws came in contact with the French, English, and finally American settlers. The Choctaw way of life was gradually changed by all these contacts, but the most profound change was caused by missionaries.

At the time of removal, the fourteenth article of the Treaty of Dancing Rabbit Creek provided that if Choctaws became citizens of the United States they could remain in Mississippi. They had to file claim for their land within six months after ratification of the treaty, and they had to live on the land for five years. Many

Choctaws remained in Mississippi. But thousands were removed to the Indian Territory (Oklahoma). It is estimated that 12,500 migrated, 2,500 died, and about 5,000 Choctaws, remained in Mississippi. Some Mississippi Choctaws continued to migrate to the Indian Territory throughout the nineteenth century.

In 1907, at the time of Oklahoma statehood, the Choctaws, in the old Choctaw Nation in southeast Oklahoma numbered 8,012, and the count in Mississippi was 1,634. Today, Choctaws in the Choctaw Nation number 9,018, and 3,779 are on the reservation in Mississippi. Their numbers are increasing, and there is a new sense of self-pride and self-determination among Choctaws.

The purpose of this book is to present a cultural history of the Choctaw Indians from the indigenous period to the present from a cultural change perspective. The methodological approach used is basically the same as that set forth by Daniel Jacobson (1954), Edward H. Spicer (1961), Jesse O. McKee (1971), and Jon A. Schlenker (1974). This methodology involves a categorical inventory of culture traits, establishing major historical events, listing specific contact groups (communities), organizing and arranging the history into specific time periods based upon culture contact, and discussing cultural trait changes brought about by specific contact communities. In summary, this approach seeks to discover changes in Choctaw culture by identifying the outside contact groups and the type and amount of change that occurred due to contact.

After thoroughly investigating the history of the Choctaws, we divided Choctaw development into five distinct periods. The order of each chapter will be to describe the major historical events and developments in each period and then to identify key changes in the social, economical, political, and technical structure of the Choctaws brought about by culture contact.

Table 1 summarizes the evolution of Choctaw cultural history and provides the framework and outline for discussion in this book. It should be noted that after the removal period the cultural history of the Mississippi Choctaws is separate from that of the Oklahoma

Introduction xvii

Choctaws. The division of the two cultures was reinforced by the dissolution of the Choctaw Nation in the Indian Territory in 1906 and the establishment of the Choctaw Agency in Philadelphia, Mississippi, in 1918.

Table 1 CHOCTAW CONTACT HISTORY

Period	Events	Contact Communities	General Change
I Indigenous, ?–1698	1540 De Soto expedition	Spanish	some change in trading patterns
II European-American contact, 1699–1800	1699 first French settlement 1702 Queen Ann's War 1720 French-Chickasaw War 1731 near extinction of Natchez tribe 1732 second French-Chickasaw War 1750 Treaty of Grandpré 1763 Treaty of Paris 1776 American Revolution 1786 Treaty of Hopewell	French, English, Spanish, American	culture influences by French
III Choctaw land cessions and acquisitions, 1801–1830	1801 Treaty of Fort Adams 1802 Treaty of Fort Confederation 1803 Treaty of Hoe Buckintoopa 1805 Treaty of Mount Dexter 1816 Treaty of Fort S Stephens 1817 Treaty of Mississippi Statehood 1818 arrival of missionaries 1820 Treaty of Doak's Stand 1825 Treaty of 1825 1826 first written constitution 1829 tribal jurisdiction abolished in Mississippi 1830 Treaty of Dancing Rabbit Creek	U.S. government MS. state government missionaries encroachment of white immigrants black slaves	political, social, religious, economical, and technological changes as a result of missionary contact

Table 1 (Continued)

Period	Events	Contact Communities	General Change
IV Removal to Indian Territory and a new nation, 1831–1906	1833 Start of ceded land sales of Mississippi 1833–45 land claim controversies in Mississippi 1834 new constitution 1837 Treaty of Doaksville 1837 capitol erected at Nanih Waiya 1838 new constitution 1843 new constitution 1845–47 additional removal from Mississippi 1855 Treaty of 1855 1857 Skullyville constitution 1860 Doaksville constitution 1861 treaty with Confederacy 1861–65 Civil War 1866 Treaty of 1866 1872 first railroad, start of coal mining 1883–84 final capitol erected at Tuskahoma 1885 citizenship to freedmen 1887 Allotment Act 1894 Dawes Commission 1897 Atoka Agreement 1898 Curtis Act 1901 United States citizenship 1902 Supplemental Agreement 1903 additional removal from Mississippi 1906 dissolvement of tribal government	U.S. government neighboring Indians white immigrants blacks	Anglo-American Acculturation
Mississippi Choctaws, 1831–1917	1833 ending of removal 1833–50 finalizing of land claims, issue of script 1845–54 additional migration to Oklahoma 1855–79 land squatter period 1879–1903 "reawakening" period 1879 Baptist missionaries renew activities 1880 beginning of switch from squatter to sharecropper 1883 arrival of Catholic missionaries 1884 land purchased—church and school established at Tucker 1892 Methodist missionaries arrive 1903 second removal to Oklahoma 1903–17 "regrouping" period 1911 New Choctaw Baptist Association	U.S. government whites missionaries Mississippi state government	limited acculturation some religious and economic changes

Introduction   xix

Table 1 (Continued)

Period	Events	Contact Communities	General Change
V Mississippi Choctaws, 1918–1979	1918 establishment of agency 1918–44 "agency and reservation" period 1934 Indian Reorganization Act (IRA) 1941 tribe organized under IRA referendum 1945 establishment of reservation 1950s shift from sharecropping to service and industrial jobs 1954 Supreme Court decision of 1954 1964 Civil Rights Act 1964 Economic Opportunity Act 1969 revision of tribal constitution and bylaws 1975 Indian Self-Determination and Education Assistance Act 1975 Indian Education Act 1975 election of Chief Calvin Isaac 1978 Indian Child Welfare Act 1979 election of Chief Phillip Martin	U.S. government Mississippi state government whites and blacks	limited Anglo-American acculturation Reassertion of Indian self-identification and self-pride
Oklahoma Choctaws, 1907–1979	1922 Albion Convention 1928 report of Institute for Government Research 1934 Indian Reorganization Act 1936 Oklahoma Indian Welfare Act 1948 Stigler Act 1948 election of Chief Harry J. W. Belvin 1951 final annuity payments 1953 Termination Act 1964 Civil Rights Act 1964 Economic Opportunity Act 1965 Oklahomans for Indian Opportunity 1975 Indian Self-Determination and Education Assistance Act 1975 election of Principal Chief David Gardner 1978 Indian Child Welfare Act 1978 election of Principal Chief Hollis Roberts	U.S. government Oklahoma state government other Native Americans whites and blacks	Anglo-American acculturation Reassertion of Indian self-identification and self-pride

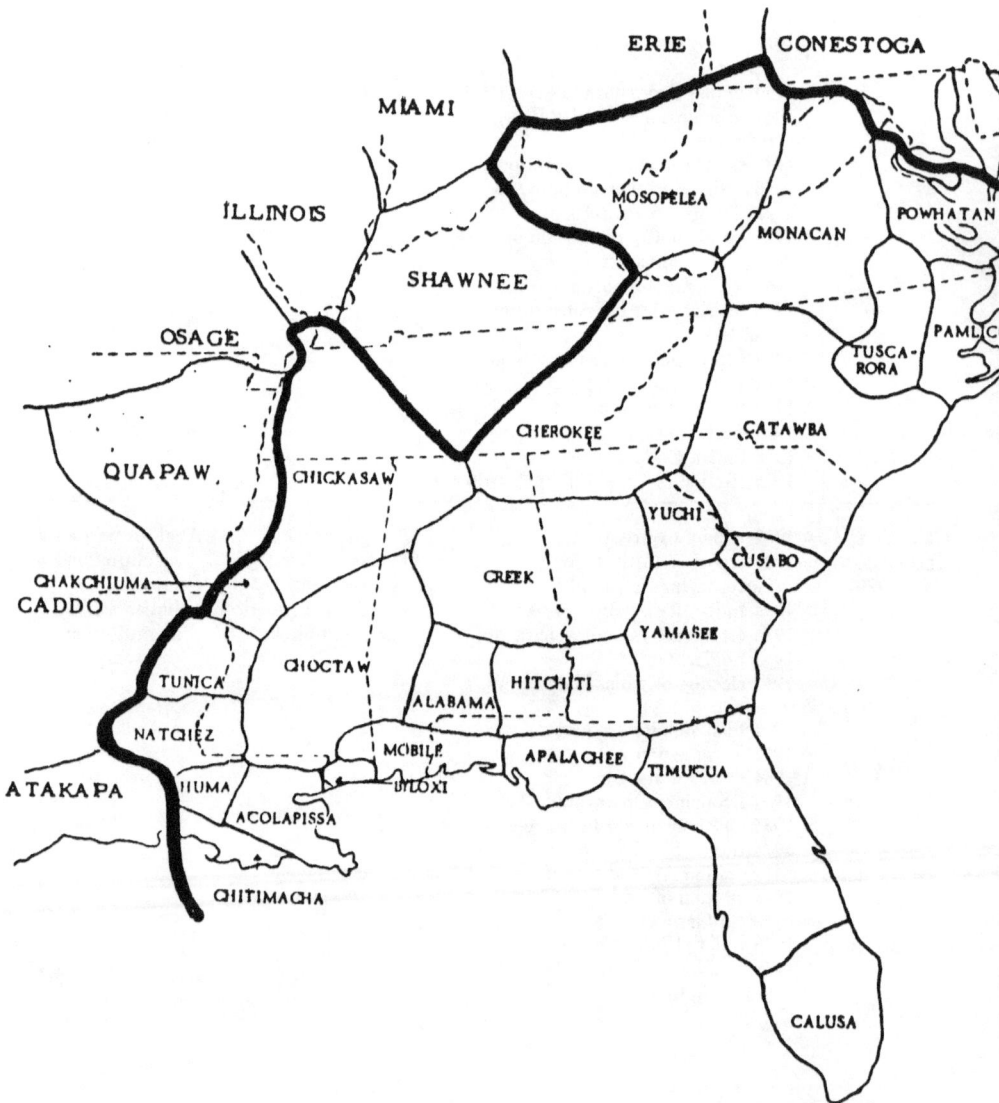

Figure 1 Location of Native Americans in the Southeast. SOURCE: Murdock, 1960

The CHOCTAWS

1

Indigenous Period ?–1698

The indigenous period of Choctaw history and culture commences with the arrival of the ancestors of the Choctaws into the present-day sand and clay hills area of east-central Mississippi and closes with the establishment of a French settlement on the Gulf Coast.

Geographical Setting

The natural landscape of an area "is the stage upon which the drama of the life of man is enacted" (Kelley, 1973:22—23). The natural landscape remains passive until the entry of man, who examines and evaluates the natural landscape and who through learned technological capabilities and other cultural traits sets about to modify the existing natural landscape. As man causes surface changes in terrain, soil, and vegetation and utilizes other resources such as water, minerals, and animal life, he slowly begins to form a cultural overlay of various man-made traits (such as housing and field types) upon the natural environment; these traits often result in a clearly distinguishable cultural landscape that differs from that of another cultural group.

INDIGENOUS PERIOD

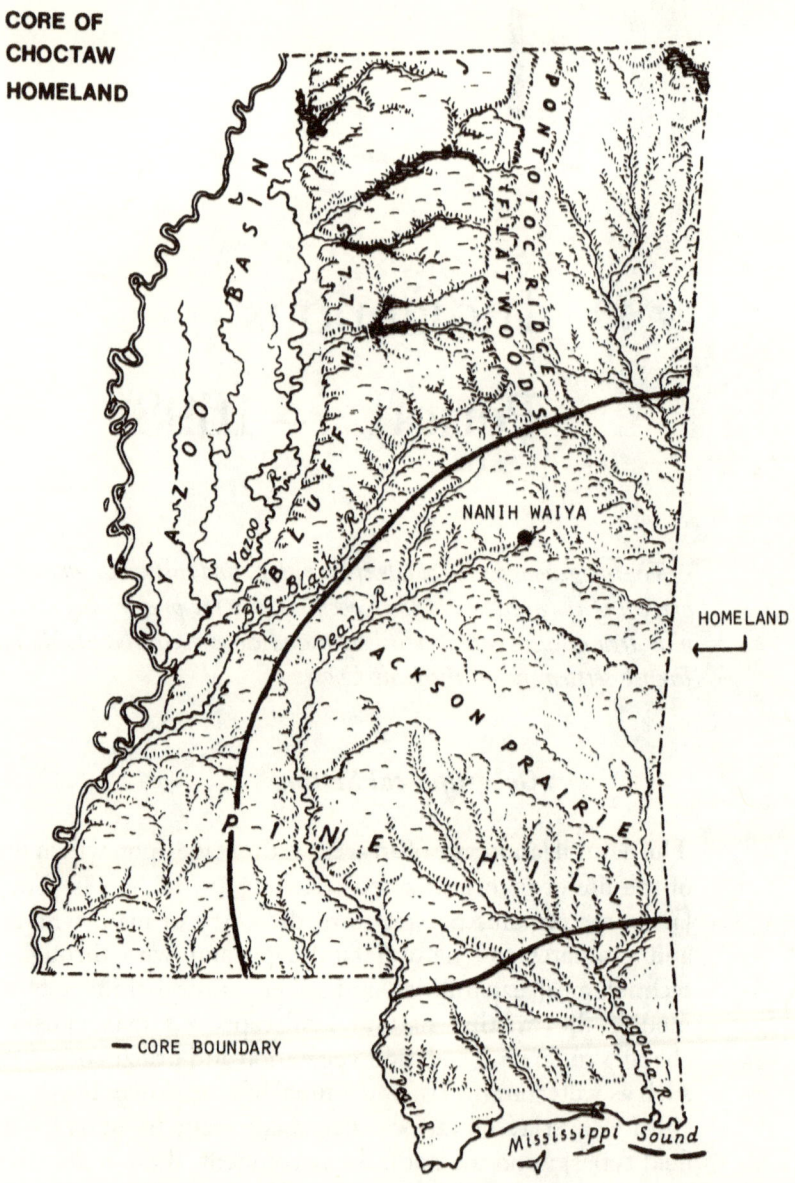

Figure 2 Base Map After Raisz, 1957

Eastern Mississippi is the ancient and present homeland of the Choctaw Indians. Classified as having a humid subtropical climate, this area has an average annual temperature of sixty-five degrees (averaging about forty-nine in January and eighty-one degrees in July). The yearly average rainfall is fifty-two inches and is rather evenly distributed throughout the year. Much of the vegetation is shortleaf and longleaf pine. Closer to the river bottoms, hardwoods prevail. The dense and extensive forests provided the Choctaws with firewood and building materials. There was also a profusion of plants to use for food and medicines, and wild game was in abundance.

Much of the soil in east Mississippi can be broadly classified as Udults, which is a suborder of the Ultisols order.[1] This soil type is more conducive to growing timber than for agricultural purposes. However, agriculture is more predominant on the river floodplains. Many Choctaw villages were located on these richer alluvial bottomlands.

According to the physiographic diagram of Mississippi, the Choctaw homeland is primarily in the Jackson Prairie and the Pine Hills landform regions (Fig. 2). The landscape in this area is slightly rolling with no formidable natural barriers. Several rivers, streams, and tributaries such as the Pearl, Noxubee, Okatibbee, and Chickasawhay drain through the old Choctaw country. Many early villages were established along these waterways. These streams helped to increase Choctaw accessibility and provided fish as a food source.

Historical Events

According to the ancient tradition of the Choctaws, their ancestors came from the West, and were probably originally from Asia.[2] The major creation myths recorded during the nineteenth century tend to lend credence to this explanation, although both Angie

[1] Ultisols are soils that are usually moist with horizon of clay accumulation and a low base or a high acid content. They are often reddish brown or light yellow in color.

[2] Cushman (1899:22), however, felt that "with regard to the migration from Asia it seems probable that educated Choctaws confused tribal tradition with what they had learned in school."

Debo (1934:3) and Thelma Bounds (1964:2) state that it is possible that these legends were partly inspired by missionaries. Nevertheless, James Adair in his 1775 *History of the American Indians* wrote "The Choctaws and Chickasaws descended from a single people called Chickemacaws, who were among the first inhabitants of the Mexican empire; and at an ancient period wandered east, with a tribe of Indians called Choccomaws; and finally crossed the Mississippi River, with a force of ten thousand warriors" (Cushman, 1899: 18).

In the past, the Choctaws held to the idea that their ancestors had migrated from some country to the west, but in more recent times the migration legend has been replaced by the creation legend—that the great mound Nanih Waiya was the birthplace of their people. Since there are several versions of the two main legends, these versions will be summarized.

Nanih Waiya, the great fortified mound located in what is now the southern part of Winston County in Mississippi, is central to most of the versions. Nanih Waiya is oblong, about forty feet high, with a base of about one acre and a summit of about one-fourth acre, and forms what archaeologists call a pyramidal mound (Halbert, 1899:223–24). The mound is on the southeastern edge of a circular rampart, which is about one and a half miles in circumference and about ten feet high and forty feet wide. Henry S. Halbert, who studied the mound, concluded that construction of Nanih Waiya probably took the continuous labor of two or three generations (1899: 232–33). And, with respect to the builders, he felt that all the evidence indicated that the Choctaws themselves built Nanih Waiya, possibly as long ago as fifteen hundred years.

H. B. Cushman related the version of the Choctaw migration legend that reportedly was given by elderly Choctaws to the missionaries in 1820 (1899:18–21). This version stated that in ancient times their ancestors lived in a distant western land, where they were persecuted by a more powerful people. Desiring to escape this oppression, they held a general council and it was decided that they would leave their homes under the leadership of two brothers, Chahtah and Chikasah. The evening before their departure, the chief medicine man and prophet placed a *fabussa* (pole) in the ground in the center of their camp. The direction that the pole was leaning in the morning would determine the direction they would proceed. In the morning the pole was leaning toward the east, so the entire population traveled in that direction. This procedure was then followed every evening and morning, with each brother alternating the task. For months they journeyed, until they reached a great river, where they had to build canoes and rafts to cross. Then, one evening, on the western bank of the Yazoo River, they set up camp and placed the pole in the center. But, unlike all other mornings, when the sun came up the pole was upright—they had arrived at their destination. To celebrate the occasion, a large mound was constructed, which when completed was leaning a little. Hence, they called it Nanih Waiya ("leaning mound"). Then, several years later, the two brothers, who were still the leaders, fell into disagreement over some tribal concern. To settle the question, they decided to play a game in which they faced one another and held a pole between them. When they let go, the direction in which the pole fell would determine where Chikasah and his followers were to go to live. When the pole was dropped, it indicated that Chikasah should take the northern part of the territory and Chahtah the southern portion. Thus, the group was divided into two tribes, each of which assumed and retained the name of its respective chief.

Another account of the migration legend was transmitted by Israel Folsom, in which the ancient ancestors of the Choctaws and Chickasaws lived in a country in the Far West, under the leadership of the two brothers Chahta and Chikasa (Halbert, 1899:228–29). In this version the population had become so large that the land was no longer able to provide sufficient food. When the prophets declared that there were fertile lands far to the east that would supply plenty of food, the entire population decided to make the journey to this bountiful land. In order to find enough supplies along the way, the people were divided into several groups, each separated by a day's travel. A prophet led the tribe, carrying a pole and planting it each night in front of the camp. Again the direction that it leaned pointed the way for the next day's journey. After many months, they arrived at Nanih Waiya, where the pole stood erect. That same day the group led by Chikasa camped across the creek from Nanih

Waiya. But that night a great storm occurred, and it rained for several days, making the waters impassable. A few days later, messengers were sent to Chikasa to tell him of the good news that they had found their destination. Unfortunately, Chikasa had already gone; he had continued on to the Tombigbee River, where he and his followers halted and consequently became a separate nation.

In writing about the origin of the Choctaws, George H. Ethridge also related a version of the migration legend (Ethridge and Taylor, 1938:522–23). He held to the tradition that the forerunners of the Choctaws and Chickasaws were continually harassed by a mighty people in the Far West. The ancestors, called the Chickamacaws, were ruled by an exceedingly wise man. Being a peaceful man, he wanted to evade their warlike enemies. Therefore, after a vision, he advised his people to migrate to the east, where they would find peace, happiness, and security. When the chief died, his two sons, Chahta and Chisca, decided to carry out his wishes. Again the sacred pole was used to direct their journey. After forty-three years, they finally came to a leaning hill, where the pole stood upright. Here they buried the bones of their ancestors, which they had carried with them on the journey. And again, a flood was responsible for the separation of Chahta and Chisca, by which Chisca decided to go on to the northern part of the territory.

Gideon Lincecum (1904:521–42) offered a version in which the origin or cause of the migration was unclear, but that presented a detailed account of the tradition of how the Choctaws settled in Mississippi. According to his version, the migrants became distressed at having to transport the skeletons of their dead. To alleviate this burden, when the pole leaned toward no direction at "Nuni Waya," the *minko* (leader) proclaimed the encampment their new home. Then a piece of sandy land was chosen for the building of a mound, in which the bones were buried.

And a last major version, which acted as a transition between the migration legends and the creation legends, was recalled by J. F. H. Claiborne (1880:518–19). The Choctaws claimed that they originally came from the West. Encouraged by their priests, they left their lands for the East. The priests traveled in the center of the

Plate 1 Choctaw—Chickasaw separation (artist conception). COURTESY Choctaw Nation Historical Society

group, carrying a sacred book. During the travel, a deadly epidemic broke out, killing all the priests except the book bearer. The dead were cremated, and their ashes were carried by the survivors. Near a great river, the tribe separated. Part of the group headed northward, under the leadership of Chickasa, a great warrior. The main portion headed south, until they came to Nane-wy-yah, the "stooping hill," where they camped and many continued to die. Finally, everyone had died except the book bearer, who was immortal. The Nane-wy-yah opened and he entered it and disappeared. Several years later, the Great Spirit created at the foot of the mound four infants, two of each sex, out of the ashes of the dead. They were suckled by a panther, and when they were strong enough, the book bearer emerged and presented them with bows and arrows and the earthen pot and said, "I give you these hunting grounds for your homes. When you leave them you die." The mound reopened, and the book bearer disappeared forever. The four then separated with one couple going in one direction and the other couple in the opposite. Thus, the two clans of the Choctaws were formed.

Among the earliest published narratives concerning the creation legend was that of the Reverend Alfred Wright (1828:181–82). According to this version, the Choctaws held that during a remote period the earth was a vast plain and that at this time a superior being came to earth near the center of the Choctaw Nation, where he created a large mound or hill, called Nunih Waiya ("stooping or sloping hill"). When this was completed, the ancestors of the Choctaws began to come out of the mound. When the superior being thought that enough people emerged, he stamped the ground with his foot, halting their emergence. Thus, the ancestors had been formed from the earth. The creator then told them that they were to live forever. But, not understanding what he had said, they asked him to repeat. This angered the creator, so he revoked their immortality. After creating the ancestors, the superior being then formed the earth to provide them with their needs.

Another version of the creation legend was recorded by Halbert (1899:229–30). In this version Nanih Waiya was looked upon as being the birthplace of the Choctaws, being referred to as *ishki chito* ("great mother"). The legend stated that the Choctaws were created in the center of the mound by the Great Spirit and that they crawled through a hole or cave to the surface. They were very wet, so the Great Spirit placed them along the rampart to dry. Shortly after the creation, the Great Spirit separated the Choctaws into two clans (*iksa*), the Kashapa Okla and the Okla in Holahta. One *iksa* was placed on the north side of the mound and the other on the west side, and the Great Spirit dictated the law of marriage—that the children were to belong to the clan of the mother and that one must always marry into the other clan.

Halbert also related the creation legend told to him by an old Choctaw at Bogue Chitto (1901_b:268–270). This version, one of the oldest, accounts for the creation of the different tribes as well as of the Choctaws. Nanih Waiya was considered the place where the creation of men occurred. The first to come out of Nanih Waiya were the Muskogees, who dried themselves on the earthen rampart and went to the east. When they arrived at the Tombigbee River, they rested and smoked tobacco, from which some fire fell. The Cherokees were next to emerge from Nanih Waiya, and after they dried they followed the route of the Muskogees. But, when they arrived at the place where the Muskogees had stopped to rest, there was a fire raging. The Cherokees, unable to follow, got lost and headed to the north, where they settled. The third people to come out of the mound were the Chickasaws. After they became dry they followed the trail of the Cherokees; when they arrived near where the Cherokees had settled, the Chickasaws settled and became a people close to the Cherokees. And the last to emerge were the Choctaws, who, when dried, remained on the land around Nanih Waiya and made it their home.

The aforementioned are the major versions of the legends dealing with the origin of the Choctaws. The main theme running throughout the migration legends is that the ancestors of the Choctaws were led from the West by the two brothers, Chatah and Chickasah. After arriving at Nanih Waiya the Choctaws became settled, while the Chickasaws continued to their new lands. The different versions deviate here as to how and why the Chickasaws left the Choctaws. One version states that they wanted to continue on because of dissatisfaction. Another holds that a disagreement and game of chance were responsible for the split. And still a third version says that a flood separated the two tribes. Likewise, the variations of the creation legend contain a common tradition—the emergence of the Choctaws from the earth, from inside Nanih Waiya.

The Choctaw migration and creation legends were traditional stories pertaining to their origin. Halbert (1899:228) cautioned that the legends had been passed from generation to generation through memories and word of mouth before the opportunity to record them presented itself in the nineteenth century. Debo (1934:3) warned that when collected the legends may have been influenced in part by missionaries. Consequently, the versions collected in the nineteenth century may have been unconsciously and unintentionally distorted to a certain degree.[3] Although the migration and creation legends are important to the Choctaws, some archeologists theorize that the Choctaws are recent inhabitants of east Mississippi and may not have built the mound at Nanih Waiya. But until it is excavated, part of the Choctaw history will remain incomplete.

The Choctaws were large in number, and once they settled in the land east of the Mississippi River they developed into a society possessing village settlement patterns, an agricultural economy, and fundamental social institutions.

They recorded practically no written detail concerning their culture, and little was recorded prior to contact with the Europeans. The earliest recorded account of the Choctaws was by the chroniclers who accompanied the Spanish adventurer Hernando de Soto. De Soto's famous three-year expedition reached Tampa Bay May 30, 1539, and proceeded to travel throughout the Southeast (Gibson, 1973:74). In late 1540 the expedition entered the territory held by the Chickasaws, which de Soto's journalists referred to as the "Province of Chicaza." The Spaniards were greeted

---

[3]Some researchers feel that the Choctaws actually came from Mexico possibly the Yucatan area. Adair stated that "the Choctaw and the Chickasaws descended from a people called Chickemacaws, who were among the first inhabitants of the Mexican Empire; at an ancient period they wandered east with a tribe of Indians called Chocmous, and finally crossed the Mississippi River with a force of 10,000 warriors." It might be inferred that *Choctaw* is a corruption of the word *Chocmous*. There appears to be some cultural likeness between the Choctaws and the Mayas (Lea, 1934:7).

Plate 2 Nanih Waiya today

by Tuscaloosa, who was evidently the chieftain of that district, as Edward Gaylord Bourne in his narratives of de Soto described him as "the suzerain of many territories, and of a numerous people" (Debo, 1934:24). At this time, de Soto demanded from Tuscaloosa various items, including carriers, women, and canoes. The carriers were provided, and, since the Choctaws had no canoes, rafts were built. Also, Tuscaloosa promised to supply women when the Spaniards advanced to Mobila (also cited as Mauvila and Mabila), near the present site of Mobile, Alabama.

On October 18, 1540, de Soto and Tuscaloosa (who was being held hostage) reached Mobila, which was described as being beside a large river on a beautiful plain, consisting of large houses, and surrounded by a high wall made of huge tree trunks (Cushman, 1899:23–24). As the two leaders entered the town they were welcomed by the Choctaws with songs, chants, and the dancing of beautiful girls. Upon arriving at the center of the town, Tuscaloosa reminded de Soto that the demands had been fulfilled and, consequently, requested his own release. De Soto hesitated in delivering an answer, and to his amazement Tuscaloosa arose and walked away. This act of defiance led the Choctaws to attack de Soto and his men. A fierce battle ensued, with the Spaniards being forced out of the town onto the plain. But, once on the plain, the Spaniards gathered their troops and counterattacked. At this point, the superiority of de Soto's forces became evident, particularly in the use of horses, armor, and lances (DeRosier, 1970:14).

In the end, Mobila was completely destroyed and both sides suffered, although the Choctaw loss was substantially greater, especially since their leader Tuscaloosa had been killed. With respect to the numbers killed, there appears to be no general consensus. An estimate by Garcellasso de la Vega places the Choctaw dead at about 11,000, while the "Portuguese Gentleman of Elvas," who was on the expedition, wrote that there were some 2,500 killed within the town alone (Cushman, 1899:26). Cushman felt the total fatalities reached some 6,000 in and outside the town. Another figure set by the Spaniards estimated that 2,500 to 3,000 Choctaws had been killed in the battle and subsequent fire, but Debo (1934:26) considers this to be grossly exaggerated. DeRosier (1970:14) gives a more conservative guess by posting the Choctaw loss at nearly 1,500. With regard to the Spanish loss, Cushman, (1899:26) wrote that 82 men and 45 horses were killed, while the Portuguese Gentleman observed that 4 men, 57 horses, and 300 hogs were lost (Claiborne, 1880:4). Debo is of the impression that 22 Spaniards were mortally wounded and another 148 were wounded but survived.

After the battle, de Soto remained at Mobila for another month to allow his soldiers to recover from their encounter with the Choctaws. Then, on November 18, 1540, he and his conquistadores began marching to the northwest, through the entire Choctaw territory and into the land of the Chickasaws (Claiborne, 1880:5). Thus concluded the first contact the Choctaws had with Europeans.

For almost a century and a half the Choctaws lived with the memory of the Europeans without having further contacts with them. But, toward the end of the seventeenth century, European explorers were once again making their way into the land of the Choctaws. Cushman stated that "as early as 1670 the English traders and emissaries had also found their way into the Choctaws,

Chickasaws, and Muscogees" (1899:28–29). And, in 1673, two French explorers, Louis Jolliet (a trader) and Father Jacques Marquette (a missionary), sailed in canoes down the Mississippi River from Canada (Claiborne, 1880:12). The Jolliet-Marquette party ventured as far as the mouth of the Arkansas River before returning to Canada, having come into contact with several Mississippi tribes (Gibson, 1973:74). Nine years later, in 1682, Robert Chavelier, Sieur de La Salle, headed a party of fifty-five Frenchmen and northern Indians in an expedition down the Mississippi River to the Gulf of Mexico. With these explorations France displayed its intention to dominate the lower Mississippi Valley.

But the English also wanted a foothold in the region to exploit the resources it had to offer. Consequently, in 1698 two English traders entered the area equipped with a supply train of goods (Gibson, 1973:74–75). They traded cloth, guns, shot, powder, knives, and hatchets with the local Indians in return for pelts and slaves. The traded items were then taken back to Charleston in Carolina.

The French became concerned over the competition from the English. As a result, the same year the French sent two missionaries to the Indians, and the following year, in 1699, Pierre Le Moyne, Sieur d'Iberville, sailed into the Gulf of Mexico and landed on the Mississippi Gulf coast. Here he established a French settlement at Biloxi, the first permanent settlement in Mississippi. European encroachment was firmly rooted at the turn of the eighteenth century, setting the stage for the second major historical period of the Choctaw Indians.

Choctaw Culture

During this initial period of Choctaw social and cultural history, the customs and traditions were observed and recorded in an unsystematic manner. The earliest Europeans to experience the Choctaws were in the de Soto expedition of 1540, and the chroniclers accompanying the expedition did not provide adequate details concerning the Choctaws. After this initial contact, the Choctaws continued a relatively unnoticed, pre-historical period. Consequently, the social and cultural characteristics covered in this section are dealt with in as much detail and documentation as possible. However, since there is some overlap in the early descriptions obtained from the major source material and since more specific detail is available concerning the European contact period, this section will provide a foundation for the development of Choctaw culture and society and a basis for a comparison of social and cultural change.

Linguistically, the Choctaws are members of the Muskogean language family, as were the Chickasaw and Natchez Indians. The Choctaws and the Chickasaws spoke practically the same language, though the Natchez tongue was quite different. And none of the tribes in Mississippi had a written language.

Likewise, the Choctaw social organization was similar to that of the other Mississippi tribes (Bettersworth, 1959:36). There were two classes of people, an upper and a lower, each possessing elaborate subdivisions. The tribe was separated into two moieties (the Imoklasha and the Iholahata), each of which consisted of several clans (Gibson, 1973:71). The clans were exogamous, the members of one clan being required to marry outside their own clan. In matters of inheritance and descent, the aboriginal Choctaws were matrilineal. The political and religious leaders of the tribe were selected from the principal clan in each moiety.

Prior to and during the eighteenth century, the Choctaws were town dwellers. Each town was controlled by a council of clan elders. The towns were joined together into a nation with a general council and three principal chiefs, each representing a geographic division of the nation. These divisions were (Bounds, 1964:7) the northwestern or western, with the "long people" (Oklafalaya); the northeastern, of the "potato-eating people" (Ahepatakla); and the southern or southeastern, with the "Sixtowns" (Oklahannali).

The government of the Choctaws was quite democratic, with little absolute authority being given to the chiefs. Each district chief or *mingo* was elected by the men within the district, so it is questionable whether any *mingo* was recognized as the leader of the entire nation (Debo, 1961:20). The district chief's position depended upon both inheritance and ability. In time of matters of great importance, as warfare, the three district chiefs ruled as one unit. The *mingo* looked after the government of the entire district; each town also had a chief, who was under the district chief and who was responsible for local control. There were likewise war chiefs, who were responsible for military authority but who were also under the district *mingo* (DeRosier, 1970:8).

Important decisions were settled in district councils, which were called by the district chief; national councils were assembled by the three district chiefs. Although the occasion was serious, a council was also the time of feasting, games, and dances. And, though it is probable that only the chiefs took an active part in the oratory and that they influenced those in attendance, the final decision was arrived at through majority expression (Ethridge, 1938: 524). Consequently, the Choctaw political organization was summarized as being an "amazingly efficient" system of "elected officials, unlimited debate, civilian rule, and local self-government" (DeRosier, 1970:9).

Thus, the few laws the early Choctaws had were the result of majority opinion and were derived through custom rather than through legislative action. Nevertheless, Choctaw law was strict, especially concerning murder, the ownership of land, and theft. When a member of the tribe killed another member, the victim's relatives apprehended and killed the murderer. If the murderer could not be found, a member of his family had to forfeit his own life (Debo, 1934:21–22). All Choctaw land was held in common by the nation, but individuals could have the right of occupancy and could use certain parts of the land (Gibson, 1973:72). With respect to the use of the land, title was strictly respected and quarrels over boundaries were nonexistent (Bounds, 1964:10–11). Other serious crimes, such as theft, blashemy, and adultery, were usually punished by public whipping and ridicule (Cushman, 1899:495).

Economically, the aboriginal Choctaws were primarily an agricultural people, focusing their efforts upon raising corn. Other important crops included beans, melons, pumpkins, peas, sunflowers, and tobacco (Gibson, 1973:73). The Choctaws cleared little plots around their cabins and land around their towns by burning the underbrush and girdling the trees (Debo, 1934:10). To cultivate their crops the Choctaws employed crude hoes made of bent sticks, bones, or pieces of flint. The women and children were responsible for tending the small cornfield of the household (Gibson, 1973:73). The Choctaws were so successful as farmers that they sold surplus corn and beans to neighboring tribes. Besides growing foodstuffs the Choctaws also gathered fruits, nuts, seeds, and roots from in the forests. These were stored in their houses, though the family's supply of corn was kept in a crib (Debo, 1934:10, 11).

Another economic activity, of secondary importance, was hunting. The Choctaw men used bows and arrows, axes, knives, tomahawks, and blowguns to kill their game, which usually consisted of deer, bear, turkey, pigeon, squirrel, otter, beaver, raccoon, opossum, and rabbit. Often the men would hunt for as long as several months, during which they would be away from the town (Bounds, 1964:6). The Choctaw hunter displayed a keen ability as a strategist and an imitator of animal cries (Cushman, 1899:138), which enabled him to stalk, entice, and kill his quarry. Deer and bear provided the main source of meat, and the skins were used for clothing. Also, deer antler tips were sometimes employed as arrowheads, and the sinew and entrails were twisted into bowstrings and thread (Gibson, 1973:73). Deer brains were used by the women to tan hides. Winter clothing was fashioned from bearskins, and moccasins and boots were made from the hides. Ornaments and necklaces were formed from bear claws; oil derived from the bear was used in cooking and rubbed on the hair and body in grooming.

Fishing was also important. Lacking hooks, which were not introduced until the coming of the white man, the Choctaws used spears and arrows to kill the fish. Another popular technique was the dragging of nets made of brush and vines through the water (Debo, 1934:11). They also poisoned the fish with winterberries, buckeye, and devil's shoestring. And, as with game, any surplus of fish was not wasted but shared with other tribes.

The close affinity with nature was particularly pronounced in the domestic economy of the Choctaws. Rivercraft were made from burned logs, the charred insides of which had been scraped out by clam shells. The frames of their cabins were fashioned from pine, and hickory was used for siding. Cane supplied the materials for baskets and mats, as well as fish traps, sieves, fences, and blowguns. Weapons were made of stone, and dishes and spoons were primarily wood, bone, or shell (Debo, 1934:11), although clay was also made into ceramic utensils.

The Choctaws had several favorite dishes. The women roasted green corn and processed ripe corn into grits, hominy, porridge, gruel, and meal for bread. One corn dish was *tafula*, which was made of boiled pounded corn and which could be mixed with beans. Another dish was cold flour, which was made of dried corn pounded finely and mixed with water. Other favorite foods included *bunaha*, made of pounded meal mixed with boiled beans and a little lye and then made into a dough wrapped in corn husks. Sometimes mashed hickory nuts were used in place of boiled beans. Cushman observed that "little pains was taken in the preparation of their food" (1899:173–74).

One of the best descriptions of the Choctaw domestic economy during this period is the account given by an eighteenth-century French writer:

> Their house is nothing else than a cabin made of pieces of wood of the size of the leg, buried in the earth, and fastened together with "lianas," which are very flexible bands. These cabins are surrounded with mud walls without window; the door is only from three to four feet in height. They are covered with bark of the cypress or the pine. A hole is left at the top of each gable-end to let the smoke out, for they make their fires in the middle of the cabins, which are a gunshot distance from each other. The inside is surrounded with cane beds raised from three to four feet from the ground on account of the fleas which exist there in quanities, because of the dirt. When they are lying down the savages never get up to make water but let it run through the canes of their bed. When lying down they have a skin of a deer or bear under them and a skin of a bison or blanket above. These beds serve them as table and chair. They have by way of furniture only an earthen pot in which to cook their food, some earthen pans for the same purpose, and some fanners or sieves and hampers to prepare their corn, which is their usual nourishment. They pound it in a wooden crusher (pile) or mortar, which they make out of the trunk of a tree, hollowed by means of burning embers. The pestle belonging to it is sometimes ten feet long

and as small around as the arm. The upper end is an unshaped mass which serves to weigh it down and to give force to this pestle in falling back, in order to crush the corn more easily. After it is thus crushed they sift it in order to separate the finer part. They boil the coarser in a great skin which holds about three or four "sceau" of water, and mix it sometimes with pumpkins, or beans, or bean leaves. When this stew is almost cooked they throw into it the finest of the corn which they had reserved to thicken the water, and by way of seasoning they have a pot hung in the air in which are ashes of corn silk, beanpods, or finally oak ashes, on which having thrown water they take the lye which has fallen into a vessel provided underneath, and with it season their stew which is called "sagamite." This serves as their principal food. . . .

They sometimes make bread without lye, but rarely, because that consumes too much corn, and it is difficult to make, since they reduce it to flour only with the strength of their arms; after which it is kneaded or they boil it in water, or wrap it in leaves and cook it in the ashes, or finally having flattened the paste to the thickness of two crowns (ecus), and the diameter of the two hands, they cook it on a piece of a pot on the embers. They also eat it with acorns. After having reduced the acorns to flour they put them in a cane sieve placed near the bank of a stream, and from time to time throw water upon them. By means of this lye they cause it to lose its bitterness, after which they put the paste around a piece of wood which they cook in the fire. When they have meat they boil it in water, however dirty it is, without washing it, saying that that would make it lose its flavor. When it is cooked they sometimes put some of the acorn flour into the broth. They also cook unpounded corn with meat, and when it is dry they pound it and reduce it to lint (charpie). They mix it in boiling with this corn. . . .

While the corn is green is the time when they hold the most feasts and they prepare it in different ways. First they roast it in the fire and eat it so. . . . When it is very tender they pound it and make porridge of it, but the most esteemed among them is the cold meal. It is corn, considerably mature, which they boil, then roast to dry it, and then they pound it; and this flour has the same effect in cold water as wheat flour put into hot water over the fire and has a taste sufficiently agreeable. . . . They also have a species of corn which is smaller than the other and which comes to maturity in three months. That they dry and then without pounding it boil it with meat. This little corn, boiled with a turkey or some pieces of fat meat, is a favorite dish with them. (Swanton, 1918:57–59).

Their domestic economy was further enhanced by trade with other tribes and booty from warfare. The Choctaws traded deerskins and bear oil for materials unknown in their territory, such as conch shells and sheet copper (Gibson, 1973:73–74). A prized item acquired in war was the slave. Women were especially valued because of the services they had to offer in and around the household.

Aboriginal Choctaws possessed a belief in a superior being. The Reverend Wright wrote that "they have no conception of a being purely spiritual. The human soul is not in their apprehension strictly a spirit, but it is what we term a 'ghost,' and is supposed to retain the human shape" (1828:179). The Choctaws felt that these ghosts were of people who had died or had been killed before they had had an opportunity to prepare for the other world and who had returned to obtain these effects (Swanton, 1918:69). They also believed that the *shilup*, or ghost, remained for some time around the body before it departed for the hereafter (Debo, 1934:4). Thus, the Choctaws held to the belief in the immortality of the spirit.

In describing the Choctaw religion, Lewis Spence stated that "it appears to consist of an admixture of Animism and sun-worship; or, more correctly speaking, the two systems may be observed side by side" (1955:567). The Choctaws had several supernatural beings, four of which were identified by Wright: *Nanapesa*, which referred to the director or judge; Ishtahullo-chito or Nanishtahullo-chito, the name given to witches; Hushtahli, which ascribed divine attributes to the sun; and Uba Pike, which pointed to "our Father above" (1828:179–80). The sun was the most important part of the supernatural forces. To the ancient Choctaws, the sun was given the power of life and death, and fire was seen as acting in harmony with the sun and as possessing intelligence. Thus, "the expression 'sun-worship' must, then, be understood to imply an adoration of all fire, symbolized by the sun" (Spence, 1955:567).

The Choctaws placed much importance upon the supernatural work of their enchanters, witches, medicine men, and prophets. This dependence upon magic was apparent on the individual level in that every warrior possessed a medicine bag full of sacred articles such as earth, ashes, and bones, as well as on the societal level in that the tribe had its sacred medicine kept by the chief (Debo, 1934:6–7). Also, certain individuals were held in high regard because of the powers they possessed. The Choctaw doctor, or *alikchi*, combined magic with the use of herbs, assisted by incantations, songs, and suction. Witchcraft was resorted to at times to account for the failings of the doctors, as well as to bring misfortune to their enemies. Another class of dignitaries among the Choctaws comprised the rainmakers or fair-weather makers, who were called upon to apply their powers and shrewdness when the tribe was in need of rain or sunshine. Of course, all those claiming to possess magical powers operated under the threat of punishment, or even death, if they failed to complete a task successfully (Ethridge, 1938:525). But, regarding their religious beliefs, Debo felt that "there is no reason to believe that the Choctaws connected them with the worship of any supernatural being" (1934:7).

According to most sources, the burial customs of the Choctaws were the most distinctive and the most popularized of their rites. When a Choctaw died, the corpse was wrapped in a bearskin or tree bark and was placed on an elevated platform, or scaffold, some five or six feet from the ground (Buckner, 1879:55). The corpse remained on the scaffold until it had nearly or totally decomposed. During this period, friends and relatives came to the platform to mourn and wail. Then a special tribal burial official was called upon to pick the bones clean of all the remaining flesh. The bone picker was a specialist who was painted and tatooed in a particular way and who had long fingernails. After the bones were picked clean, they were placed in a prepared box, and the scaffold was burned (Cushman, 1899: 165–66). The box was then placed in a bone house, after which the bone picker presided over a feast. The bone house was emptied several times a year, and the bones were interred in a burial mound, accompanied by a general funeral ceremony.

Aboriginal Choctaws had a vague idea of future rewards and punishments. Various versions of the Choctaw afterworld have been recorded. Six major accounts were reviewed by T. N. Campbell (1959$_b$:149–51), and a composite version was devised. According to Campbell's collection, each Choctaw was supposed to possess two souls that survive after death. One was the *shilombish*, an outside shadow that follows him in life and remains in the area to frighten his survivors. The other was the *shilup*, an inside shadow or ghost that goes to the afterworld after death. The Choctaw afterworld was located on the earth, a great distance away, and consisted of two adjoining lands, one good and the other bad. The good afterworld, a pleasant and delightful land, was rewarded to those of good behavior. The bad afterworld was a place of misery and discomfort, where individuals of bad behavior, such as those who committed murder or divorced a pregnant wife, were sent.

Being a peaceful, agricultural people, the Choctaws devoted a considerable amount of time to recreational activities, primarily ball games, dances, and feasting. Their native ball game, called *ishtaboli*, was similar to the French game lacrosse and the Natchez Indian game *chunky*. There are many descriptions of the Choctaw ball game, but one of the oldest, which describes the game as it was played in ancient times, was related by Cushman (1899:123–30):

> The intervals between war and hunting were filled up by various amusements, ball plays, dances, foot and horse races, trials of strength and activity in wrestling and jumping, all being regulated by rules and regulations of a complicated etiquette.
>
> But the tolik (ball play) was the ultimatum of all games. . . .
>
> When the warriors of a village wearied by the monotony of everyday life, desired a change that was truly from one extreme to that of another, they sent a challenge to those of another village of their own tribe, and not infrequently, to those of a neighboring tribe, to engage in a grand ball-play. If the challenge was accepted . . . a suitable place was selected and prepared by the challengers, and a day agreed upon. The hetoka (ball ground) was selected in some beautiful level plain. . . . Upon the ground, from three hundred to four hundred yards apart, two straight pieces of timber were firmly planted close together in the ground, each about fifteen feet in height, and from four to six inches in width, presenting a front of a foot or more. These were called aiulbi (ball posts).
>
> The night preceding the day of the play was spent in painting . . . dancing with frequent rubbing of both the upper and lower limbs, and taking their "sacred medicine."
>
> In the meantime, tidings of the approaching play spread on wings of the wind from village to village and from neighborhood to neighborhood for miles away; and during the first two or three days preceding

the play, hundreds of Indians . . . were seen wending their way through the vast forests from every point of the compass, toward the ball-ground; with their ponies loaded with skins, furs, trinkets, and every other imaginable thing that was part and parcel of Indian wealth, to stake upon the result of one or the other side.

On the morning of the appointed day, the players, from seventy-five to a hundred on each side, strong and athletic men, straight as arrows and fleet as antelopes, entirely in a nude state, excepting a broad piece of cloth around the hips, were heard in the distance advancing toward the plain from opposite sides, making the heretofore silent forests ring with their exulting songs and defiant hump-he! (banter). . . .

Then came a sudden hush—a silence deep, as if all Nature had made a pause—the prophetic calm before the bursting storm. During this brief interval, the betting was going on and the stakes being put up. . . . This being completed, the players took their places, each furnished with two kapucha (ball-sticks), three feet long, and made of tough hickory wood thoroughly seasoned. At one end of each ka-puch-a a very ingenious device, in shape and size, very similar to that of the hand half closed, was constructed of sinews of wild animals, in which they caught and threw the ball. . . . In taking their places at the opening of the play, ten or twenty, according to the number of players engaged, of each side were stationed at each pole. . . . In the centre, between the two poles, were also stationed the same number of each party as were stationed at the poles, called middle men, with whom was a chief "medicine man," whose business was to throw the ball straight up into the air, as the signal for the play to commence. The remaining players were scattered promiscuously along the line between the poles and over different portions of the play-ground.

All things being ready, the ball suddenly shot up into the air from the vigorous arm of the medicine man, and the wash-o-ha (playing) began. The moment the ball was seen in the air, the players of both sides, except the falamolichi and hattak fabussa, who remained at their posts, rushed to the spot, where the ball would likely fall, with a fearful shock. . . .

They threw down and ran over each other in the wild excitement and reckless chase after the ball, stopping not nor heeding the broken limbs and bruised heads or even broken neck of a fallen player. . . . The object of each party was to throw the ball against the two upright pieces of timber that stood in the direction of the village to which it belonged; and, as it came whizzing through the air, with the velocity comparatively of a bullet shot from a gun, a player running at an angle to intercept the flying ball, and when near enough, would spring several feet into the air and catch it in the hands of his sticks, but ere he could throw it, though running at full speed, an opponent would hurl him to the ground, with a force seemingly sufficient to break every bone in his body. . . .

From ten to twenty was generally the game. Whenever the ball was thrown against the upright fabussa (poles), it counted one, and the successful thrower shouted: "Illi tok," (dead) meaning one number less. . . .

To any one of the present day, an ancient Choctaw ball-play would be an exhibition far more interesting, strange, wild and romantic, in all its features, than anything ever exhibited in a circus from first to last—excelling it in every particular of daring feats and wild recklessness. In ancient ball-play, the activity, fleetness, strength and endurance of the Mississippi Choctaw warrior and hunter, were more fully exemplified than anywhere else. . . . The education of the ancient Choctaw warrior and hunter consisted mainly in the frequency of . . . muscular exercises which enabled him to endure hunger, thirst and fatigue; hence they often indulged in protracted fastings, frequent foot races, trials of bodily strength, introductions to the warpath, the chase and their favorite tolih.

The women from each opposing side often played a ball game after the men had completed their game (Debo, 1934:9). The action and ability of the women in these games resembled that of the men. Thus, the ball game was a social event in which everyone took part—men and women, young and old.

Among the other games played by the Choctaws was *ulth chuppih*, in which only two players were involved at the same time. In this game an alley with a hard, smooth surface, about two hundred feet long, was made on the ground (Cushman, 1899:130–31). To begin the game, a rounded stone about six inches in diameter was rolled down the alley. Each player had a tapering pole about eight or ten feet long, which was thrown at the rolling stone. The object was to hit the stone of the opponent, while he attempted to keep his opponent's pole from hitting his stone. It was, of course, difficult to strike either the small stone or the flying pole.

The other major diversions among the Choctaws were their

dances, which were usually considered important, and the accompanying feasts. Debo stated that these dances and feasts "seemed to be more recreational than ceremonial and religious" (1934:7); the most important were the green corn dance, the war dance, the scalp dance, the ball-play dance, and the dance of the young people. Minor dances carried the names of animals, such as the dances of the turkey, bison, bear, and alligator (Swanton, 1918:68–69). At any rate, the dances were performed in an open space in the center of the village, during which time the dancers painted themselves and wore their finest clothes. They danced around a drummer, who beat on a drum "constructed from a section cut from a small hollow tree, over the hollow part of which was stretched a fresh deer skin . . . which became very tight when dried; and when struck by a stick made a dull sound . . . (but which) was considered an indispensable adjunct as an accompaniment to all their national and religious ceremonies" (Cushman, 1899: 155). The accompanying feasts involved elaborate preparations, in which the hunters supplied meat and the women cooked corn and other vegetables (Debo, 1934:8).

Physically, the aboriginal Choctaws were a small people, characterized by a graceful, active body form. The men were handsome and well proportioned, and the women with long, black, wavy hair, were also beautiful in form, but with a tendency to be stout in later life (Debo, 1934:23; Cushman, 1899:113, 209). Deformity was virtually unknown in their primitive state, as Swanton wrote, "One seldom sees among them a crooked or humpbacked person" (1918:59).

Both the men and the women had long hair, and the men had sparse beards (Debo, 1934:14). Cushman observed that the male faces were "as smooth as a woman's because the men plucked the hair from their faces" (1899:146). Another characteristic custom of the Choctaws was their practice of flattening heads. Infants' heads were encased in wood and compressed by a sandbag placed on the forehead. For this reason they first became known to the white man as Flat Heads (Cushman, 1899:177). Still another early Choctaw custom was tattooing, with each clan having its own particular pattern (Bounds, 1964:3).

In their personalities the Choctaws were described as honest and trustworthy in their dealings with one another and with other tribes and possessing integrity—"Despotism, oppression, avarice, fraud, misrepresentation in trade, were things absolutely unknown in all their own tribal relations, and in their dealings with neighboring tribes" (Cushman, 1899:14)—highly regarded for their skill and invincible bravery; being good friends and bad enemies in that they never forgot a favor or forgave an injury (Guyton, 1952:11); good spouses and loving parents; great imitators; hospitable and mannerly; patient; and curious. They were also regarded for their ability to endure pain (Cushman, 1899:90, 109, 111, 154, 155, 209). Thus, as Swanton summarily indicated, the Choctaws "never become angry, love much, and will sacrifice themselves for their friends, are very patient in suffering, and endure the death penalty without complaint" (Swanton, 1918:59).

With regard to their dress, the Choctaws were fond of their clothes and ornaments, taking many hours to adorn themselves with paint, plumes, jewelry, and clothes made of deerskin. The men always wore a belt and breechclout. Their upper garments were often woven from feathers and the bark of mulberry trees. In the winter the men, wore leggings and moccasins. Usually, they went barefooted at home (Debo, 1934:13–14). The women wore short skirts of deerskin and in winter supplemented their clothing with shawls and moccasins. Nuts, wood, seeds, berries, bones, stones, and shells were used to make brightly colored ornaments. Often, jewelry was worn in pierced ears and noses, and feathers were placed in the hair.

As previously stated, the Choctaw social organization consisted of a complex system of moiety, clan, and local divisions. The tribe was divided into two large moieties, the Imoklasha and the Iholahata. Members of a given moiety were forbidden to marry within their own moiety. Descent was from the female side of the family, which separated the Choctaw family into two groups, with the mother and children belonging to one and the father belonging to the other. Each moiety was then divided into six or eight clans, or *iksa*. Also there were local groups that permeated through several towns or a single town or that separated a given town into several bands. Thus, the formal social organization of the Choctaw Indians was based upon "matrilineal exogamous moieties divided into non-totemic clans, a territorial division into three of four groups of 'towns,' and four social classes" (Eggan, 1937:35).

In aboriginal times the Choctaws had a Crow Indian type of kinship system, in which "the father's sister's son and *his* descendants through *males* are classed as 'fathers,' whereas the children of the father's sister's daughter (who is classed with the father's sister) become 'brothers' and 'sisters' " (Eggan, 1937:37–38). John Edwards (1932:400–01), in a concise and excellent account of the early Choctaw kinship structure, wrote:

> With them, my father's brothers are all my fathers, and my mother's sisters are all my mothers, and their children are my brothers and sisters; but my mother's brother is my uncle, and his sons and daughters are mine; and my father's sister is my aunt, her son is my father, her daughter is my aunt, and *her* daughter is my aunt, and her daughter is my aunt, and so on, as far as it is possible to go. This is what they call *aunts* in a row. The farthest removed of one's kindred by consanguinity are aunt, uncle, nephew, and niece. The line of relationship, after turning aside thus far, returns into the direct line, and becomes that of father to son, or grandfather to grandson.

Among the early Choctaws, childbirth was one of the tasks the Choctaw wife was expected to perform with a minimum of disruption to the household (Cushman, 1899:174–75). Little assistance was given to the woman, and to have had a male in attendance would have offended her modesty. The custom of adopting related or orphaned children also was quite common (Claiborne, 1880:523). Even those who already had several children of their own were known to adopt one or more children. Adopting was a simple process, completed through the symbolic act of permitting the child to eat from the family bowl (Debo, 1934:16–17). After this, the adopted child took an equal part in the family with the other children.

When a child was born, he or she was given a mare and colt, a cow and calf, and a sow and pigs. According to custom none of these, or its offspring, could be sold or given away, so that when the child had grown the entire stock formally became his or hers with which to begin adulthood. After birth, the infant was customarily placed in a receptacle, called *ullosi afohka* and was kept there for almost a year (Cushman, 1899:169, 175–76). This container allowed the mother to carry the child on her back, place it upright, or hang it from a tree. When the child began to crawl, the *ullosi afohka* was no longer used, but he was still carried on his mother's back in a blanket apparatus. When he had grown too large to be carried in this manner, the child was fastened to the back of a pony for transporting. Finally, when the child was about four or five years old, he was placed on the pony by himself, free to ride.

The names of Choctaw children during this period were usually the same as the words applied to animals, often with reference to some attribute of the animal (Cushman, 1899:46). Many times they were named after some event that had occurred at the time of birth (Debo, 1934:17). Later in life, however, a Choctaw acquired another name, or a succession of names, as a result of some adventure, exploit, or personal characteristic. According to custom, a Choctaw seldom, if ever, spoke his own name. This name-speaking taboo was also extended to the wife not being permitted to speak her husband's name and to the complete restriction placed upon the speaking of names of the dead (Claiborne, 1880:519–20).

Children were reared in an atmosphere of relative freedom. Because they belonged to the clan of the mother, they received their status from her. The girl was taught by the mother to perform domestic household chores, as well as field work (Cushman, 1899:308–09). The fact that the women would ridicule men who undertook such labor indicates that there was a fine demarcation in the tasks performed by men and women. As for the young men, their training fell into the realm of three activities: war, hunting, and ball playing. The mother's brother was responsible for their training and control. Accordingly, boys were exposed to many physical tests, which involved much suffering, and lectures pertaining to bravery, truth, and sincerity.

When the time came to select a mate, the Choctaw young man and woman seem to have had the opportunity to choose their own partner, as long as they married outside their own moiety, of course. Choctaw courtship was quite brief, and, according to several writers, there were established courtship customs. Cushman (1899:309–11) described the ancient practices in which the young man went to the residence of the one he had selected and while there made advances toward the girl by slyly tossing a small stick or pebble to her. She, knowing the meaning, threw the item back if she wanted to marry him. If she refused to reciprocate, she simply sprang up and left the room. Upon being accepted, the prospective bridegroom returned in a few days with presents for her parents, in order to gain their approval. A wedding date was then set, friends were invited, and a feast was prepared. When all the guests were assembled, a symbolic game was played in which the bridegroom had to catch the bride. When she was caught, the women friends gave her wedding gifts and the feast and dance took place, the two young people now being one. Then a few days later the new husband, with the aid of several other men, built a cabin in which the newlyweds would live.

Another version of Choctaw courtship was related by Claiborne (1880:516), in which the young man asked the maternal uncle for the girl and paid an agreed-upon price to him. Again a chase took place, but this time the bride-to-be was pursued by the female relatives of the prospective husband. If she agreed to the marriage, she allowed herself to be caught; otherwise, she ran to the safety of the woods. But, if apprehended, the bride was given presents and that night she was united with the bridegroom.

Swanton also wrote that the young man gave gifts to the parents of the girl he wished to marry, the father receiving a breechcloth and the mother some strings of beads (1918:60). Debo, however, indicated that the young man's mother negotiated with the girl's mother's brother to obtain permission for the marriage to take place (1934:16).

A peculiar custom which followed after the marriage was the mother of the bride being forbidden to look upon her son-in-law, although they could speak to one another. If they were to remain in the same room, a small screen or partition was placed between them (Swanton, 1918:60). If no screen was available, she was obliged to cover her eyes (Cushman, 1899:144).

The Choctaws practiced both monogamy and polygamy, with the toleration of polygyny. Usually the plural wives were sisters, or at least close relatives. This allowed the man to establish one residence rather than several separate ones (Gibson, 1973:72). Although separation was permitted, it seldom occurred (Debo, 1934:16). Marriages tended to last only as long as it was agreeable to the husband and wife, and either could dissolve it at will (Claiborne, 1880:517). If a separation or divorce occurred and the couple had children, it was the right of the wife to keep the children to help her. With regard to adultery, it was unusual for a Choctaw woman to be guilty of unchastity. If adultery did occur, however, the wife was usually punished by her husband (Swanton, 1918:61).

In conclusion, the general social and cultural characteristics of the Choctaw Indians during the period of their history before the coming of the white man is best summarized by Debo (1934:23):

> In attempting to evaluate the characteristics of the aboriginal Choctaws it is hard to differentiate between those common to all primitive people and those traits that were distinctive. But compared with other Indians they seem to have been distinguished for their peaceful character and their friendly disposition; their dependence on agriculture and trade; the absence of religious feeling and meaningful ceremonial; and their enjoyment of games and social gatherings. A mild, quiet, and kindly people, their institutions present little of spectacular interest; but to the very extent that they were practical minded and adaptable rather than strong and independent and fierce, they readily adopted the customs of the more advanced and more numerous race with which they came in contact.

2

European–American Period, 1699–1800

The eighteenth century was marked by the increase in European intrusion into Indian territory in the lower Mississippi Valley. The beginning of the new century was represented by international and intertribal conflict.

Historical Events

From the beginning of their settlement in the region, the French attempted to befriend the Choctaws with presents and honors, and both the French and the English sought to keep the Choctaws at odds with their neighboring tribes (Debo, 1934:27). But in 1702, Jean Baptiste Le Moyne, Sieur de Bienville, as commander of the French at Mobile, secretly contacted both the Choctaws and the Chickasaws in an attempt to develop friendly relations, as well as trade partnerships (Cushman, 1899:30). And, in Louisiana, Iberville wanted "to use the Choctaws and Chickasaws as a buffer between the French in Louisiana and the British in Carolina" (Holmes, 1973:120).

In 1702, war broke out between the French and the English (known as Queen Anne's War in the New World), and the flirtations with the Indians were heightened. The Spanish sided with the French, as did the Choctaw Indians, but the Chickasaw and

Creek Indians allied with the British. British strategy used the Chickasaws to fight the pro-French Choctaws; in 1704 the Choctaw War, which had been terminated two years before, was rekindled. Choctaw retaliation was related by Bernard de La Harpe, who wrote, "In January, 1704, Bienville induced several war parties of the Choctaws to invade the country of the Indian allies of the English" (Cushman, 1899:30). But the Choctaw reliance upon French protection was short-lived, because in the fall of 1705 a force of Chickasaws and Creeks swarmed into Choctaw lands, and French support proved nonexistent. Then, in 1708, weary from war, the Choctaws agreed to peace with the English (Cotterill, 1954:18). In May, 1711, however, as a result of English pressure, the Choctaws and the Chickasaws once again began fighting.

According to A. M. Gibson, a French-Chickasaw war began in 1720 and was prompted because the Chickasaws continued to allow English traders to frequent their towns (1973:77). The French employed Choctaw mercenaries to attack the Chickasaws. In return, the Chickasaws raided Choctaw settlements and French shipping on the Mississippi River. The French and the Chickasaws remained at war until 1725, when French officials declared a truce.

Meanwhile, during the second and third decades of the eighteenth century, the French were encountering the Natchez Indians in Mississippi. French traders had carried on commercial relations with them since 1713, but in 1714 several Natchez killed four French traders during a dispute (Gibson, 1973:76). Because of this, the French built Fort Rosalie on the bluffs at what is now Natchez, Mississippi. Growing resentment by the Natchez culminated in an attack on the French in 1722, which saw the French as the victors. Little opposition was shown by the Natchez until 1729, when they destroyed several French settlements, killing some 250 and capturing nearly 300 women and children. The enraged French, along with Choctaw mercenaries, struck back, killing many Natchez and scattering the survivors. In the end, the Natchez Indians were nearly annihilated by 1731.

Another employment of Choctaw mercenaries by the French occurred in 1732, in what Gibson referred to as "the second French-Chickasaw war" (1973:77). The main reason for this confrontation was identical to the previous one in 1720, namely, the

Chickasaw refusal to sever economic ties with the English. The French also wanted the Chickasaws to give them Natchez survivors who had sought refuge among the Chickasaws. Again the French and Choctaws, as well as the Illinois Indians, attacked the Chickasaws. And again the Chickasaws retaliated by raiding the Choctaws (and the Illinois) and French shipping on the Mississippi River.

In an attempt to settle the Chickasaw problem once and for all, Bienville in 1736 planned to attack the Chickasaws with two forces, one consisting of 400 French and Indians and the other having 600 French regulars and 600 Choctaws (Gibson, 1973:78). Unfortunately for the French, the two forces arrived at different times and the fortified Chickasaw towns were able to stave off the charge (Cotterill, 1954:25). The French made two more unsuccessful campaigns against the Chickasaws, one in 1739 and the last in 1752, before 1763, when the French surrendered their American possessions to England.

In the first years of the 1740s the Choctaws and the Chickasaws attempted to resolve their differences. Among the Choctaws a peace faction emerged under the leadership of Shulush Homa ("Red Shoes"). Chief Shulush Homa's wife had been seduced by the French, so he therefore leaned toward the English (Debo, 1934:27). Then, in 1744, when the Choctaws and the Chickasaws were closest to peace, the French governor of Louisiana succeeded in defeating the negotiations because he feared that the Chickasaws would coerce the Choctaws into an alliance with the English and consequently against the French (Claiborne, 1880:86). It became his plan to subdue the Chickasaws and to unite the Choctaws under French control (Bounds, 1964:16), but he failed to receive support from France.

These events brought about the division of the Choctaw Nation into two factions: one supporting the English and the other remaining loyal to the French. By 1748 the two groups had become so hostile toward one another that they entered into a civil war (Claiborne, 1880:87). The losses to both Choctaw factions were heavy, and both came to realize that they were destroying their own nation for the sake of two foreign rivals. The warring Choctaws therefore agreed to a council, at which it was decided to assassinate Shulush Homa in order to reunite the Choctaw Nation (Debo, 1961:28). This decision was carried out, but the English continued the fight with the brother of Shulush Homa as the head of the English partisans. The French countered under the efficient leadership of Grandpré by defeating and dispersing the pro-English faction in 1750 (Claiborne, 1880:87–88). Peace was ultimately achieved in 1750 by the Grandpré Treaty, which placed the Choctaws under French rule.

For the next dozen years the French and the Choctaws played a continual cat-and-mouse game, in which the French dealt cautiously and suspiciously with the Choctaws, and the Choctaws sporadically threatened to ally with the English (Debo, 1934:28–30). Then without warning, on November 3, 1762, a secret treaty was signed in Paris, by which the king of France ceded the territory in the New World known as Louisiana to the King of Spain. J. F. H. Claiborne related the following account for the transferral: "There had been no negotiation whatever—no overtures on the part of Spain. It was an absolute gift, tendered through the Spanish ambassador, and only accepted by him on the condition that his royal master should approve the act. Given by one king, from sheer inability to maintain it out of his treasury or to defend it against his enemies, and accepted by the other without any demonstrations of satisfaction" (1880:89).

Another agreement was arrived at the following year, when a treaty of peace (known variously as the Treaty of Paris, Peace of Paris, or the Proclamation of 1763) was signed by France, Spain, and England. According to this treaty, France gave up its territory and Spain ceded the land that now makes up Florida to England. Thus, with this treaty the colonial ambitions of the French in the New World came to an end, and the Choctaws, unknowingly and perhaps unwillingly, became part of the British Empire (Debo, 1934:30).

Realizing that control of the Indian groups in their newly acquired territories would present problems, the British decided to invite the various tribes to a council at Augusta, Georgia, in November, 1763. In attendance were representative chiefs of the

Choctaws, Chickasaws, Cherokees, and Creeks, as well as the governors of Virginia, the two Carolinas, and Georgia (Cushman, 1899:36).

Another meeting was held at Mobile in March, 1765. At this conference George Johnstone, the British governor, made a treaty with the Choctaws that defined their southern and eastern boundaries and prohibited the encroachment of English settlers (Debo, 1934:31). But, while at the meeting, the Creeks attacked the Choctaws, killing ten and capturing others. This act of hostility and violence led to a six-year war, which found the Choctaws, Chickasaws, and Cherokees pitted against the Creeks (DeRosier, 1970:17).

The British control of the Indians was rather short-lived, because in 1775 the colonists on the Atlantic coast rebelled against their mother country. British officials in West Florida hoped to deter the advancement of the Americans by distributing arms, powder, and shot to the Chickasaws and Choctaws and by instructing the Indians to defend their region (Gibson, 1973:82). Nevertheless, the only active part played by the Choctaws in the American Revolution took the form of scouting for the Americans, especially under George Washington, Anthony Wayne, Daniel Morgan, and John Sullivan (Debo, 1934:31). But for the most part the Choctaws were indifferent to the war.

With the end of the Revolution and with the Americans emerging victorious, the Choctaws faced an age-old problem, but with different parties involved. That is to say, the Spanish held the lands and position the French had in the past, while the Americans occupied the territory previously controlled by the English. Again the Choctaws became the object of a rivalry.

The Spanish wanted to create a buffer zone between them and the Americans with the Choctaw lands. In order to solidify their relations with the Choctaws, Chickasaws, and Creeks, Spain developed trading alliances with the Indians. And, in the summer of 1784, Spain made treaties at Pensacola agreeing to forbid traders from entering Indian territory who did not buy a Spanish license (Debo, 1961:32). In return, the Indians identified themselves with Spanish protection. As usual, a major aspect of the treaties was the continuation of the custom of giving the Indians presents each year (Holmes, 1973:165).

Likewise, the Americans wished to establish amiable relations with the southern Indians and of course wanted to counter the Spanish influence upon them. To this end the Americans organized a conference in late 1785 at Hopewell, South Carolina. This meeting resulted in the first treaty made with the Choctaws by the United States government, which was signed January 3, 1786 (Cushman, 1899:46). The Treaty of Hopewell contained eleven articles, the highlights of which are outlined by Debo: "It established perpetual peace and friendship . . . it gave the United States the right to establish three trading posts within the Choctaw Nation . . . it defined, but did not survey, the eastern boundary along the line fixed by the British treaty of 1765; and it provided that a citizen of the United States who should settle within the Choctaw Nation would forfeit the protection of his government and become subject to tribal jurisdiction" (1934:32). Thus, the first American treaty with the Choctaws and the Chickasaws covered commercial trade relations, boundaries, rights and duties, the particulars of American-Indian relations, and the proclamation of peace among the tribes by placing the Indians "under the protection of the United States of America, and no other sovereign whosoever" (Gibson, 1973: 82–83).

The Spanish reciprocated by inducing the Choctaws to allow them to have a tract of land at the mouth of the Yazoo River, where they began in 1791 to build a fort, known as Nogales (DeRosier, 1970:20). Then in 1792 at Fort Nogales the Spanish completed a treaty of friendship with the Choctaws, Chickasaws, Cherokees, and Creeks (Debo, 1961:33). Also at this time, the Spanish obtained from the Choctaws another tract of land located on the Tombigbee River in the eastern section of the territory. On this site the Spanish constructed a second fort, Fort Confederation, so named to serve as a reminder of the treaty agreed upon at Nogales.

After several clashes between the Chickasaws and the Creeks (one in 1793 and another in 1795), in which the Chickasaws with U.S. arms and supplies defeated the pro-Spanish Creeks, the United States and Spain signed the Treaty of San Lorenzo, "by which Spain agreed to evacuate to the Americans all of Mississippi north of thirty-one degrees" (Gibson, 1973:83–84).

This treaty permitted the United States to formulate a program to deal with the southern Indians. Samuel Mitchell became the U.S. agent for the Choctaws and Chicksaws in 1797. It was his responsibility to enforce federal laws within Indian Territory and to "civilize" the Indians (Gibson, 1973:84). Mitchell was replaced as the agent for the Choctaws in 1799 by John McKee (Cotterill, 1954:134). Thus, at the end of the eighteenth century it was the Americans and their governmental programs and treaties with which the Choctaws had to contend, after a full century of European intrigue.

Choctaw Culture

After the first contact with Europeans in 1540, the Choctaw social institutions did not undergo any extreme changes for another two and a half centuries. But this stability began to be broken at the beginning of the eighteenth century. As Gibson emphasized, "The European intrusion . . . provoked drastic change among the Mississippi tribes and ultimately destroyed their aboriginal life style" (1973:74). As will be shown, the Choctaws readily accepted the idea of trading with the Europeans, and they were anxious to obtain the domestic plants and animals, as well as the superior tools and weapons, that the foreigners had to offer. Thus, when Iberville established the first permanent French settlement at Biloxi in 1699, the full thrust of European influence upon the Choctaw cultural and social systems began.

As in the previous period, three geographical divisions among the Choctaws were recognized by the eighteenth-century Europeans, but John R. Swanton felt that a careful scrutiny of the towns revealed four divisions. He wrote that the Choctaws in the southern part of the territory were the Sixtown Indians (Okla Hannali), who were partly linguistically and partly culturally different from the other Choctaws. Another group, the central division, containing the towns in which the principal leaders of the entire nation lived, was known as the Big People (Okla Chito). The other clusters of towns were the Long People (Okla Falaya) in the west, whose speech became recognized as the standard Choctaw language, and the People of the Opposite Side or Party (Okla Tannap). Toward the end of the eighteenth century the central division, which was absorbed by the eastern and western groups, ceased to exist as a separate entity (Swanton, 1931:54–55).

Frederick Hodge estimated that in 1700, when the French came into contact with the tribe, there were between 15,000 and 20,000 people (1907:289). In 1730 the French reported the Choctaw population at about 15,000 or 16,000 (Wright, 1951:99). Swanton guessed that between the years 1702 and 1814 the Choctaw population ranged between 700 and 16,000. Thus, it might be inferred that the Choctaw Indian population comprised about 15,000 people throughout the eighteenth century.

During the 1750s African slaves were brought to the Choctaws and Chickasaws by European traders and settlers (Gibson, 1973:81). Slave labor was adopted primarily by the mixed bloods and whites within the Indian Territory. Gibson cited three important influences that the presence and ownership slaves had upon the Choctaws: "slavery fed the aristocratic pretensions of the owners in their drive to emulate white planter neighbors," which created feelings of superiority and a form of social stratification; "the slave performed labor generally scorned by Indians such as clearing the wilderness and opening fields for agriculture, building roads and bridges, and performing other useful labor which enhanced the value of Indian properties and improvements"; and "slaves purchased from English-speaking planters learned the Indian language, served as an important communication bridge, and played a substantive . . . role in tribal acculturation."

Similar to the Chickasaw Indians, the Choctaws were divided into two great moieties, the Inhulahta and the Imoklasha or Kashapa Okla (Swanton, 1931:76–77). The moieties were strictly exogamous, and the children belonged to the mother's group while the father stood alone within the family. These great groups were separated into three smaller clans, making six in all (Wright, 1828:179–80). The subdivisions coexisted in the same town and neighborhood while maintaining an awareness of their membership in both the larger and the smaller group.

It is generally held that the Choctaws of this period did not have totemic clans or *iksa*, although it is probable that there were "nontotemic divisions corresponding to the Chickasaw totemic clans and differentiated in some manner from the smaller geographical bands." The remaining groups of the Choctaws apparently fell into the category of local groups, or "house names" (Swanton, 1931:79, 81–82). These local groups appear to have consisted of all sizes and levels of importance. Often they spanned several different towns and many times were identified with a given town. Thus, the Choctaws comprised matrilineal exogamous moieties that were divided into nontotemic clans; during historic times the moieties ceased to exist and the clans assumed the function of exogamy (Eggan, 1937:35).

Each of the Choctaw towns had a chief, a war chief, two lieutenants under the war chief (*tascamingoutchy*), and a *tichou-mingo* (assistant chief), who was responsible for arranging ceremonies, feasts, and dances and for speaking for the chief (Swanton, 1931:90–92). Within the village the inhabitants were divided into four orders: the grand chief, village chief, and war chief; the beloved men (*atacoulitoupa);* the warriors; and the supporting people (*atac emittla*). Swanton stated that the head chiefs were not from any particular town and that leadership was dependent upon merit and popularity. Figure 3 shows the early tribal organization.

As mentioned previously, Choctaw towns were divided into four geographical divisions. Later, as the central division merged with the western and eastern, there were three. Swanton once compiled a list of 115 towns that existed in the various geographical divisions. However, they were not all occupied at the same time (Fig. 4).

The aboriginal domestic and intertribal economy of the Choctaws has been described. It was seen that agriculture was their primary economic interest, with hunting and fishing secondary. But, with the European intrusion, the Choctaws were exposed to different consumer goods. When Iberville settled Biloxi in 1699, the Indians of the Gulf region came into contact with French administrators, missionaries, and traders. At first, the Choctaws (as

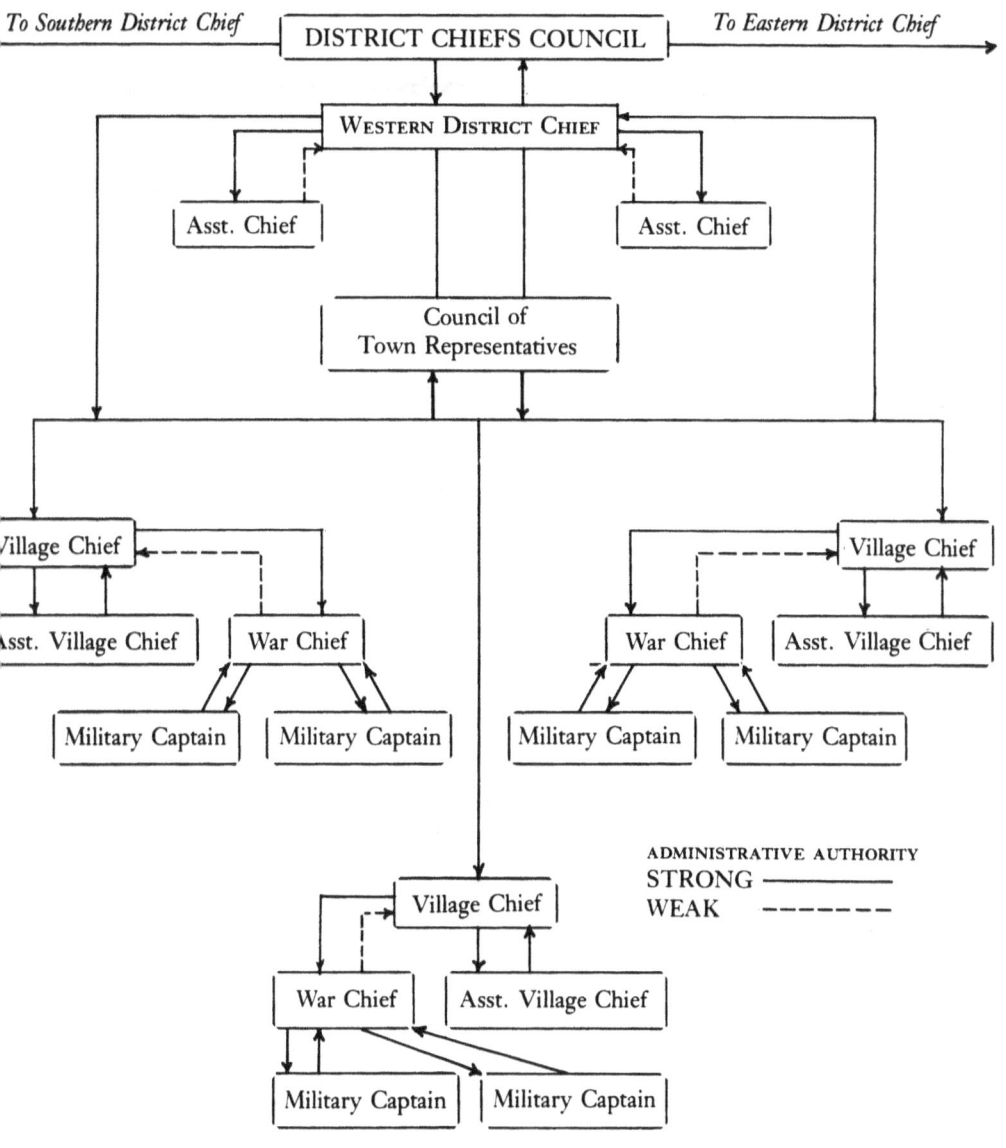

Figure 3 Early Mississippi Tribal Organization. SOURCE: Kiamichi Economic Development District, 1974

Figure 4 The Old Choctaw Country, Mississippi   C,F,S,W.—Towns belonging to the Central, Eastern, Southern, and Western divisions of the nation, respectively. The dotted lines indicate the boundaries between the three latter divisions in the early part of the nineteenth century. SOURCE: Swanton, 1931

well as the Natchez and Chickasaws) appeared to be willing to accept the French. They readily recognized the advantage and importance of trading with these newcomers. The Choctaws were quick to trade for new plants, weapons, implements, clothing, and domestic animals (Bounds, 1964:14). Also at this time the Choctaws were receiving goods from the English located along the Atlantic coast. But the French offered many new items of trade, such as calico, sugar, coffee, flour, and weapons. In return, the Choctaws offered furs, bear's oil, honey, beeswax, and groundnuts.

During much of the eighteenth century, the Choctaws were the object of a series of intrigues with the French, English, Spanish, and Americans, in which the goal was political and economic control of the lower Mississippi Valley. The conflict between the French and the English brought several changes to the Indians of this area. Tribal ways were transformed or replaced by European traits, and European goods affected the simplicity and self-sufficiency of the tribal economy. Ultimately, the reliance upon French and English implements, weapons, and fabrics altered the economic emphasis within the tribes from growing and hunting to trading. The impact of European contact is reflected in the fact that by 1763 only two tribes, the Choctaws and Chickasaws, remained in Mississippi, while the others, including the Natchez, were virtually nonexistent (Gibson, 1973:75–76).

When the British gained control of the Mississippi Indians with the signing of the Treaty of Paris in 1763, the Choctaws and Chickasaws continued to hunt for furs, which were used to trade for the European goods that had become necessary and valued to the Indians. Among these esteemed possessions were guns, ammunition, tools, and cloth. As Gibson stated, "This trade led to an abandonment of ancient self-sufficiency derived from the products of nature and simple local technology" (1973:80–81). The Choctaws also acquired livestock and poultry from the traders, and the Spanish introduced the horse, which became useful as a beast of burden.

When competition for Indian trade and land increased among the European intruders, the British took full advantage of their situation. Accordingly, British traders employed the Choctaws and

Chickasaws as intermediaries between their land and Spanish Louisiana, in which the commerce of other Europeans was forbidden. The British developed Indian towns in Mississippi into trading posts, where British goods were exchanged to the Choctaws and Chickasaws, with the purpose that the goods would then be traded to the tribes west of the Mississippi River. The British consequently were able to export their trade items to groups that were formerly the exclusive trade partners of the Spanish.

When the United States entered into the Treaty of Hopewell in 1786, American trading posts were established in Choctaw territory. Ten years later, an American law permitted the United States to develop factories throughout the area with the intention of creating trade relations with the Indians (Bounds, 1964:20). An agent was appointed to handle the trade conducted at each trading post, and it was his responsibility to report all transactions to the secretary of war.

Thus, through European and American contact, the Choctaws began experiencing changes to their economy. Although agriculture remained supreme, trade was increasing in importance. American influence was to become more apparent after the turn of the nineteenth century.

As with the previous period, the Choctaws believed in the existence of a deity, which they referred to as "the Great Spirit, the Giver of Breath," who made and ruled all things (Claiborne, 1880:492). They believed that the Great Spirit possessed supernatural power and was omnipresent but that he did not require or expect any form of worship from them (Cushman, 1899: 300–02). The Choctaws also believed in future rewards and punishments. The reward of pleasure and enjoyment was given to those of virtue, honesty, and truth. According to their ideas, heaven was located in the southwestern horizon. Their place of punishment was a land of pain and suffering.

The Choctaws believed in the work of witches and sorcerers. They also had privileged classes of specialists: the rainmaker, who was called upon to save the crops during time of drought; the medicine man, who interpreted dreams, charmed away spells, and cured the ill; and the prophet or seer, who saw into the future (Claiborne, 1880:502).

Respect and reverence for the dead were foremost among the values of the Choctaws, and they had no fear of death, since it was conceived of as a journey to a better hunting ground (Claiborne, 1880:503). The dead were placed on a scaffold and allowed to deteriorate before the bone picker cleaned the remaining flesh off the bones. Then the remains were placed in the charnel house in the village. When the bone house became full, the bones were buried in a mound.

These beliefs and customs remained relatively the same until the full influence of the missionaries upon the Choctaws began in the second decade of the nineteenth century. Then the traditional religious practices became fused with or replaced by Christianity.

Early accounts of the Choctaws by European observers remarked that the children received little guidance or training. Little restraint, parental or otherwise, was placed upon them. "In all that concerns the child, the oldest maternal uncle, or if he is dead, the nearest male relative in that line is consulted" (Claiborne, 1880:517).

From infancy the boys were taught the use of weapons, especially the bow and arrow, for hunting and warfare and how to play their ball games. To become physically fit for these activities, the boys wrestled, ran races, lifted and threw weights, and endured various other exercises and contests. The young men's training was designed to make them good warriors, hunters, governmental figures, and producers of houses and wooden and stone implements (Swanton, 1931:139). The girls received training in the various tasks that women carried out in and around the village, such as caring for the household and the crops.

As with the previous period, the "two-stick racket" game (ball game), or *toli*, was the most important. From the different accounts by the early visitors to the Choctaws during this period, it appears that the method of play varied or was interpreted differently. Nevertheless, the main elements tended to be in agreement and were much the same as the description of the ball game offered in the preceding chapter. No further description will be given here, except to note that because of the importance of this form of amusement it remained relatively unchanged. In fact, there were accounts of the ball game being used to decide disputes, such as the one that occurred between the Choctaws and the Creeks over a beaver pond around 1790 (Swanton, 1931:148).

Besides the varieties of ball game, another game played by the Choctaws was the "moccasin game," or *naki lohmi* ("hidden bullet"), which was described as follows:

> Twelve men were required in playing this game. They knelt or sat on the ground in two rows, or sides, facing each other, six players in each row. Seven hats were placed on the ground in a line between the two rows of players.
>
> The player who was to start the game and who was always at one end of his row held in one hand a small stone or shot. With his other hand he raised all the hats in order, placing under one of these the stone or shot; during the entire performance he sang a particular song. After the stone or shot had been placed, the player sitting opposite him guessed under which it lay. If he did not succeed in three guesses, the leader removed the object and again hid it under either the same or another hat. Then the second player on the opposite side had three guesses. If a player guessed under which hat the object was hidden, he in turn became the leader.
>
> . . . the side having the greater number of points made by the six players combined, won. (Swanton, 1931:158)

Dancing and feasts continued to be main forms of recreation during this period. And all the towns had a public square where the various dances took place.

In aboriginal times all Choctaws, men and women, wore their hair long. As late as 1771, both sexes still allowed their hair to grow long, with the exception of some young men (Swanton, 1931:57). Some twenty or more years later, however, the northern Choctaws had their hair cut similar to the Creeks.

The Choctaw Indians were identified previously as originally possessing matrilineal exogamous moieties, though in historic times the moieties went out of existence and the nontotemic clans took over the function of exogamy. By 1763 there had been a rapid increase in mixed-blood families, since the French and British had been living for several generations among the Mississippi tribes. This growth of the mixed-blood community "confused and disturbed the ancient system of family relationships, reduced social control of the clan system, and eventually corrupted tribal values" (Gibson, 1973:79–80). Thus, the native social system based on clans was being eroded by the time of the American takeover of Choctaw lands at the end of this historic period.

Among the Choctaws, a woman was required to separate herself completely from her family during her menstrual period. (Swanton, 1931:115–16). She immediately left her house for a designated place, where she built a fire. During this time the husband did not live with his wife, and the woman had to remain out of the sight of the men. The husband prepared his own food or went to the home of a neighbor.

When a woman became pregnant, the husband abstained from eating salt and pork, which were thought would harm the child. As the time of delivery approached, the husband ate only after sunset. After the birth, if the child was a girl, the husband continued his fast for eight more days.

When the time of delivery arrived, the woman never gave birth in the cabin, but retired to the woods, where she had her baby without assistance. After the delivery, she cleaned the baby and returned to her daily routine. Mothers also practiced the custom of head deformation by applying a small bag of sand on the head, from the top to the eyebrows, in order to flatten the forehead. Children were not weaned until they grew tired of the breast, which might not be for several years.

The traditional Choctaw courtship and marriage customs were described in the preceding chapter, and the source materials available for this period provide descriptions that coincide with the aforementioned accounts. It is adequate here to restate that Choctaw courtship and marriage were quite flexible, provided that the prospective partner was a member of the opposite moiety. The marriage ceremony was rather simple, with a feast and dance, and the couple lived together as long as it was agreeable to both. If the spouses became displeased with one another, they simply parted, with the children remaining with the wife. Polygamy was permitted, but it was not universal. A Choctaw man might have had from one to six wives, each usually residing in a separate cabin, unless they were sisters, in which case they usually shared the same yard (Claiborne, 1880:520).

In the last half of the eighteenth century French and British settlers were mating with the Mississippi Indians, giving rise to mixed-blood families (Gibson, 1973:79–80). Cushman (1899: 314–15) related the traditional story told concerning the first marriage between Choctaw and white:

> A white man at an early day, came into their country, and in course of time married a Choctaw girl and as a natural result, a child was born. Soon after the arrival of the little stranger, (the first of its type among them), a council was called to consider the propriety of permitting white men to marry the women of the Choctaws. If it was permitted, they argued, the whites would become more numerous and eventually destroy their national characteristics. Therefore it was determined to stop all future marriages between the Choctaws and the White Race, and at once ordered the white man to leave their country, and the child killed. A committee was appointed to carry the decision into execution, yet felt reluctant to kill the child. In the meantime, the mother, hearing of the resolution passed by the council, hid the child, and when the committee arrived they failed to find it, and willingly reported that the Great Spirit had taken it away. The mother kept it concealed for several weeks, and then secretly brought it back one night, and told her friends the next morning that the Great Spirit had returned during the night with the child and placed it by her side as she slept. The committee had previously decided, however, that if ever the child returned it might live; but if it never came back, they then would know that the Great Spirit had taken it. The boy was ever afterwards regarded as being under the special care of the Great Spirit, and became a chief of their Nation. The law was repealed; the father re-called and adopted as one of the tribe; and thus the custom of adopting the white man originated and has so continued from that day to this.

The changes apparent from the increase of mixed bloods among the Choctaws did not reach full velocity until the time of removal, but gradually the mixed bloods, who identified more with their European fathers than their Choctaw mothers, rose to become a type of aristocracy in the tribe, as the Le Flore line attested with such leaders as Greenwood Le Flore. Nevertheless, during the eighteenth century, control of the clan family system was still in the hands of the full bloods (Gibson, 1973:80).

The burial and funeral customs of the eighteenth-century Choctaws were not always conducted in the same manner in every locality and during each decade, but there were similiarities, which were dealt with in detail in the previous chapter. The practice of scaffolding and bone picking was to continue until after the end of this historical period, although different communities might have had their own slight variations, as reflected in the major source material (Swanton, 1931; Buckner, 1879; Halbert, 1901; Claiborne, 1880; Cushman, 1899).

During this period (1699-1800), the Choctaws came into contact with several foreign powers—the French, English, Spanish, and Americans. The French influence was the most pronounced, particularly with regard to the many alliances entered into by the two groups in opposition to the Natchez, Chickasaws, and English. During the eighteenth century, many French cultural traits became acquired or modified by the Choctaws. But on the whole the Choctaw social and cultural systems remained much as they had been during their prehistorical period. Although the Americans were only beginning to obtain a foothold in the Choctaw territory toward the end of this period, their influence was to become increasingly apparent during the first three decades of the nineteenth century.

3

Choctaw Land Cessions and Acquisitions, 1801–1830

The first thirty years of the nineteenth century found the Choctaw Indians faced with new experiences. Particularly identifiable with this period of their history were the major treaties and land cessions between the Choctaws and the U.S. government and the entrance and influence of missionaries. Among these outstanding events, of course, is the admission of Mississippi as a state of the Union. Thus, this period characteristically continued the encroachment of non-Indians into Choctaw territory and the subsequent threat of the annihilation of the Choctaws as an ethnic community in Mississippi.

Historical Events

The first Choctaw-U.S. government treaty occurred in 1786 at Hopewell, South Carolina. The second treaty entered into by the Choctaws and the United States was signed at Fort Adams, on the Mississippi River, in December, 1801. To negotiate the treaty at this conference, President Thomas Jefferson sent General James Wilkinson, Benjamin Hawkins, and Andrew Pickens (DeRosier, 1970:28–29); the Choctaws were represented largely by those seeking refuge from a famine created by a poor hunting season (Cotterill, 1954:134). As a result, to receive compensation for ceded lands, the Choctaws were quick to agree to terms. By the Treaty of

Fort Adams, the Choctaws' eastern boundary established by the treaty with the English was reaffirmed; the United States received the right to build a road through the Choctaw Nation from Natchez to Nashville; and the Choctaws ceded the triangular Old Natchez District in the southwestern territory (Fig. 5), which consisted of "2,641,920 acres of valuable land from the mouth of the Yazoo River south to the thirty-first parallel" (DeRosier, 1970:29). In return for these concessions, the Choctaws were granted "two thousand dollars in money and merchandise, and three sets of blacksmith's tools to the Choctaws whose homes had been in the ceded land" (Debo, 1934:34).

With the Treaty of Fort Adams, the Choctaws felt that the U.S. government would not make demands upon them for many years to come. But this was not to be the case. Scarcely one-half year later, General Wilkinson received orders to negotiate a new treaty dealing with the northern and eastern boundaries of the Choctaw lands. At first the Choctaws refused to listen, but at the insistence of Governor William C. C. Claiborne they finally agreed to establish the boundaries. By the Treaty of Fort Confederation in 1802, the eastern boundary was defined according to the British treaty of 1765 and the Choctaws gave up a small tract of land north of Natchez in present-day Jefferson County. This treaty involved no compensation, and the Choctaw chiefs signed reluctantly. They also made it quite evident that they desired no more treaties with the government (DeRosier, 1970:30).

Again, in less than a year, the United States demanded more land to accommodate the influx of American settlers. President Jefferson had General Wilkinson contact the Choctaw chiefs, and Wilkinson gathered the chiefs together at Hoe Buckintoopa, an Indian village. The chiefs refused to negotiate. But, when Wilkinson reminded them of Choctaw debts incurred with the British suppliers Panton, Leslie & Company and requested immediate payment, they were forced to confer with the Americans (DeRosier, 1970: 30–31). Thus, with the exchange of debts for land, the Choctaws signed the Treaty of Hoe Buckintoopa on August 31, 1803. The Choctaws lost another 853,760 acres of land north of Mobile to the American government. And each chief who signed the treaty received a bribe of "fifteen pieces of strouds, three rifles,

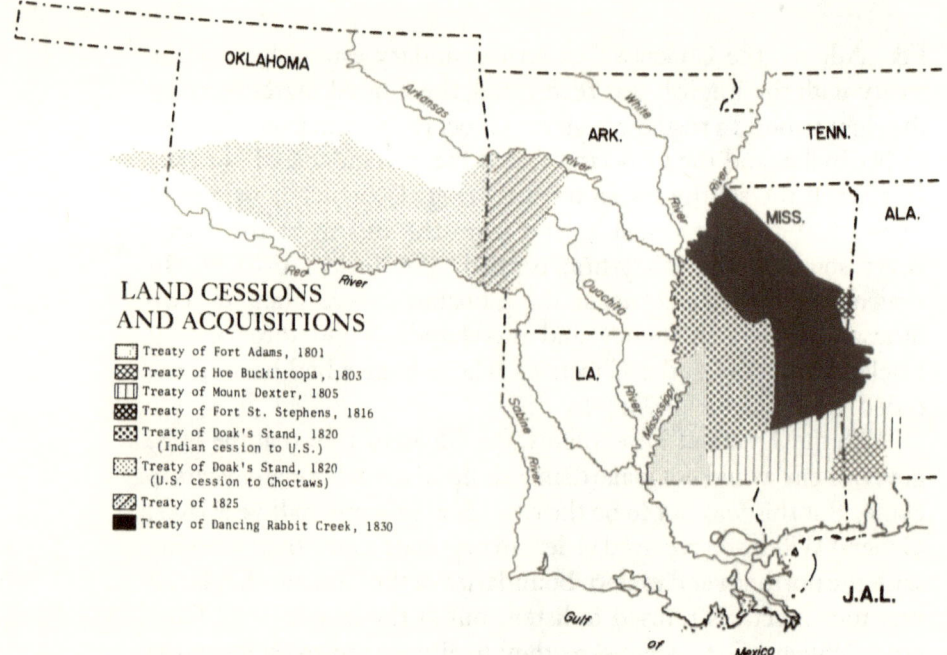

Figure 5 Land Cessions and Acquisitions. After DeRosier, 1970

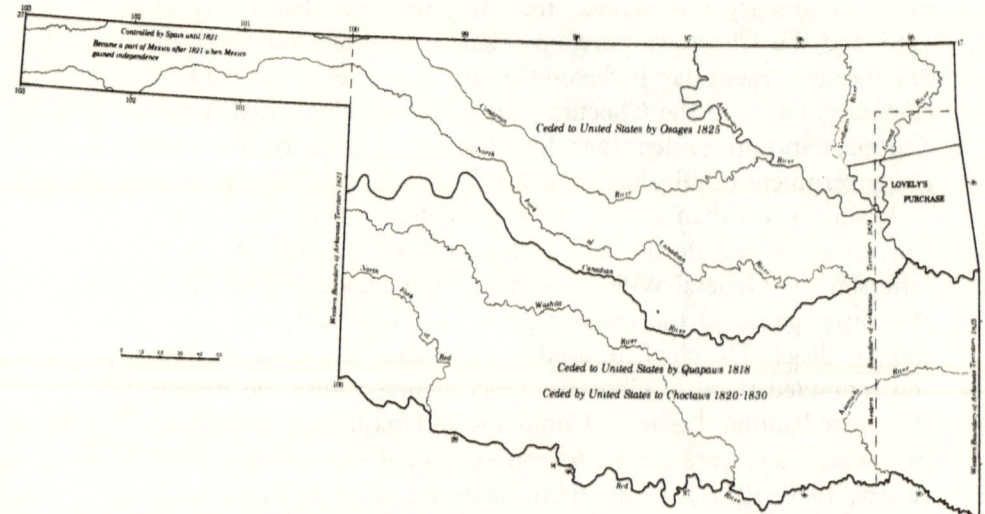

Figure 6 Indian Territory, 1803-1830. From *Historical Atlas of Oklahoma*, Second Edition, by John W. Morris, Charles R. Goins, and Edwin C. McReynolds. Copyright 1976 by the University of Oklahoma Press

one-hundred fifty blankets, two-hundred fifty rounds of powder, two-hundred fifty pounds of lead, one bridle, one man's saddle, and one black silk handkerchief" (Debo, 1934:34).

But, as the future was to show, these first three treaties were relatively minor and unimportant compared with those yet to come. The first of the major treaties concerned with land cession was the Treaty of Mount Dexter, also referred to as the First Choctaw Cession. The conference convened on November 6, 1805, and was completed on November 16, when the Choctaws again unwillingly signed the treaty. According to the agreement, the Choctaws gave up from their southern lands a large tract that stretched from the Natchez District to the Tombigbee District (Bounds, 1964:21) and that contained 4,142,720 acres of fertile land (DeRosier, 1970: 32). For this land the Choctaws received $50,500 in cash ($48,000 to be paid to Panton, Leslie & Company for debts owed by the Choctaws and $2,500 to be paid to John Pitchlynn, a white interpreter, to compensate for losses derived in Choctaw territory). The Choctaws were also given their first permanent tribal income in the form of $3,000 a year, which was to be dispensed as the chiefs saw fit. In addition, the treaty of 1805 provided "that the District Chiefs, Apukshunnubbee, Pushmataha, and Moshulatubbee, should receive salaries of $150 a year during their continuance in office, and $500 each in consideration of their past services to the Nation; and it reserved 5,120 acres of the ceded tract for the benefit of Aliza and Sophia, daughters of Samuel Mitchell, a white man, and Molly, a Choctaw woman" (Debo, 1934:36).

The Treaty of Mount Dexter ceded more land than the previous three treaties combined. It likewise marked the beginning of several other distinct features:

> The Choctaws were bargaining with their last possession—land. They had lost their monopoly on the fur trade to the long hunters, and there were others who knew the forests and could act as guides or scouts now. The chiefs were corrupted through this system of treaty making. Gifts and favors were given to the chiefs for their services and influence with the tribe. Debts to certain traders and other individuals were paid by treaties. (Bounds, 1964:21)

Therefore, as some sources have indicated, "when Pushmataha signed the Treaty of Mount Dexter, in 1805, it was the beginning of the end for the Mississippi Choctaw" (Choctaw Agency, n.d.:2).

During the War of 1812, the Choctaws demonstrated their loyalty to the United States, in spite of the fact that in 1811 the Shawnee chief Tecumseh visited the three districts of the Choctaws to get them to join his Indian confederacy in a war against the United States. The leading chief at that time, Pushmataha, listened to Tecumseh's arguments and then urged the Choctaws to support the United States (Gibson, 1973:85). A second indication of loyalty came in the war itself, when Pushmataha led a group of Choctaws to fight with General Claiborne and General Andrew Jackson: they took an aggressive part in several engagements, including the battle of Holy Ground, the battle of Horseshoe Bend, and the battle of New Orleans. Many Choctaws served as scouts and messengers in the army.

After proving their loyalty in the War of 1812, the Choctaws enjoyed two years of relatively good relations with the government and with white settlers. Then in 1816 the Choctaw chiefs and U.S. representatives met at St. Stephens to settle boundary difficulties created by the Creek War. Through this treaty, the United States gained a small area of land east of the Tombigbee River. In return, the Choctaws were paid $6,000 a year for twenty years, as well as $10,000 in merchandise (Bounds, 1964:29–30). It was agreed that the annual payment would be held by the government and that the interest earned would be used for Indian education. The United States also guaranteed always to be friendly toward the Choctaws (DeRosier, 1970:37).

The following year saw the U. S. Congress approve the constitution of Mississippi on December 10, 1817. This marked the state's official admittance to the Union.

One of the most important developments in the history of the Choctaw Indians was the formal arrival of missionaries in 1818. Actually, tradition had held that several Roman Catholic missionaries were among the Choctaws in 1735 (Cushman, 1899:70) and that the Reverend Joseph Bullen visited and preached among the Mississippi tribes as early as 1799 (Gibson, 1973:86). But formal mis-

Plate 3 Lithograph of Push-ma-ta-ha, a Choctaw warrior. COURTESY of Western History Collections, University of Oklahoma Library

sionary work with the Indians began in 1817 with a mission among the Cherokees near Chattanooga, established by the American Board of Commissioners for Foreign Missions (Bounds, 1964:30–31). The board was nondenominational, but the Congregational and Presbyterian churches of New England supported it. Having heard of the missionaries' work, particularly the schools, the Choctaws requested missions for themselves. To accommodate the request, the board sent two New England missionaries, Cyrus Kingsbury and Cyrus Byington, to the Choctaws in 1818.

In August of that year Kingsbury and his Christian helpers built the Eliot Mission School on the Yalobusha River, about thirty miles above its junction with the Yazoo River (near the present site of Grenada, Mississippi). This school was named for John Eliot, the famous Massachusetts "Apostle to the Indians" (Bettersworth, 1959:265). Within a year the mission had a school, a model farm, and several buildings. Although they were hesitant at first, the Choctaws soon offered their services, and the chiefs turned over the $200 they received annually from the federal government and the Choctaw people donated eighty cows and calves and $500 to be paid annually (Lucas, 1973:376). In 1820 the Choctaw council agreed to give $6,000 a year for seventeen years for the mission's support. Thus Eliot was financed by three sources—the federal government, the mission board, and the Choctaws themselves.

A second mission was established among the Choctaws in October, 1820, when Kingsbury and some of the missionaries moved to Oktibbeha Creek (near the present town of Osborn) to found Mayhew Station, named after a noted New England missionary family (Bettersworth, 1959:265). By 1822 Mayhew consisted of "a frame dining room, four log houses, four cabins, three storehouses, a joiner-and-blacksmith shop, three stables, and two cribs" (Cotterill, 1954:227–28). Kingsbury lived at Mayhew, from where he supervised all the other missions and schools, ten in all (Love, 1911:376).

The Reverend L. C. Williams then established a third mission, called Newell Station, in 1821 and a fourth, called Bethel, in 1822 (Lucas, 1973:376–77). The popularity of and attendance at the missions and schools by the Choctaws were high; nearly half the Choctaw population took advantage of the services rendered by the missionaries. The number of missions established also indicates the Choctaw identification with them. There were three missions founded by 1820, and another eighteen were created by 1826

(Cotterill, 1954:227). Aubrey Lucas noted that at least thirteen were established by 1830 but that no more than eleven were operating at one time (1973: 376–77).

In spite of the relative satisfaction the Choctaws derived from the missions and schools, in 1830 the government decided to withdraw all financial support. Because the missions had taught the Indians that their land could not legally be taken from them, the War Department and the citizens of Mississippi pushed for government reprisal. The consequent financial strain placed upon the missions made their operation difficult (DeRosier, 1959:182).

After the War of 1812 and the admission of Mississippi as a state, a steady flow of Americans into Choctaw and Chickasaw lands began. More pressure for the Choctaws to cede their fertile lands followed. In January, 1820, Governor George Poindexter spoke to the Mississippi legislature in favor of purchasing Indian lands with the goal of removal in mind (Fortune, 1973:260–61). Previous attempts to acquire Indian territory had failed in 1818 and 1819, but the pressure became so great that John C. Calhoun, President James Monroe's secretary of war, was forced to act. As a result, Calhoun accepted an offer from Andrew Jackson to serve as head of a government negotiation team. Jackson had criticized Calhoun's policies and favored western removal, but he agreed to deal fairly and honestly with the Indians.

Mississippian General Thomas Hinds was appointed a commissioner to assist Jackson. Representing the Choctaws were Chiefs Pushmataha and Moshulatubbee. The site selected by Jackson for the conference was a tavern on a flat, grassy area on the Natchez Road near the Pearl River (in the southeast corner of what is now Madison County), known as Doak's Stand. The preliminary gathering of the Choctaws carried an atmosphere of distrust toward the proposals and intentions of the government, but by the time the formal discussion began on October 10, 1820, much of the tension had been replaced by friendly feelings and even the playing of games and drinking (DeRosier, 1970:63).

After a period of discussion, arguments, and threats, the Choctaws finally submitted to the will of Jackson and reluctantly signed the Treaty of Doak's Stand on October 18, 1820. By this treaty,

Jackson proposed to trade the Choctaws approximately thirteen million acres of land in Arkansas and the future Indian Territory for over five million acres (or about one-third) of the remaining Choctaw holdings in Mississippi, located chiefly north and east of the Natchez District (Figs. 5, 6). Jackson also was to arrange for each Choctaw man who was removed to receive "a blanket, kettle, rifle gun, bullet moulds and wipers, and ammunition sufficient for hunting and defense for one year plus enough corn . . . for one year" (Fortune, 1973:262). Another stipulation made by Jackson was the provision for schools, stores, blacksmith shops, and agents in the new lands (DeRosier, 1970:65).

With the signing of the Treaty of Doak's Stand, new land in Mississippi was opened to settlement by Americans. Jackson and Hinds were lauded as heroes by the government, people, and press (DeRosier, 1970:66–67). In fact, Jackson was later immortalized when the new capital of Mississippi (coincidentally located in the center of the cession of 1820) was named after him: the county in which it is located was named Hinds County. As for the Choctaws, once again they were involved in the transaction of a treaty in which they came away feeling betrayed and disappointed.

Before the provisions of the treaty could be carried out, many difficulties were encountered. One difficulty was that the Choctaws were reluctant to relocate across the Mississippi River (Fortune, 1973:262–63). Another problem resulted because of the inaccuracy of the maps possessed by the commissioners. Also, white settlers in the land given up in Arkansas by the United States were unwilling to abandon their lands to the Choctaws. When the Choctaws were requested to renegotiate a revised treaty, they refused. Then, in 1824, the Choctaws agreed to send representatives to meet with Calhoun in Washington, D. C. Selected to make the journey were the three district chiefs, Pushmataha, Moshulatubbee, and Puckshenubbee. They were accompanied by David Folsom, who served as interpreter (Bounds, 1964:35). Unfortunately, Puckshenubbee died the day before the delegation arrived in Washington, so the Choctaw delegates appointed Robert Cole as his successor (Cushman, 1899:70). After their arrival in Washington another tragedy occurred—the death of Pushmataha on December 24, 1824. He received a distinguished military funeral and was buried in the Congressional Cemetery in Washington.

Meanwhile, the terms of the new treaty were debated for several weeks, until both parties arrived at a compromise. The signing of the Treaty of 1825 took place on January 20, and the major conditions included:

> (1) a $6,000 per year perpetual annuity to be sold to the government for a lump sum settlement or continued permanently any time after twenty years, (2) an additional $6,000 a year for sixteen years as promised in the Treaty of Doak's Stand, (3) government waiver of all claims to back debts owed by the Choctaws, (4) government compensation to all Choctaws who fought in the War of 1812, and (5) Choctaw evacuation of most Arkansas lands after the completion of a careful survey. (De Rosier, 1970:82)

The treaty of 1825 proved to be a bright spot in Choctaw dealings with the government of the United States.

But, like the Treaty of Doak's Stand, the Treaty of 1825 failed to offer a permanent solution to the problems of land cession and removal. Discontent was felt on both sides: the Choctaws once again displayed an unwillingness to move west of the Mississippi River, and the government wanted to obtain the Indian lands through another cession. As in the past, however, the Choctaws were not forced to migrate to the new lands in the West, primarily because of the moderate policies of Calhoun and Thomas L. McKenney, chief of the Bureau of Indian Affairs. The Choctaws always had been permitted to choose their own course—to migrate or not to migrate. Generally, their decision was not to migrate: it is estimated that only as many as fifty Choctaws emigrated before 1829 (DeRosier, 1970:98).

This policy of moderation came to a halt in 1829, when Andrew Jackson took office as president of the United States. He had previously advocated Indian removal, and his supporters, especially those favoring removal, expected him to continue pressing for Indian relocation. The Mississippi legislature, taking a cue from Jackson's election, on February 4, 1829, attempted to eliminate the Indian nations in the state by prohibiting the rule of the chiefs,

Plate 4   Greenwood Le Flore. COURTESY Oklahoma Historical Society

abolishing tribal government, and including the Indians as citizens of the state (Bounds, 1964:38). Although not enforced, these laws did add to the insecurity of the Indians (Fortune, 1973:264). The Mississippi Indians were now being pressured by both the federal and Mississippi governments into making another decision concerning their future.

In the meantime, the Choctaws called a general council to discuss the alternatives available to them. Two of the three Choctaw chiefs, Greenwood Le Flore and David Folsom (both mixed bloods), favored removal. Their opinions and actions almost prompted a civil war in the tribe; to hold the nation together, Le Flore was elected chief of the entire nation. His election thus opened the door to Choctaw removal from Mississippi, particularly when he immediately proposed a removal treaty, which was delivered by special messenger to President Jackson (DeRosier, 1970:114).

Jackson first rejected Le Flore's proposed removal terms but realized that the Choctaws were ready to be approached with a final removal treaty. Jackson therefore instructed Secretary of War John H. Eaton to ask the Choctaw leaders to join him in conference at Franklin, Tennessee, during the summer of 1830. The Choctaws, who refused to meet with Jackson outside their lands, asked him to send reliable men to talk to them in the Choctaw Nation (DeRosier, 1970:117–18).

Jackson decided to send Eaton and General John Coffee to meet with the Choctaws and negotiate a removal treaty. The site selected was between the two prongs of Dancing Rabbit Creek (in what is now Noxubee County), and the conference was scheduled to begin in mid-September. When the delegations arrived at Dancing Rabbit Creek, the Choctaws were represented by almost 6,000 people under the leadership of Chiefs Le Flore, Moshulatubbee, and Nitakechi (Bounds, 1964:40). Major John Pitchlynn, a mixed blood, was the interpreter, and George S. Gaines was responsible for furnishing supplies during the conference. With all the preliminary arrangements made, the treaty negotiations were formally opened on September 18 with the usual atmosphere of entertainment and speechmaking. But this gathering was unusual in some respects, as the following demonstrates:

> It must be recorded, that a large portion of the white people at Dancing Rabbit were not the best characters, being mainly rowdies, gamblers and saloon-keepers—in short, the bad element of the American frontier. . . .
>
> The dissipation and revelry at Dancing Rabbit was not confined to

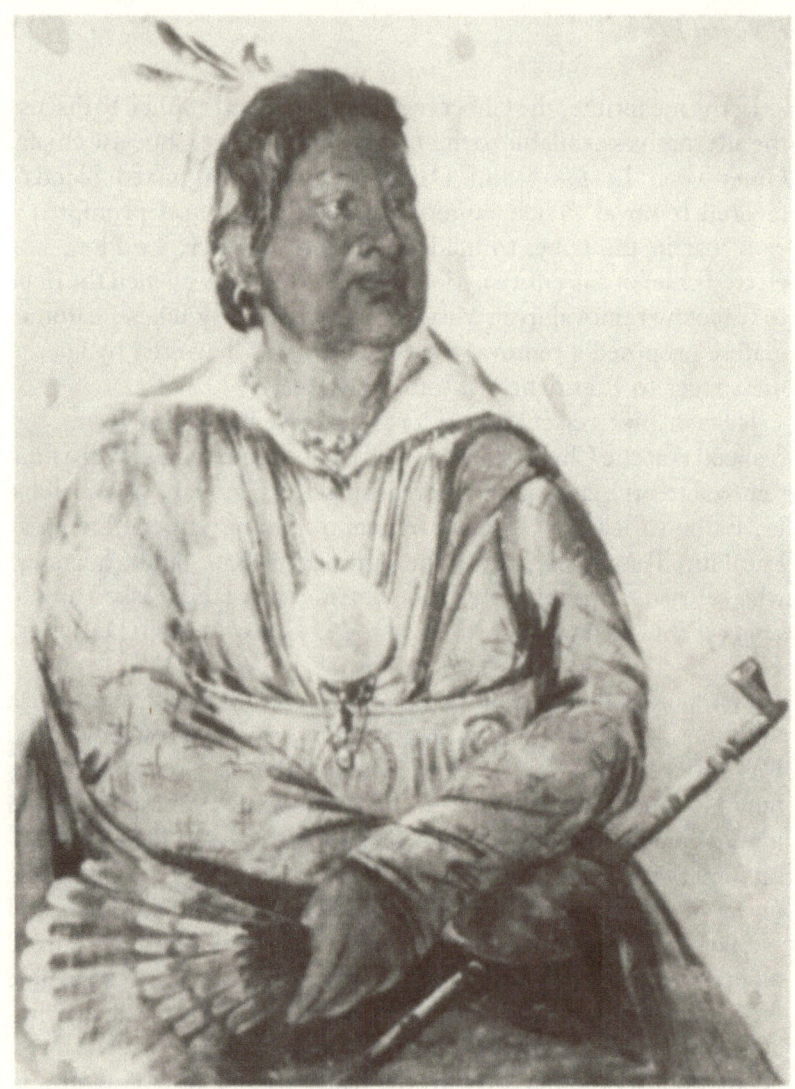

Plate 5 Moshulatubbee (He-who-puts-out-and-kills) By Catlin, 1834. COURTESY Oklahoma Historical Society

the day time alone, for every night somewhere on the ground, there was a big Indian dance, which was always protracted to a late hour. . . .

Two unpleasant duties confronted the commissioners on their arrival at the treaty ground of Dancing Rabbit. One was to allay the discontents and dissatisfactions prevailing among the Indians so that they would assemble peaceably in council. The second was . . . with the missionaries, who greatly desired . . . to be present during the progress of the negotiations. . . . The missionaries finally yielded to the positive demands of the commissioners that they should not come upon the treaty ground (Halbert, 1902 $_a$:377–78)

Then, after proposals and counterproposals by both sides and especially after the threats by Eaton and Coffee, a compromise in the form of the Treaty of Dancing Rabbit Creek was signed on September 27, 1830, by 172 Choctaw leaders and Eaton and Coffee. The content of the twenty-two articles of the new treaty is concisely summarized by Arthur DeRosier (for the full text, see Appendix 1):

> The new treaty stipulated that the Choctaw Nation would be within the following boundaries: "Beginning near Fort Smith, where the Arkansas boundary crosses the Arkansas River; running thence to the source of the Canadian fork, if in the limits of the U.S., or to those limits; thence due South to Red River, and down Red River and to the W. Boundary of the territory of Arkansas; thence N. along that line to the beginning." In return for their western lands, now reduced in acreage, the Choctaws must cede to the United States all of their remaining 10,423,130 acres of land east of the Mississippi River.
>
> The balance of the twenty-two articles of the treaty pertained to four areas. The first group related to the actual removal itself, providing that once each year for three years, a group made up of approximately one-third of the tribe would be transported to Indian Territory so that by the end of 1833 all emigrants would have been removed. The government of the United States promised to underwrite the moving of the Indians and all their possessions, including livestock; to furnish all necessary transportation facilities and supplies; and to provide full subsistence for twelve months after arrival in Indian Territory.
>
> The second group of articles concerned federal protection of the Indians in their new home. The United States would guarantee domestic tranquility in the nation and protection from foreign invasion. No whites, especially traders, would be allowed to enter the nation without the consent of the Choctaw government, except for an Indian agent who would be appointed by the president every four years. The treaty also promised to ban all alcoholic beverages from the nation.
>
> The third category listed the payments promised by the United States to the Choctaws: (1) continuation of all annuities in force before the Treaty of Dancing Rabbit Creek; (2) an annuity of $20,000 per year

for twenty years; (3) payment by the United States of all costs incurred in educating forty Choctaw children a year for twenty years; (4) an annual payment of $2,500 to be used to employ three teachers for Choctaw schools; (5) a donation of $10,000 to erect a centrally located council house in the nation, a church, and schools; and (6) a gift, after removal, of 2,100 blankets, 1,000 axes, 400 looms, and enough rifles, ammunition, hoes, and other personal articles for all.

The fourth and most important group of articles concerned land gifts to the Choctaw chiefs and land reservations for those members of the tribe who wished to remain in Mississippi. Each chief was to receive four sections of land, plus $250 annually as long as he remained in office. The captains, subcaptains, and principal men were to receive lesser amounts of land without gifts of money. ARTICLE 14, a significant part of the treaty, stipulated that if any Choctaw families or individuals desired to remain in Mississippi they might do so by registering with the Indian agent within six months after ratification of the treaty. Each adult male and female who registered was entitled to 640 acres of land; each child over ten who was living with a family was to receive 320 acres; each child under ten living with a family, 160 acres. If an Indian failed to register within six months, or if he went to Indian Territory and then returned, he was forever barred from registering under ARTICLE 14. (1970:124-26)

By the end of 1830, the federal government had finally succeeded in acquiring all of the Choctaw lands in Mississippi. As will be described in the next chapter, the removal was to take place beginning in the fall of 1831 and was to be completed in 1833. It is estimated that some 5,000 Choctaws remained in Mississippi and received their defined allotments by taking advantage of Article 14 (Gibson, 1973:88). These Choctaws became known as the Mississippi Choctaws in order to distinguish them from those who emigrated to the Indian Territory.

Choctaw Culture

Prior to the end of the eighteenth century, the Choctaws experienced relatively little change in their basic social institutions, although they readily accepted European domestic plants and animals, weapons, and implements. From the beginning of the nineteenth century, however, the Choctaws openly accepted many of the social institutions of the white man; and, during the first thirty years of that century, they created Christian churches, schools, and a constitutional government. Debo emphasizes the historical and cultural significance of this acceptance:

> Although the Choctaws had been subject to . . . [the European and American] intrigues for a century, the series of land treaties with the United States indicates that for the first time in their history they were being seriously crowded by settlers. But this contact also brought a definite decision to adopt the white man's institutions, and the same generation that saw them driven from their ancient homes also marked the period of their greatest educational, religious, and political development.
>
> A strong factor in this decision was the influence of a few intermarried white men of great ability and force of character, who identified themselves fully with their adopted people. . . . These men settled among the Choctaws during the last quarter of the eighteenth century, and their sons became leaders of progress and education within the tribe.
>
> Another source of white influence was the increasing activities of traders, and the construction of roads in the Choctaw country. The most important trading post was St. Stephen's, established by the United States in 1802. . . . The Choctaws brought bears' oil, kegs of honey, beeswax, bacon, groundnuts, kegs of tobacco, and all kinds of furs, which they traded for the cloth, iron tools, arms and ammunition, and plows kept in stock by the Federal Government. (1934:37)

White influence was dramatically illustrated by the two major events that occurred during this period, namely, the series of government treaties and the entrance of missionaries to the Choctaw territory in 1818. These caused modifications in the Choctaw social and cultural systems.

In social organization the old native system based on clans was gradually eroded by the growth of the mixed-blood population among the Choctaws. The early missionaries, who were particularly concerned about the fact that under the matrilineal system of inheritance the women worked in the fields and the father was not responsible for his children, introduced the idea that the man should be the head of the family (Eggan, 1937:41–42). Another change involved the leaders being chosen by the adult males in the district to represent only the male population and not the clan, as it had been in the past.

Thus, the push was on for a change from a matrilineal to a patrilineal society. Of course, those who were responsible for creating this change had no idea that the effect on the social organization would be the breakdown of the clan structure, with emphasis placed upon the territorial bond. Consequently, the pattern of descent shifted from the father's sister to the father or, in other words, from the female to the male line.

One thing did not change. As in the past the Choctaw Nation maintained its geographical distribution into three main districts even after missionary contact (McKee, 1971:127).

The effects of extended contact with the white man became evident in the modifications the Choctaws made in their government. Initially, the Choctaws were insulated to a degree from outside influence and exploitation through restrictions placed upon white intruders by the federal Indian Intercourse Acts of 1790, 1793, 1796, and 1802 (Debo, 1961:38–39). But the U.S. government sent an Indian agent to regulate the execution of treaty agreements, as well as to entice the Choctaws to accept some of the white man's "civilized" ways. The Indian agent became the catalyst in several changes in Choctaw customs.

One such modification involved the Choctaws' ancient law of retaliation and revenge. According to custom, a murderer was punished by the victim's relatives, and, if the murderer could not be apprehended, a member of his family served as a substitute to be punished or even put to death. When the American Indian agent observed this practice, he decided a change was necessary. Debo relates the incident:

> Some white hunters had wantonly murdered a peaceful Choctaw in the Chickasaw country, and the Choctaws, in accordance with their old custom, had satisfied the demands of justice by killing an innocent white trader. Agent Dinsmore then demanded the life of the man who

had retaliated upon the trader. A conference was called in September, 1812, at the Chickasaw council house, at which Apukshunnubbee, Moshulatubbee, and other Choctaw leaders were present, as well as John Pitchlynn and other interpreters, and the Chickasaw agent with two Chiefs of that tribe. This Council abandoned in principle the law of retaliation by agreeing to the death of the Choctaw who had killed the trader; but the Chiefs cannily delayed the execution of the sentence until the white people should have punished their murderer. A treaty was made, however, between the Choctaw leaders and a group of Cherokees who had migrated to the region beyond the Mississippi, by which if a murder were committed by a citizen of one tribe against a citizen of the other, only the guilty person, and not any innocent member of the offending tribe, should be subject to the law of blood revenge. The Chickasaws also subscribed to the same agreement. (1934:39-40)

Soon after the missionaries settled among them, other important changes were introduced to the Choctaws. In place of the blood revenge, the Choctaws were encouraged to establish a body of law enforcement officers. Accordingly, Greenwood Le Flore and David Folsom organized a mounted patrol in each district, known as the "light horsemen" (Claiborne, 1880:505). The light horsemen continually rode throughout the district, serving the residents in a threefold manner as sheriff, judge, and jury (Cushman, 1899:157). The right of trial by jury was extended to all offenders, replacing the customary action of retaliation and revenge. Soon irregular courts were provided for the Choctaw people, and a legal code patterned after that of the white man was developed (Bounds, 1964:33).

Methods of punishment differed. Murderers were generally put to death. The rifle invariably was the instrument of execution (Claiborne, 1880:506), since the Choctaws thought that a person who was hanged could not enter the good hunting land (Cushman, 1899:158). For minor violations, the lash was the major form of punishment. Claiborne observed that "this punishment was not known until [the Choctaws] fell, more or less under white influence," especially the missionaries (1880:506). No matter what the offense or the punishment, the Choctaw violator never attempted to escape the punishment and always voluntarily appeared at the appointed time and place.

After Mississippi became a state in 1817, legislation was enacted that increasingly pointed to the continual and inevitable cession of Choctaw lands and the tribe's ultimate removal from Mississippi. In 1820 the legislature "abolished all tribal rights, privileges and immunities enjoyed by the Indian within the limits of the State" (Claiborne, 1880:507). This act declared that any person functioning as a chief would be prosecuted. Because the Indians became citizens of Mississippi, they were bound to follow the laws of the state. To preside over them, judges and constables were appointed, and the territory was joined to the adjacent counties. Then, in 1826, the Choctaws adopted a system of elective chiefs (Bounds, 1964:33). Placing the Choctaws under state control created major stress within the tribe, since those opposing removal had to decide whether to follow the path of removal or that of the dissolution of tribal government (Peterson, 1970_a:14).

With intensified contact with the Americans, the material culture of the Choctaws became greatly developed. They had learned not only how to grow cotton, but also how to spin and weave the fiber into clothing, which became the characteristic material for clothes (Debo, 1934:40). The economic advances made by the Choctaws during this period are related by Gibson, who relied upon the 1830 report of a federal agent dealing with the Mississippi Indians:

> Thus the Indians of Mississippi were "compelled to subsist by a different means than that of the chase. They have a plenty of horses of superior quality. . . . They have large herds of cattle, swine, sheep and goats, and poultry of every description. . . . Cotton, beef and pork are the principal articles for exportation." He estimated that Chickasaw nation planters would export 1,000 bales of cotton during the year. From the proceeds of farm produce and livestock sales the Indians purchased "necessaries and luxuries of life" as well as slaves, sugar, coffee and "dry goods to render them comfortable and ornament their persons. The time has come when they no longer depend upon the rifle for support, but it is used more for their recreation and amusement than for the means of sustenance. Every family cultivates the earth more or

less as his thirst for gain, or his imaginary or real wants increase. . . . For the last eight years, the practice of the men requiring the women to perform all the labor in the field is much changed—the men now (with few exceptions) cultivate the earth themselves, while the female part of the family is engaged in their household affairs. They spin, weave and make their own clothing." The women made butter and cheese and kept themselves "decent and clean and in many instances particular attention is paid to fashions that are in use by the whites. It is their constant practice to appear in their best apparel at their public meetings, also when they visit the country villages in the white settlements." (1973:85–86)

The Choctaw economy of this period reflected the influence of the white man, but the central endeavor still involved the agricultural activities of raising corn, beans, and other crops. And their houses consisted of two rooms instead of one.

Although the main influx of missionary activity began in 1818, some exploratory missionary visits to the Mississippi Indians occurred before that time. One of the first missionaries to come during the American contact period was the Reverend Joseph Bullen in 1799 (Gibson, 1973:86). After an examination of the religious status of the Mississippi tribes, missionary helpers were brought in to attempt to convert Choctaws and Chickasaws to Christianity. Visitation and preaching were the techniques applied, but no schools or churches were established.

The first to succeed in Christianizing the Choctaws were the Presbyterians under the leadership of Cyrus Kingsbury and Cyrus Byington at Eliot Mission in 1818 and at Mayhew Station in 1820. By 1820 Methodist and Baptist missionaries were among the Choctaws, but they did not follow the Presbyterian model of mission settlements and neither was able to achieve the success of the Presbyterians (DeRosier, 1959:176,180). Nevertheless, missionary activity continued in Mississippi until removal. The Baptist Board of Foreign Missions sent the Reverend John A. Ficklin and the Reverend Stark Dupuy to the Choctaws and Chickasaws in 1819 and established the Choctaw and Chickasaw Mission in 1825 (Gibson 1973:86–87). In 1827 the Mississippi Conference of the Methodist church founded a mission among the Choctaws and Chickasaws, of which the Reverend Alexander Talley was the most noted missionary.

Between 1818 and 1830 over one thousand Choctaws were converted to Christianity, and many others learned to respect the Christian beliefs and practices as taught by the missionaries (DeRosier, 1959:184). Missionary influence caused the death of many traditional Choctaw superstitions. The missionaries demonstrated that the medicine man, rainmaker, and prophet were imposters, and consequently belief in their powers was undermined (Claiborne, 1880:503). This questioning of the validity of the powers of their "doctors" led to the passage in 1829 of a tribal law, which gave a person accused of witchcraft the benefit of trial rather than putting that individual to death (Debo, 1961:46–47). Also resolved by this law was that no doctor should have the power to impose the death penalty upon such witches or "wizzards," thus placing judical functions into the hands of the light horsemen.

Other laws affecting Choctaw religion were enacted by the chiefs between 1826 and 1830 as a result of missionary suggestion. One such law stated that "all persons shall be allowed liberty of conscience and be permitted to worship God in their own way and manner which they may see proper"; another held that "any neighborhood that should wish to build churches for the purposes of worshipping God, that privilege is herewith granted it" (De Rosier, 1959:184).

During this period many Choctaws began to accept Christianity, while the traditional religious practices and beliefs, such as the belief in witchcraft, underwent change. Many missionaries, however, may have believed that the Choctaws were completely accepting their ministrations without understanding that some of the Choctaw cooperation may have been strategy to exploit missionary know-how in education and other techniques. By educating their youth in mission schools, the Choctaws might become more adequate and effective adversaries of the predaceous whites for land and other Indian properties.

In 1818 the U.S. Congress suggested that the annual payments previously made to the Indians to promote civilization by subsidizing missionaries, paying agents and annuities, and providing domesticated animals and implements should be spent to support schools among them. The following year funds were directed to establish Indian schools, and John C. Calhoun, the secretary of war, was appointed to administer the spending of these funds (Bounds, 1964:30). It was Calhoun's decision to offer a subsidy to mission schools, and as a result many were created among the Indians. By 1825 over forty mission schools had been opened to serve the Indian tribes east of the Mississippi River, of which thirteen were for the Choctaws (DeRosier, 1959:180). Most of the schools duplicated the educational program instituted at the Eliot and Mayhew missions, which were among the most successful until around 1830, when governmental support was abandoned.

The major figures promoting the establishment of schools among the Choctaws were Greenwood Le Flore, David Folsom, Cyrus Kingsbury, and Pushmataha (Bounds, 1964:31). Through their efforts the first school was opened at Eliot in 1819, with financial support coming from three areas: the federal government, the mission board, and the Choctaws themselves. Because the Eliot Mission had facilities to care for only eighty students, most of the over three hundred who applied for admission had to be turned away (DeRosier, 1959:176–77). At any rate, at the boarding school the students were taught not only basic studies, but farming, housekeeping, and a trade as well.

In October, 1820, Kingsbury opened a similar mission school at Mayhew. The operation and effect are described by DeRosier:

> They worked in the fields and taught the aborigines the latest agricultural techniques. They taught the Indians how to care for livestock and firearms, as well as how to read, write, and study the Bible. In other words, they presented a practical program that would appeal to an industrious people.
>
> The idea of practicality was also carried into the schools by the Presbyterians. They decided at the outset that such subjects as the classics, languages, and higher mathematics were not suitable for a curriculum in the Indian nation, so they concentrated their efforts on a vocational type of education. Elementary courses in English, spelling, arithmetic, and religious instruction were presented to all of the Indian students. Male students were also required to take such subjects as

farming, trading, bookkeeping, hunting with firearms, and an elementary study of American law; while the females studied cooking, sewing, spinning, knitting, and other domestic labors. Also, the missionaries required the Indian students to remain at the mission as boarding students. This was done in an effort to keep the students from returning to the old tribal habits that were practiced at home. (1959:178–79)

In addition, some adult Choctaws were taught to read and write their native language. At first the missionaries attempted to instruct the Choctaws in English; when the older Choctaws objected, the missionaries decided to learn the Choctaw language instead (Bounds, 1964:32). In fact, Cyrus Byington, with the assistance of the Folsoms, translated hymns and parts of the Bible into Choctaw, composed a Choctaw grammar and dictionary, and wrote a speller and an almanac in Choctaw (Debo, 1961:43).

In 1821 three white men, who had Choctaw families and whose children had attended the mission school at Eliot, set out to establish schools in their own neighborhoods, if the American Board of Commissioners for Foreign Missions would supply the teachers (Debo, 1961:43). Newell Station thus was created with an enrollment of fifteen students. By this program the students could live at home and still attend school. From this beginning, more neighborhood schools were established, with some of the teachers being graduates and former students of the mission schools (Bounds, 1964:32). Also of educational importance was the Choctaw Academy for boys, located in Kentucky, the result of an agreement between the Choctaws and Colonel Richard Mentor Johnson. It was in operation from 1825 to 1841.

By 1830 there were eleven schools in the Choctaw territory. Reports showed that there was a total of 29 teachers and 260 students. Some 250 adults also were being taught to read the Choctaw language at these schools. Added to these figures was the total of 89 boys at the Choctaw Academy. Consequently, during this period, the Choctaw educational system was begun, which "was to be the greatest pride of the Choctaws during all the rest of their tribal history" (Debo, 1961:45).

During this period, the Choctaws still played their traditional ball games, but they were not quite as physical or violent as they had been. They also participated as in the past in many of the same ceremonies and dances, which had undergone little change or modification.

The clan system of kinship continued in use, although it was being influenced by missionary and governmental activities. The missionaries introduced the new idea that the man, rather than the woman, was the head of the family. Thus there occurred a shift from a matrilineal to a patrilineal system of inheritance, with the effect that the clan structure was being transformed into a territorial structure.

The custom of the wife receiving no assistance during childbirth continued. Under missionary influence the children began to receive English names. The custom of head-flattening ceased to be practiced during this time (Cushman: 1899:177). Parents also began to acquire more control over the rearing and education of the children, whereas the maternal uncle had assumed this responsibility in the past. Thus the old system of family relationships was being altered.

Within the family there were several values that were admired by the missionaries. They remarked that the Choctaws respected old age and that they exhibited a tenderness toward their elderly and infirm (Cushman, 1899:95). The home was considered a sacred institution, in which the parents and ancestors were placed in high regard.

A major change in Choctaw culture involved the mourning rites, one of their most important ceremonies. Shortly after the coming of the missionaries, the practice of placing the dead upon the scaffold was abandoned, but not without much opposition. This custom was replaced by the burying of the body in a sitting position, along with several of the dead person's favorite possessions (Debo, 1961:39). A new funeral ceremony was adopted, in which "seven men were appointed whose duty it was to set up each a smooth pole (painted red) around the newly made grave, six of which were about eight feet high, and the seventh about fifteen, to which thirteen hoops (made of grape vines) were suspended and so united as to form a kind of ladder, while on its top a small white flag was fastened. This ladder of hoops was for the easier ascent of the spirit of the deceased to the top of the pole, whence, the friends of the deceased believed, it took its final departure to the spirit land." Then for a specified time the family came to the grave to weep and cry. At the end of the mourning period, the friends and relatives of the deceased gathered at the grave for a final ceremony, which consisted of a "pole-pulling" (Swanton, 1931:177, 183). All who were present indulged in a feast that officially signified the end of mourning.

Another distinctive funeral practice went out of existence at this time, namely, the custom of bone picking. Henry Halbert held that the bone-picking custom "fell into misuse in the early years of the nineteenth century" (1900:356), and George Ethridge and Walter Taylor noted that the practice lasted until the Creek War of 1813–1815 and, among the lower Choctaws, until their removal (1938:524). It is probable that some communities did abandon the practice later than others but that it was no longer used at all by the end of this period.

During the land cessions and acquisition period the Choctaws became involved in a series of treaties with the U.S. government that resulted in a progressive loss of their lands to the encroaching Americans and ultimately in their removal to western lands. Social and cultural changes began with the arrival of the missionaries, who "introduced the gospel, erected churches for worship, established schools for educating Indian youth, conducted special classes to make Indian adults literate, and set up programs of vocational education which included instruction and training in the mechanical arts, agriculture, animal husbandry, and home making" (Gibson, 1973:86). And, as Debo concludes, "It is apparent that the Choctaws' support of the missionary activities was due to their educational and economic, rather than their religious interests" (1934:45).

4

Tribal Separation and Divergence, 1831–1917

This historical period of the Choctaws begins with the enactment of the provisions in the 1830 Treaty of Dancing Rabbit Creek and ends with the dissolvement of tribal government in 1906 in Oklahoma. The movement of the Choctaws from their homeland in Mississippi and their subsequent relocation and adjustment to a new life in a new territory are examined. Attention is also paid to those Choctaws remaining in Mississippi; for them, this historical period closes in 1917 just prior to the establishment of the Choctaw Agency in Philadelphia in 1918.

Historical Events

The Treaty of Dancing Rabbit Creek was ratified on February 24, 1831. As stipulated in Article 3, "as many as possible of their people not exceeding one half of the whole number shall depart during the falls of 1831 and 1832, the residue to follow during the succeeding fall of 1833" (DeRosier, 1970:175). Under the provisions of Article 14, any Choctaw who desired to remain in Mississippi would receive allotments if he registered within six months. As Thelma Bounds states, "This is the beginning of two stories—

one is the story of the people who migrated; the other of those who remained in Mississippi" (1964:42).

A count of the Choctaw population before removal indicates that there were 19,554 Choctaws. When the removal was completed it is estimated that 12,500 had migrated, 2,500 had died, and 5,000 to 6,000 persons remained in Mississippi (McKee, 1971:129). Only about 6,000 emigrated during the first winter removal of 1831–1832, probably consisting mainly of those who were both willing and prepared to make the journey. In the second winter of removal, primarily because of increased pressure from white settlers, the number of Choctaws leaving Mississippi had risen to about 7,500 (Tolbert, 1958:57). Consequently, some 6,200 Choctaws were still in Mississippi by August, 1833, mostly those who were determined to stay. To encourage and/or persuade as many of these as possible to move to the Indian Territory (Oklahoma), removal agents traveled throughout the ceded lands during the summer and fall of 1833. Only about 900 were induced to emigrate, however, thus leaving some 5,000 Choctaws in Mississippi.

Some Choctaws began migrating in the 1820s and the latter part of 1830, before the official movements were scheduled to occur. It was their idea that by leaving early they would be able to claim the best land in the Indian Territory. According to General George Gibson, almost 1,000 emigrants wanted to move before ratification of the Treaty of Dancing Rabbit Creek (DeRosier, 1970:129). The early migration was silently sanctioned by Secretary of War Eaton, who appointed Lieutenant J. R. Stephenson to arrange for their journey. But only about 400 Choctaws departed in December (DeRosier, 1970:132).

Another preremoval event involved fulfillment of Article 14 of the treaty. Choctaws who wanted to receive a reservation in Mississippi had difficulty registering for their claims. William Ward, the agent, was strongly opposed to allowing any Indian to remain in Mississippi and delayed the registration as long as possible (DeRosier, 1970:135). Even those few persons who were able to register were often defrauded by him.

The government nevertheless moved ahead in making arrangements for the first scheduled removal proposed for the fall of 1831.

The first task was taking a thorough census, which would indicate the precise number of Choctaws eligible for removal. In late February, the census taker William Armstrong reported that the nation contained 17,963 Indians, 151 whites, and 521 slaves (DeRosier, 1970: 137). With the population identified, the government determined that the first group should consist of about 6,000 people, or approximately one-third of the nation.

The planning and preparation for the first group of emigrants began in the spring of 1831 with the removal agents—George S. Gaines in the East and Captain J. B. Clark in the West—meticulously caring for each detail of the journey. But by midsummer the organization began to show signs of confusion, as controversy and disagreements developed among the removal agents. Then, to complicate the matter, Secretary of War Eaton resigned and was ultimately replaced by Lewis Cass, who knew little about the removal, but who expressed disagreement with Eaton's efforts (DeRosier, 1970:141–42). After realizing his inability to manage the removal, especially after many incorrect personnel changes, Cass turned the project over to George Gibson. Gibson placed the removal under civilian rather than military direction, with Gaines as the field director. By October people began to be gathered for the removal.

Although the original plan was to use the overland route to the Indian Territory, unusually heavy rainfall necessitated using steamboats to transport the Choctaws as far as possible. As of November 4, Gaines had secured five steamboats, the *Walter Scott*, the *Brandywine*, the *Reindeer*, the *Talma*, and the *Cleopatra*. The Choctaws of the northeastern district consequently traveled to Memphis to the river, while the others went to Vicksburg. Again confusion surrounded the preparations, and makeshift revisions by Gaines sent the emigrants on the five boats following various routes and plans (DeRosier, 1970: 143–45).

One group from Vicksburg went north on the Mississippi River to the Arkansas River, then on to Arkansas Post, Little Rock, Washington, and the Indian Territory (Foreman, 1953:54). One group from Memphis went south to the Arkansas River and then followed the same route as the Vicksburg group to the Indian

Territory. Another Vicksburg group went south and turned up the Ouachita River to Ecore à Fabre. Another group from Memphis went south to the Red River, then up the Ouachita to Ecore à Fabre (DeRosier, 1970:144). Captain L.T. Cross, while at Ecore à Fabre, learned that still another group was stranded at Lake Providence. He eventually brought them to Ecore à Fabre via Monroe. From Ecore à Fabre, the route went to Washington, Arkansas, then north along Little River to the Indian Territory (Fig. 7). Figure 8 shows the physiography of the removal route.

Much of the journey was marred by misery and suffering, particularly because the cold and severe weather caused much sickness and death. Finally, at the beginning of March, 1832, five months after they had left Mississippi, all the parties arrived in the Indian Territory. On April 30, Lieutenant Stephenson reported that 3,749 Choctaws were located at four stations: Fort Towson, Horse Prairie, Old Miller Courthouse, and Mountain Fork (DeRosier, 1970:147). Thus, the first stage of the removal was complete, with many of the Choctaws sick, tired, and discouraged in their new land.

The War Department considered the first removal a failure, especially financially. As a result, George Gaines and the other civilians were released from their duties, and the project was made the responsibility of the U.S. Army. Under the new organization, Captain William Armstrong was appointed agent east of the Mississippi River and Major Francis W. Armstrong served as agent west of the Mississippi. Preparations began for the second removal in August, 1832, and by September it appeared that more than 9,000 Choctaws wanted to emigrate. But by October less than two-thirds that number (5,317) actually signed up for relocation (DeRosier, 1970:149–50, 153).

At the outset, the second removal seemed to be progressing rather well—the planning had been better, the people were in good spirits, and the supplies were adequate. But a cholera scare spread panic throughout the emigrating parties, and several parties experienced heavy rainfall. In spite of the inconveniences and disruptions, 5,538 Choctaws arrived in Indian Territory in January and

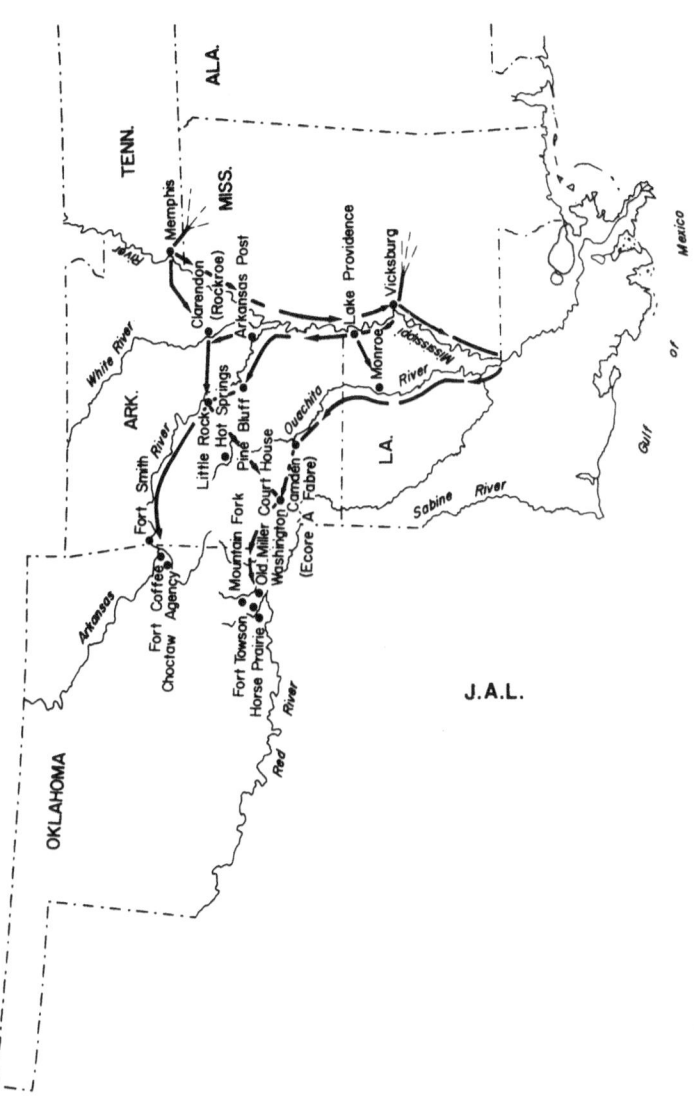

Figure 7 Major Choctaw Removal Routes. SOURCE: After Foreman, 1953, and De-Rosier, 1970

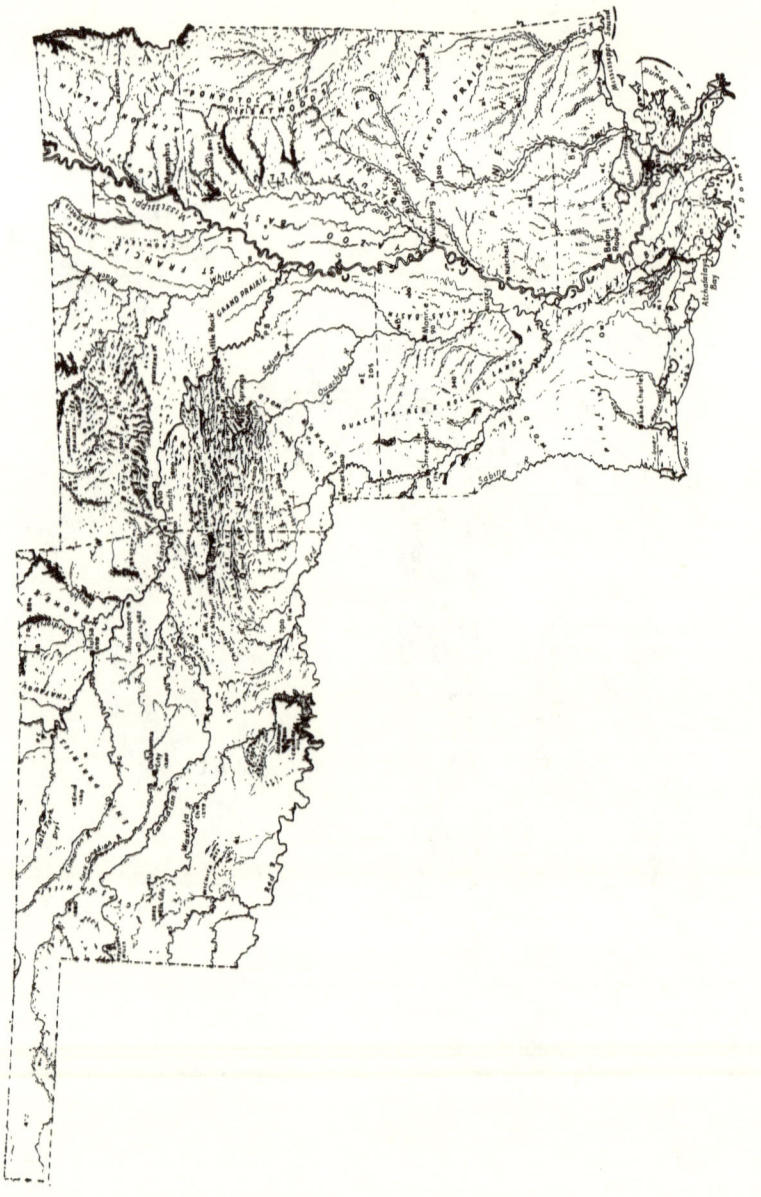

Figure 8 Physiography of Removal Areas. SOURCE: After Raisz, 1957

February, 1833, of which 1,000 had made the journey independently (DeRosier, 1970:157–58).

Plate 6 Site of the Treaty of Dancing Rabbit Creek in Noxubee County, Mississippi. Burial sites, mostly of children, surround the stone marker. COURTESY *Choctaw Community News*

Memphis and Vicksburg were again departure points. From Memphis one group went by land to Rockroe and another went by boat down the Mississippi and then north on the White River to Rockroe. From Vicksburg the emigrants traveled north by steamboat to Rockroe. From Rockroe the Choctaws traveled overland to Little Rock, then followed the Arkansas River to Fort Smith and on to the Indian Territory. Others left Little Rock and went southwest to Fort Towson (DeRosier, 1970: 155–57).

With the second removal accomplished, the War Department began preparing for the third and final removal under the treaty of 1830. The removal agents, however, had difficulty getting commitments from any of the more than 6,000 Choctaws remaining in Mississippi. In fact, only 813 left Memphis in October for the

Plate 7 A characteristic river scene during Indian removal, taken from an early print. From *Indian Removal: The Emigration of the Five Civilized Tribes of Indians*, by Grant Foreman. Copyright 1932, 1953 (new edition), and 1972 by the University of Oklahoma Press

Plate 8 Remains of the Choctaw "Trail of Tears" at Washington, Arkansas

Plate 9 Cypress swamp in Arkansas through which the Indians struggled for thirty miles frequently up to their waists. COURTESY Jas. E. Thompson Company, Knoxville, Tenn.

Plate 10 Cypress swamp in Arkansas today

Indian Territory, where they arrived by December 20, 1833 (DeRosier, 1970:161–62). Like those before them, they left Memphis, went south on the Mississippi River, then north on the White River to Rockroe, then west to Little Rock, and arrived finally in the Indian Territory. This small group was followed by emigrants who journeyed on their own after the beginning of 1834. Thus, between 1831 and 1834, some 12,500 Choctaws had been relocated to the new territory. The U.S. Senate declared that the total cost of removal and subsistence was $813,927 and that the total cost of meeting all the provisions of the Treaty of Dancing Rabbit Creek was $5,097,367.50 (DeRosier, 1970:163). For the sale of the ceded Choctaw lands to white settlers the United States government received $8,095,614.89, or a profit of $2,998,247.39. But this profit was turned over to the Choctaws in a "net proceeds" case in federal court, and most of it then went to lawyers' fees. The Choctaws not only were removed from their homeland, but also paid for this removal themselves.

The new land in the West originally secured by the Treaty of Doak's Stand was bounded on the north by the Canadian and Arkansas rivers, and on the south by the Red River. Encompassing an area of 20,000 square miles, it was situated between 94.5 degrees and 98 degrees west longitude. A small section in the southwest was in dispute with Texas (Fig. 9).

Permanent settlement in Choctaw Indian Territory from 1831 until 1855 was in three general areas (Fig. 10): in the northeast along the Poteau and Arkansas rivers; in the southeast along the Little River and its tributaries and along the Red River; and in the west along the Kiamichi River and westward, plus settlement near the Red River (Wright, 1951:105). With a new constitution written in 1834, these were organized into three districts (Fig. 11). To the west a fourth district, the Chickasaw District, was established in 1837; Choctaws could also settle there. Some of the early towns to spring up were Boggy Depot, Skullyville, Eagletown, Perrysville, and Doaksville, which was the largest (Debo, 1934:59).

After the initial shock of removal had lessened, the Choctaws began to adjust and prosper in their new lands. In addition to a new constitution in 1834, they signed the Treaty of Doaksville in 1837

Historical Events 85

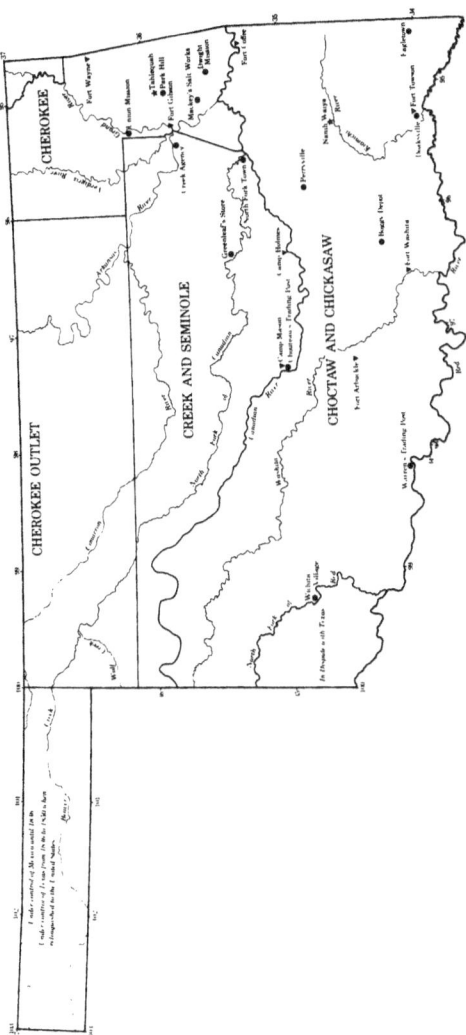

Figure 9 Indian Territory, 1830–1855, From *Historical Atlas of Oklahoma*, Second Edition, by John W. Morris, Charles R. Goins, and Edwin C. McReynolds. Copyright 1976 by the University of Oklahoma Press

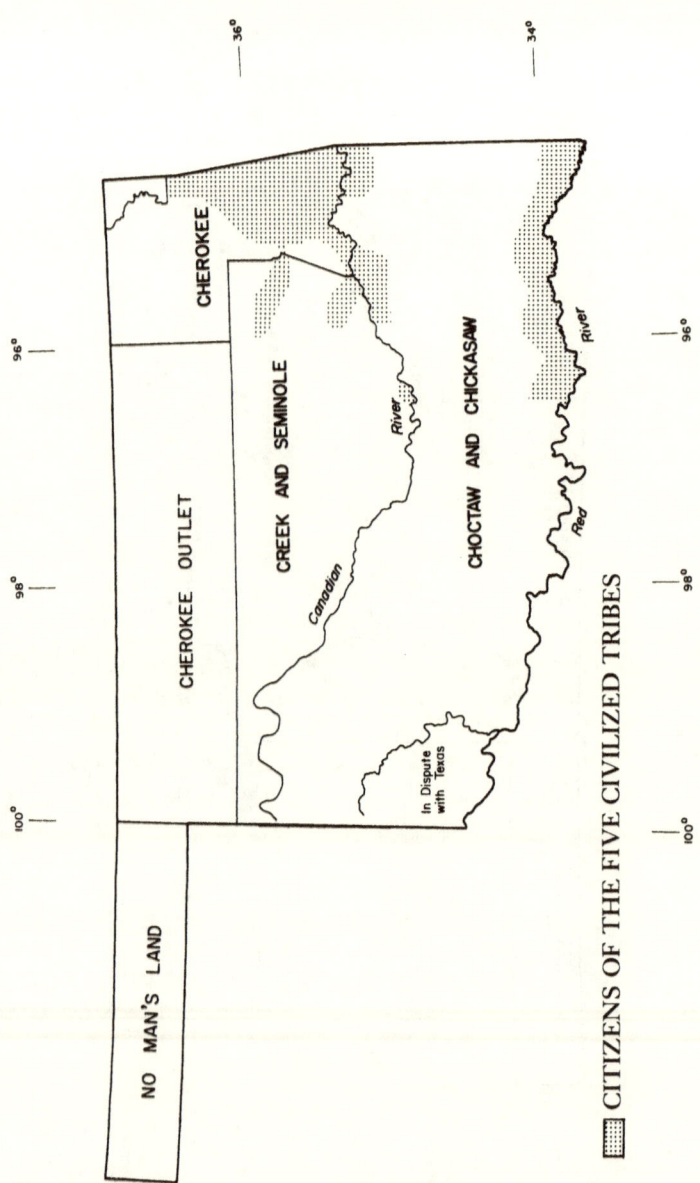

Figure 10 Settled Area to 1845. SOURCE: After Doran, 1976

Figure 11 Choctaw Districts. SOURCE: After Debo, 1961

with the U.S. government, which relocated the Chickasaws in the western part of the Choctaw Nation in Indian Territory (Gibson, 1973:89). The Treaty of 1855, signed by the Choctaws, the Chickasaws, and the U.S. government, separated the Chickasaw from the Choctaw (Debo, 1934: 71; Fig. 12). Figure 13 shows the Choctaw population density in 1855.

The 1840s were marked by renewed attempts to induce the remaining Indians to leave Mississippi. In 1845 Congress passed an act providing for the issuance of scrip for one-half the claims remaining, with scrip for the other half to be received upon arrival in Oklahoma (Tolbert, 1958:65). Between 1845 and 1854 some 5,700 Choctaws left Mississippi for the Indian Territory.

The Choctaws drew up a new constitution in 1838 and modified it in 1843. Because of the difficulty amending it, in 1860 they adopted a new constitution that provided for the retention of the district organization with its district chiefs. It also represented a democratic form of government consisting of a national government, a principal chief, executive officers, a general council of two houses, and a supreme court (Debo, 1934:74, 75). This constitution was the fundamental law of the Choctaw Nation until dissolvement of the tribal government in 1906.

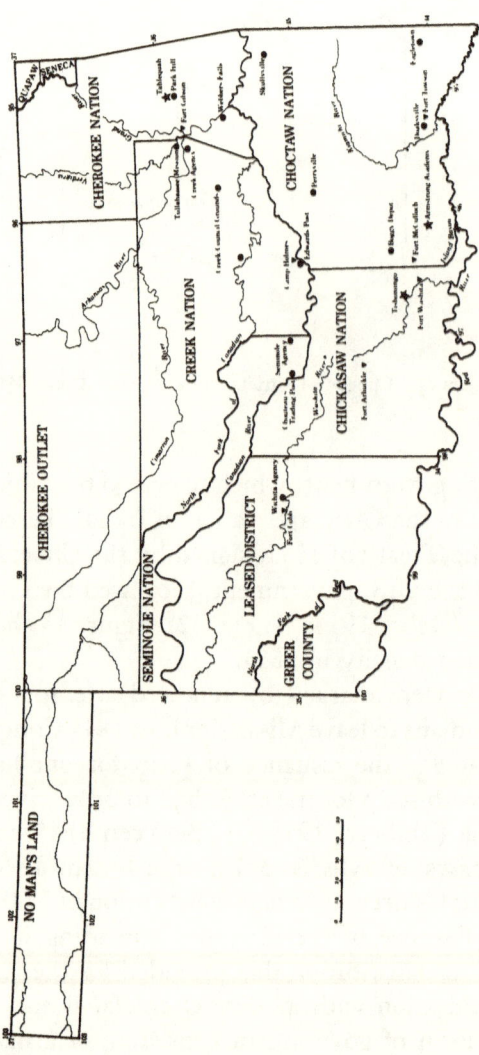

Figure 12 Indian Territory, 1855–1866. From *Historical Atlas of Oklahoma*, Second Edition, by John W. Morris, Charles R. Goins, and Edwin C. McReynolds. Copyright 1976 by the University of Oklahoma Press

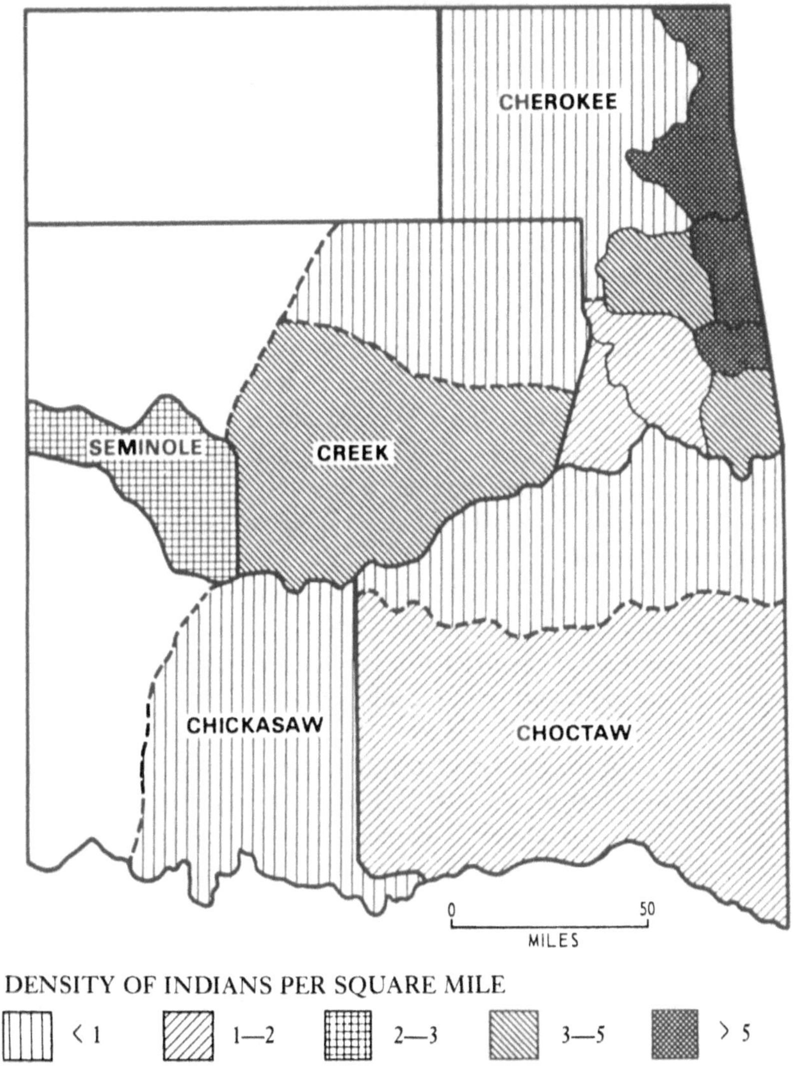

Historical Events

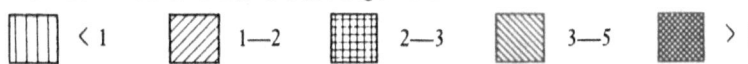

Figure 13 Five Civilized Tribes in Indian Territory, circa 1855. SOURCE: Roark, 1976

The first tribal council was held on the Jacks Fork, near the Military Road that went from Fort Smith to Horse Prairie. A large, log council house was erected here in 1837, and the capital was named Nanih Waiya (Wright, 1951:105). During these early years the Choctaw capital was moved from there to Doaksville, Skullyville, Fort Towson, and Boggy Depot (Debo, 1934:76). In the fall of 1863 the council met at Armstrong Academy and established it as the capital with the name Chahta Tamaha. Then in 1883–1884 a brick capitol was constructed at Tuskahoma, about two miles northeast of old Nanih Waiya (Wright, 1951:105).

In 1861 the Choctaws signed a treaty with the Confederacy and during the Civil War supported the Confederate cause. When the South lost, the Choctaws requested assistance from the U.S. government to protect them not only from white intruders, but also from Unionist Indians. This brought about the Treaty of 1866, which established peace and allowed tribal government to continue. The Choctaws geared themselves to rebuild their nation, but the war obviously had caused a major break in economic continuity and development.

From 1840 until the Civil War has frequently been referred to as the "golden years" for Indians in Oklahoma. During this time the Choctaw and other Civilized Tribes were basically left alone by the U.S. government and white immigrants.

According to Michael Doran, the population of the Choctaw Nation in 1860 comprised 13,666 Indian citizens (81 percent), 804 whites (5 percent), and 2,349 black slaves (14 percent), for a total of 16,819. The Choctaw national census of 1867 also is helpful in determining the number of persons in the Choctaw Nation. "In 1867, the Choctaw summary of the census recorded native population resident within fourteen of the sixteen counties extant at that time totaling 13,161 persons" (1975–76:501, 509). Michael Roark (1976:13), after checking the *Roll of 1867*, has the Indian population (mostly Choctaws) totaling 14,237 (Table 2). Figure 14 shows the spatial density of the population in 1867.

After the Civil War, white immigration increased. Coal mining began near McAlester and later in the vicinity of Lehigh. The Missouri, Kansas & Texas Railroad was constructed in 1872, and

Table 2 CHOCTAW CITIZEN CENSUS OF 1867				
County	Indian	Intermarried Whites	Black Freedmen	Total
Atoka	1,089	9	85	1,183
Blue	1,609	17	258	1,884
Boktucklo	713		71	784
Cedar	900		33	933
Eagle	944	3	136	1,083
Gaines	541	3	33	577
Jacks Forks	1,009	2	53	1,064
Kiamitia	1,606	13	245	1,864
Nashoba	648	1	35	684
Red River	872	2	273	1,147
San Bois	578	1	24	603
Skullyville	1,003	33	186	1,222
Sugar Loaf	710	5	3	718
Tobucksy	398	4	56	458
Towson	1,119	9	265	1,393
Wade	498	2		500
Total	14,237	104	1,756	16,097

SOURCE: Roark, 1976

three other railroads were built within the next twenty years (Wright, 1951:109). Thus, economically, the Choctaw Nation was developing. At the same time white immigration and intermarriage increased.

In general, after 1866 and particularly after 1868, freedmen "were treated as United States citizens, and were therefore rendered the criminal jurisdiction of the Federal district court at Fort Smith and entirely outside any civil jurisdiction." For nearly twenty years after the Treaty of 1866, however, the legal status of freedmen was not clearly defined. Finally, in 1883, "the Choctaws passed a law adopting their freedmen." This law stated that all former slaves were to be granted the rights, privileges, and immunities, including the right to vote, of citizens of the Choctaw Nation, "except in the annuities[,] moneys, and the public domain" of the nation (Debo, 1961:102, 105). Freedmen declining to become citizens were subject to removal.

The Choctaw census of 1885 shows a population of 12,816

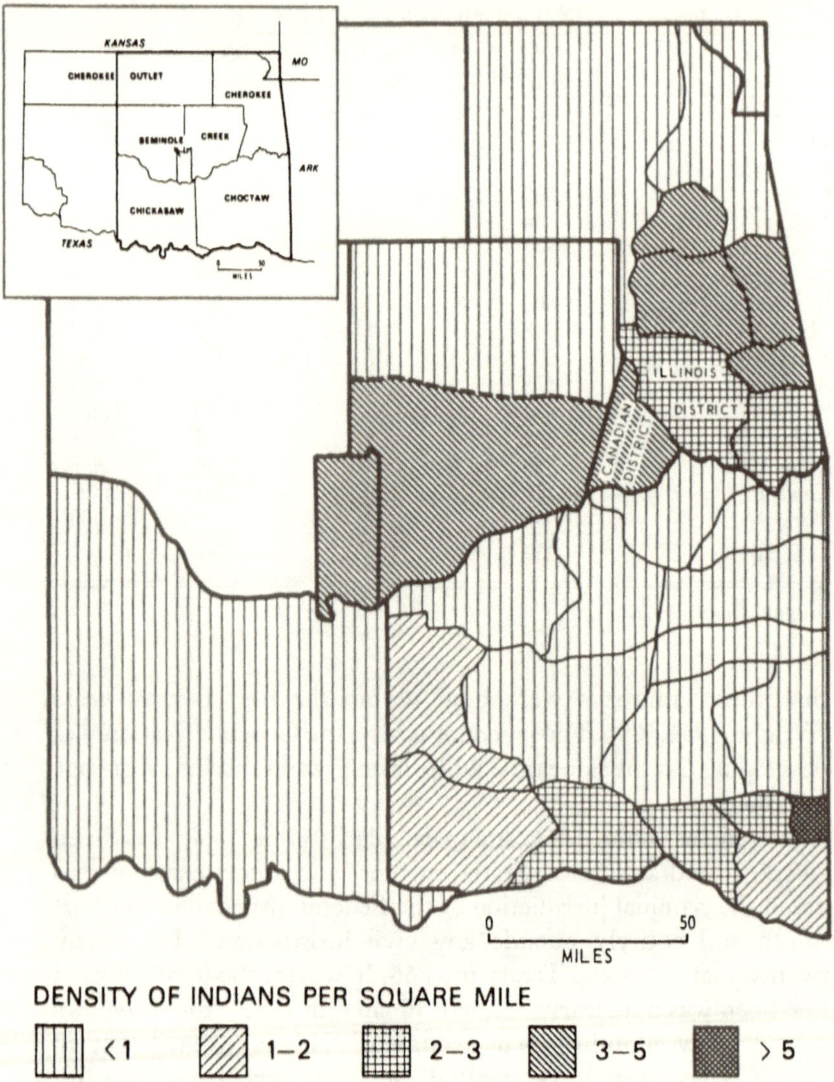

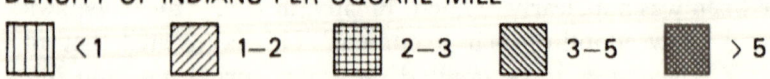

Figure 14 Five Civilized Tribes in Indian Territory, circa 1867. SOURCE: Roark, 1976

Table 3 CHOCTAW CITIZEN CENSUS OF 1885

County	Indian	Intermarried Whites	Black Freedmen	Total
Atoka	1,160	70	17	1,247
Blue	1,647	90	3	1,740
Boktucklo	327	1		328
Cedar	555			555
Eagle	742	2		744
Gaines	687	11	4	702
Jacks Forks	697	6	1	704
Kiamitia	1,188	55	7	1,250
Nashoba	792		5	797
Red River	804	4		808
San Bois	726	38		764
Skullyville	738	26		764
Sugar Loaf	856	35		891
Tobucksy	838	83	1	922
Towson	470	6		476
Wade	589			589
Totals	12,816	427	38	13,281

SOURCE: Roark, 1976

Indians, 427 intermarried whites, and 38 black freedmen for a total of 13,281 (Table 3). In 1890 the Indian citizen population in the Choctaw Nation totaled 11,057; 32,751 were counted as non-Indian citizens (Doran, 1975–76:511). Figure 15 shows the population density of the Choctaw Nation in 1890.

The Allotment Act (Dawes Act) was passed by Congress in 1887 preceding the creation of the Dawes Commission in 1894 (Wright, 1951:110). The act was intended to break up Indian reservations into individual allotments and to open the surplus land to white settlement. But many Choctaws were opposed to allotment of lands. The major purposes of the Dawes Commission (actually authorized by the president in 1893) were to encourage the abandonment of Indian self-government among the Five Civilized Tribes in Oklahoma in order to clear the way for Oklahoma statehood and to induce Choctaws still east of the Mississippi River to migrate to Oklahoma. In 1897 Congress ordered the commission to determine whether the Mississippi Choctaws qualified as Choctaw citizens (Peterson, 1970a:91).

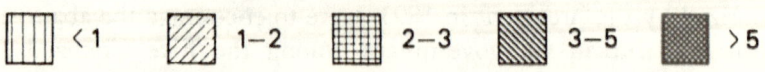

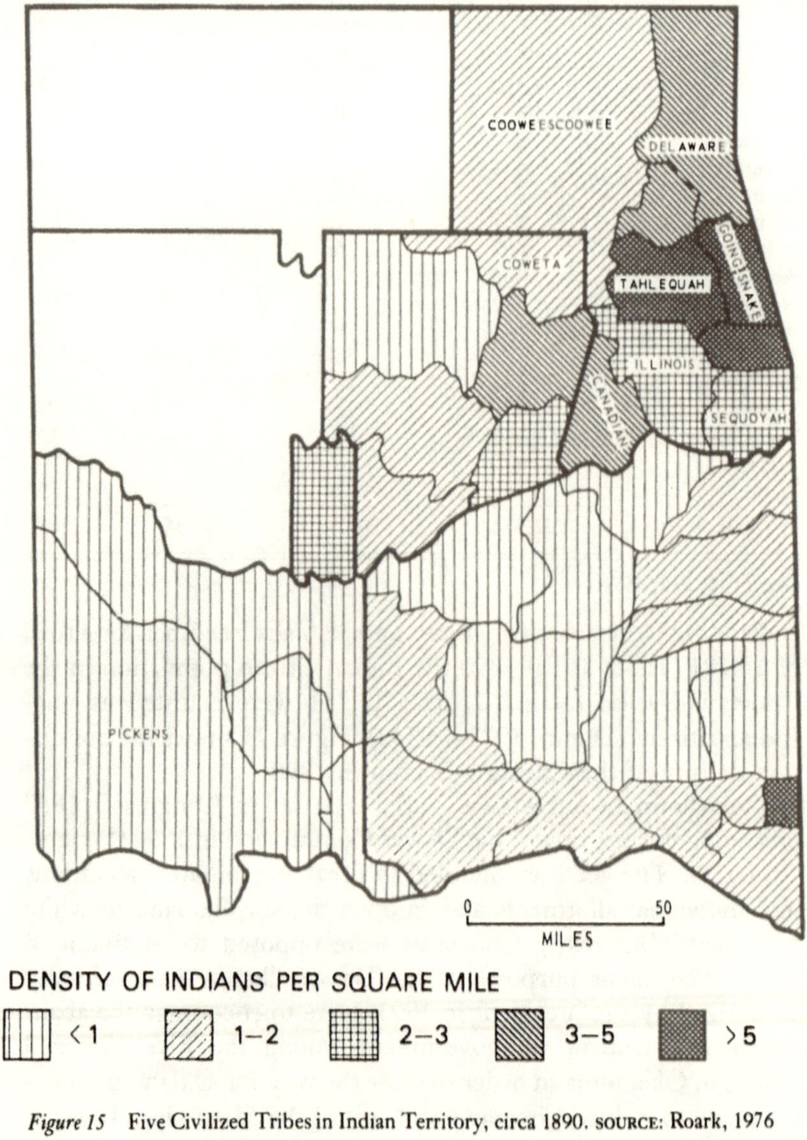

Figure 15 Five Civilized Tribes in Indian Territory, circa 1890. SOURCE: Roark, 1976

The commission had little success with allotment and determination of eligibility enrollment until the signing of the Atoka Agreement in 1897. This agreement provided for a fair allotment of land to each enrolled Choctaw and Chickasaw and for the deeding of all tribal lands to the United States. The Curtis Act of 1898 established the manner in which the Atoka Agreement should be ratified (Debo, 1934:262), as well as a time limit for the existence of the Choctaw government. The act basically stated that the tribal government was to be dissolved in 1906 and provided for a more rigorous identification of those eligible for enrollment on the tribal roll and for land allotment. To be eligible, Choctaws, even those remaining in Mississippi, had to take up residence in the Choctaw Nation. Still, problems existed in determining citizenship. Therefore a supplemental agreement was negotiated and signed by the president in 1902. This discussed the rights of Mississippi Choctaws and further determined eligibility for citizenship rolls (Wright, 1951:111).

In 1901, one year prior to the supplemental agreement, Congress granted United States citizenship to every Indian in the territory. Of course the Atoka Agreement had set citizenship as a future goal. Finally, in 1906, the tribal government of the Choctaw was dissolved. At that time the Choctaw population consisted of 18,981

Table 4 CHOCTAW POPULATION, 1906

Oklahoma Choctaws		
Full bloods	7,076	
Mixed bloods, three-fourths or more	706	
Mixed bloods, one-half to three-fourths	1,636	
Less than one-half, including whites	9,563	
Total		18,981
Freedmen		5,994
Mississippi Choctaws		
Full bloods	1,344	
Mixed bloods, three-fourths or more	85	
Mixed bloods, one-half to three-fourths	27	
Less than one-half, including whites	183	
Total		1,639
Grand Total		26,614

SOURCE: Debo, 1961

Oklahoma Choctaws and 1,639 Mississippi Choctaws, for a total of 20,620 in Oklahoma and Mississippi (Table 4). In Oklahoma, full bloods and mixed bloods of one-half or more Choctaw amounted to 9,418 persons. In Mississippi, these persons numbered 1,456.

The period 1831–1918 was a trying time for those who chose not to migrate and remain in Mississippi. From the end of removal until 1854 the Choctaws tried to exercise their rights to land claims designated to them in Article 14 of the Treaty of Dancing Rabbit Creek, but the federal government through Colonel Ward was recalcitrant about registering legitimate land claims by Choctaws. As early as 1829, the Mississippi legislature had declared Choctaw Indians to be citizens of Mississippi, and by 1830 "tribal governments were abolished, all rights under tribal laws were revoked." The rights of Choctaws to be Mississippi citizens was further clarified in the Treaty of Dancing Rabbit Creek. Thus, those Choctaws remaining in Mississippi were attempting only to enact the provisions of the 1830 treaty. It appears, however, that representatives of the government were working to ensure the migration of full bloods to the Indian Territory and to encourage only mixed bloods who could more easily assimilate into Mississippi society to remain. Since only sixty-nine heads of Choctaw families (only thirty family heads were full bloods) were recorded and transferred by Colonel Ward to the War Department as intending to remain in Mississippi, the land claims of many Choctaw families remained unregistered (Peterson, 1970a:13, 17, 19).

Because of the confusion over land titles, Congress in 1845 issued scrip that encouraged Choctaws to migrate to Oklahoma. Statistics show that 1,182 Choctaws left Mississippi for the new Choctaw Nation in 1845. Subsequently in 1846, 1847, and 1849, respectively, 1,768, 1,623, and 547 persons left for the Indian Territory (Peterson, 1970a:24). In 1853 and 1854, 500 more made the long trek westward. These figures total 5,720 persons, leaving approximately only 1,000 Choctaws in Mississippi in 1854. Since there were about 5,000 Choctaws in Mississippi in 1833, natural population increase together with reverse migration help to explain the population growth during this twenty-one year period.

Presumably only the hard-core Choctaws resistant to migration remained, and their history is hard to trace between 1855 and 1879. Peter Folsom, a Baptist missionary who in 1879 came to the Mississippi Choctaws from the Choctaw Nation in the Indian Territory, recorded some of this history. It is assumed that most Choctaws lived as squatters and eked out a rather poverty-stricken existence.

The time from 1879 to 1903 is thought in some ways to be a reawakening period primarily because of contact with missionaries, some of whom were Choctaw. It is also a period of economic transition, when Choctaws changed from living as squatters to living as sharecroppers (Peterson, 1970a:57). Although some Choctaws were skeptical of the returning missionaries, fearing it would result in another removal, the missionaries were instrumental in setting up institutions, such as churches and schools, which were sorely needed after years of neglect.

The next period, 1903 to 1918, is frequently referred to as the second removal and its aftermath. In 1903, in accordance with the Dawes Commission and the supplemental agreement, the final move of Mississippi Choctaws to the Indian Territory took place. Congress made an appropriation to assist full-blooded Choctaws in removal (Bounds, 1964:45). The Choctaws considered in this removal were from thirty counties in east-central Mississippi, but mostly from Neshoba, Kemper, Winston, Lauderdale, Newton, Leake, and Scott counties. By June 30, 1903, the commission had identified 1,738 Mississippi Choctaws eligible to receive land allotments and entitled to other rights of Choctaw citizenship in the Choctaw Nation (Beckett, 1949:46). More than 20,000 other persons were refused Choctaw citizenship. By the end of June, 1904, 508 additional persons were identified as being "full-blood Mississippi Choctaws." Thus, a total of 2,246 Mississippi Choctaws were identified as being eligible for Choctaw citizenship. However, not all of these registered claimants journeyed west. But on August 13, 1903, "a special train arrived at Atoka Indian Territory with [264] full-bloods" (Beckett, 1949:46). In addition, 26 identified full-blooded Mississippi Choctaws were removed to Fort Towson, Indian Territory, on October 9, 1903.

By the end of June, 1905, the commission identified an additional 394 Mississippi Choctaws eligible for the citizenship rolls. Of the total 2,640 persons registered, only 1,639 were certified for entry on the final roll because they migrated and took up residence in the Choctaw Nation. Thus 1,000 to 1,500 Choctaws remained in Mississippi. The 1910 census for Mississippi indicates that there were 1,253 Indians in Mississippi, most of these obviously Choctaw. "By 1907 the second removal of the Choctaws was completed" (Beckett, 1949:48).

When Oklahoma achieved statehood in 1907, the Bureau of Indian Affairs then shifted its interest to the Mississippi Choctaws. A special agent was sent by the commissioner of Indian affairs to Philadelphia, Mississippi, in 1908 to report on conditions (Bounds, 1964:53). Another agent was sent to Mississippi in 1916. Both reports drew attention to the poor health, lack of education, and low economic status of the Mississippi Choctaws. In 1918 an influenza epidemic struck, causing many Choctaw deaths, perhaps as many as several hundred (Choctaw Agency, n.d.: 5) The two investigations and the epidemic brought attention to the plight of the Mississippi Choctaws, who were living mainly in Neshoba, Leake, Newton, Scott, Jones, Winston, and Noxubee counties (Bounds, 1964:53). Then, in 1918, the U.S. Senate established the Choctaw Indian Agency of the Bureau of Indian Affairs at Philadelphia, Mississippi.

It should be noted that some Choctaws remained in Louisiana. Dominique Rouquette has been one of the few persons to write about these Choctaws during the nineteenth century. While the Dawes Commission was working in Mississippi to encourage final migration west, some Louisiana Choctaws were moved westward. Not all of them migrated, however, and many of their descendants remain in such parishes as Terrebonne and Lafourche.

Choctaw Culture

Removal of the Choctaw Indians to Oklahoma represents the most disruptive event in their history. Old traditional ways of doing things were rapidly replaced by new and different ways of life. These changes were especially apparent in their religious, educational, economic, political, and familial institutions. Those Choctaws who migrated to the new Indian Territory were not only geographically dislocated, but were socially and culturally dislocated as well. Even those Choctaws who remained in Mississippi were not isolated from major disruptions to their way of life.

In Mississippi in 1830, the three district chiefs were Greenwood Le Flore of the northwestern or western district (Upper Towns), Moshulatubbee of the eastern or northeastern (Lower Towns), and Nitakechi of the southern or southeastern (Six Towns). After removal, those of Le Flore's district were to settle on the east side of the Kiamichi River, those of the southern district were to settle on the west side of the Kiamichi, and those of the northeast district were to settle in the northern part of the new Choctaw country along the Arkansas River (Wright, 1929:396). In Mississippi the three districts had been largely based upon clans; but during removal the people within the different clans were separated, and therefore the three districts in the Indian Territory had Choctaws belonging to different clans. This disruption helped to dissolve the clan system.

Once in the Indian Territory the three districts were given names. The northern district along the Arkansas and Canadian rivers was called the Moshulatubbee District. The southwestern district was called Pushmataha, and the southeastern district bounded by Arkansas on the east, the Kiamichi River on the west, and the Red River on the south was called Oklafalaya or Red River District, though it was later changed to the Apukshunnubbee District (Wright, 1929:396).

From removal to 1861, the Choctaw record in Oklahoma is one of orderly development in government, agriculture, and early towns and villages. Schools and missions were opened, and by 1836 "eleven schools enrolled 238 children" (Jordan, 1976:32).

As stated before, most of the Choctaws were recorded in the Indian Territory at Horse Prairie, Fort Towson, Mountain Fork, Old Miller Courthouse, and the Choctaw Agency. The establishment of post offices indicates settlement patterns. Some of the early post offices were at Miller Courthouse in 1824, Fort Towson in 1832, Choctaw Agency in 1833, Eagletown in 1834, Fort Coffee in 1835, Spencer Academy in 1844, Wheelock in 1845, Doaksville in 1847, and Boggy Depot in 1849 (Foreman, 1928:5). Doaksville, near Fort Towson, consisted mainly of white traders in the early years (Foreman, 1934:26).

Most of the early villages, if not near a railroad when the railroads were constructed in the latter part of the nineteenth century, became rather insignificant. Most of the settlements throughout the tribal government periods were concentrated near the river valleys. Small-scale ranchers and farmers occupied the hill country. With the coming of the railroads, the opening of the mines, and the utilization of the timber resources, many new towns sprang up in association with these economic activities (Fig. 16).

During this period the exogamous moieties and clans became nonexistent. The largest recognizable kinship unit became the bilateral family of immediate kin members (Spoehr, 1947:196). In addition, matrilineal descent gave way to patrilineal descent, in which the inheritance of personal property was derived from the father rather than from the maternal uncle.

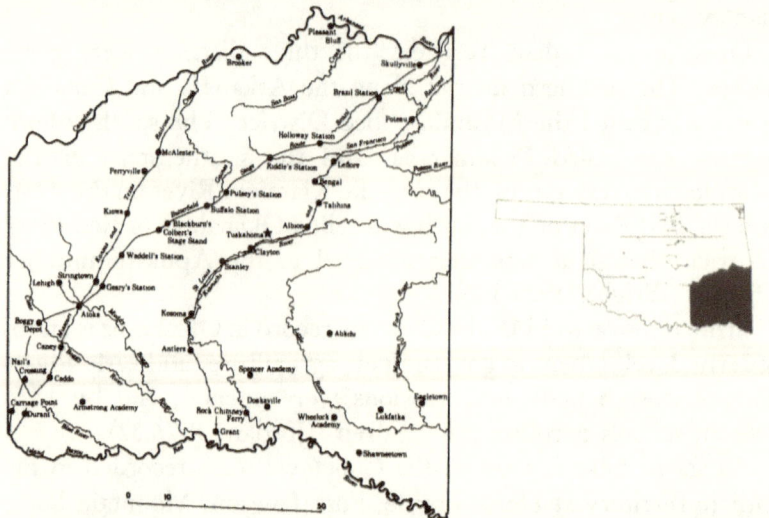

Figure 16 Choctaw Nation: Important Places. From *Historical Atlas of Oklahoma*, Second Edition, by John W. Morris, Charles R. Goins, and Edwin C. McReynolds. Copyright 1976 by the University of Oklahoma Press

Plate 11 First Choctaw chief's house in Oklahoma Territory

Plate 12 Red River

Plate 13 Giant cypress tree, a favorite council place of the Choctaws. Largest tree in Oklahoma, west of Eagletown. COURTESY of Western History Collections, University of Oklahoma Library

Plate 14 Eagletown, an early Choctaw town

Plate 15 Eagletown today

Plate 16 Doaksville, capital of the old Choctaw Nation in Indian Territory 1851–1860, was on its way to oblivion when this picture was taken, for its prinicpal businesses consisted of the above: a blacksmith shop on the far left and a barber shop in the tent on the right. The large building in the center appears to have been a store, as the sign on the front advertises "Your money back if you don't like Best Tobacco." Clothing worn by the men suggests that this picture was made about 1890–1900. COURTESY Oklahoma Historical Society

Plate 17 Remains of downtown Doaksville

Plate 18 Remains of Fort Towson

Plate 19 Marker of early Choctaw town

Plate 20 Skullyville cemetery

For the decades following removal, John Peterson offers a general outline of Choctaw social organization in Mississippi (1970a:34–36). During this period the local residence groups of the Choctaws consisted of "one or more closely related extended families." These groups were connected through marriage to other nearby groups into "local communities" of fifty to one hundred persons. There were three main forms of social interaction among members of the different local groups. The first consisted of informal visiting between related households, which was the most prevalent kind of social interaction in the Choctaw community, as it had been in the past. Another major form of social interaction occurred at the time of family celebrations, such as births, marriages, and deaths. The last type was the taking part in nonfamily activities, such as stickball games and dances. Despite this social interaction within Choctaw groups, the groups tended to be scattered. This separation partially explains why there are distinguishable differences in the way Choctaw is spoken in the various Mississippi Choctaw communities today.

Shortly after their arrival in the new territory, the Choctaws adopted a new constitution on June 3, 1834. The tribal council met "at the crossing of the military road from Fort Smith to Horse Prairie, on the Jacks Fork, where a commodious log council house was erected in 1837" (Wright, 1951:105). This first seat of government was called "Nvnih Waya"[1] (Nanih Waiya). It was about two and one-half miles southwest of the present capital Tuskahoma.

> Under the provisions of the constitution of the Choctaw Nation, each of the three political districts was governed by a chief elected every four years by the people of his district, the incumbent being eligible to succeed himself for a second term only. The General Council, or legislative body, consisted of the three chiefs and twenty-seven council members who were chosen in annual elections by the people in each district and trial by jury was guaranteed, the jurors being selected in the ordinary way. The fourth, or military department was composed of a general, elected by the people, and thirty-three captains from each district, the latter having been chosen under the provisions of the fifteenth article of the Treaty of Dancing Rabbit Creek (Wright, 1929:396).

Because the Choctaws and Chickasaws were related ethnologically, government officials urged that the Chickasaws settle in the western part of the Choctaw country. The two tribes were united by the Treaty of Doaksville in 1837. Choctaw signers were Thomas Le Flore of the Oklafalaya (Apukshunnubbee) District, Nitakechi from Pushmataha, and Joseph Kincaid from Moshulatubbee. But constitutional changes had to be made in 1838. Problems later developed over finances and geographical distribution of the population, which involved representation. So additional changes were required in 1843:

> From that time, the General Council was made up of two branches, a senate and a house of representatives. Each district had an equal number of senators. Members in the lower house of the Council were chosen in annual election upon the ratio of one representative for every one thousand inhabitants, an additional member being allowed for a

---

[1] Nvnih Waya is from the Choctaw words *nunih* meaning "mountain," and *waya* meaning "to produce," literally, the "mountain that produces" (Wright, 1929:396–97).

fractional number of five hundred or more inhabitants. All officials in each district were to be selected from the citizens living within its boundaries. (Wright, 1929:400)

In 1850 additional changes were made in the constitution with regard to the judicial system:

> The judicial power of the Nation was vested in a supreme court, district circuit courts, and county courts. The General Council, by a joint vote, elected four supreme judges, one from each district, every four years; it likewise elected four district judges every two years. The Supreme Court had appellate jurisdiction only, under such regulations as were prescribed by law. It met once a year at the capital of the Nation, usually during the session of the General Council. The District Circuit Court had original jurisdiction over all criminal cases in the district, not otherwise provided for by law; exclusive original jurisdiction over all crimes amounting to a felony, and original jurisdiction in all civil cases not cognizable before the county judges. District Court was held four times a year in each district. . . .
> . . . The whole nation was divided into nineteen counties, each of which had a judge, elected by the people every two years, and an inferior court that took cognizance of all minor offences, tried cases in which the amount did not exceed fifty dollars, and held the preliminary trials in criminal cases. It also had jurisdiction in all matters relating to disbursement of money for county and district purposes. All cases tried by the county courts could be appealed to the higher court in the usual order. The nineteen counties, according to districts were: Mosholatubbee District, Skullyville, Sugar Loaf, Sans Bois, and Gaines Creek counties; Apukshunnubbee District,—Wade, Nashoba, Eagle, Red River, Bok Tuklo, Towson, and Cedar counties; Pushmataha District,—Kiamichi, Tiger Spring, Jacks Fork, and Shappaway counties; Chickasaw District,—Panola, Wichita, Caddo, and Perry counties. (Wright, 1929:403–04)

In 1854 Tiger Spring County was changed to Blue County, Shappaway became Atoka, and Tobaksi was created in the Moshulatubbee District (Fig. 17).

Further problems developed because the Chickasaws thought they had too few representatives and very little power in influencing elections or holding office (Wright, 1929:401). In 1855 two

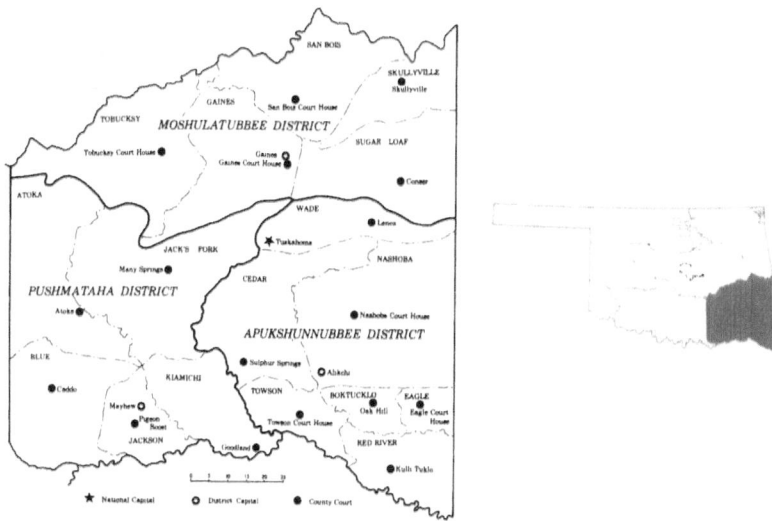

Figure 17 Choctaw Nation: Political Divisions. From *Historical Atlas of Oklahoma*, Second Edition, by John W. Morris, Charles R. Goins, and Edwin C. McReynolds. Copyright 1976 by the University of Oklahoma Press

treaties were signed, one between the Choctaws and Chickasaws and the other among the Choctaws, the Chickasaws, and the United States (Bonnifield, 1973:386).

> Four leading issues were involved in these negotiations. The Government sought a relinquishment from the Choctaws of all their claims to any territory west of the hundredth meridian. It also wished to secure a lease from the Choctaws and Chickasaws of all their common territory between the 98th and 100th meridians for the settlement of other Indian tribes thereon. The Chickasaws demanded that a separate district be assigned them where they could establish their own government. The Choctaws held out for a settlement of their Net Proceeds claim from the United States. (Wright, 1929:408)

With this treaty the Choctaws lost a large amount of land to the west originally ceded to them by the United States. Land between the ninety-eighth and hundredth meridians was leased to the U.S. government for settlement of the Wichita and other Plains tribes (Bonnifield, 1973:386). The building of railroads and telegraph lines across the Choctaw Nation was also provided for.

Just prior to the Civil War, the Choctaws were thinking about becoming a state in the Union. But would they be a free or slave state? The idea of Indian statehood inspired the Choctaws to write a new constitution more in line with those found in the United States. Twenty-eight delegates, meeting at Skullyville, produced a new constitution in 1857. It provided for judicial, executive, and legislative divisions of government and incorporated a bill of rights. "The constitution established the office of governor, thus abolishing the title of principal chief and the offices of district chiefs. Representation in the house and senate was based on population and counties; thus, the traditional Choctaw districts were eliminated" (Bonnifield, 1973:395). The constitution recognized slavery as lawful, but stated that slaves should be treated humanely. The Choctaw people, however, were opposed to the new constitution, with the most intense resistance coming from Doaksville and Blue County. Because of this opposition, a new constitution was drafted at Doaksville in 1860.

The Doaksville constitution reinstated the title principal chief instead of governor. Moreover, districts and district chiefs were reestablished (Bonnifield, 1973:395). Legislative, judicial, and executive branches remained intact. The General Council of the Choctaw Nation still comprised a senate and a house of representatives. Members were elected from the counties. The judicial system had a supreme court, circuit courts, and county courts. Executive power was vested in the principal chief and three district chiefs. Their terms were for two years, and they were eligible for only two terms in succession (Wright, 1929:413). Different from the Skullyville constitution, the 1860 document made no provisions for humane treatment of slaves. Land west of the ninety-eighth meridian, known as "leased land" or the "leased district," was named Hotubbee District, but is was never formally organized.

Powers of the district chiefs were weakened. For example, district chiefs would provide a list of nominees for appointment as light horsemen, but the principal chief would grant commissions (Bonnifield, 1973:397). This constitution remained basically unaltered until tribal dissolvement in 1906.

No neutral solution of the slave question was possible. The Doaksville constitution, which was different from the more liberal one at Skullyville, pushed the Choctaws closer to the Confederate States of America. In 1861 the Choctaws signed a treaty with the Confederacy, which admitted the Choctaw Nation into the Confederacy on equal terms with the other states (Bonnifield, 1973:386).

Although some Choctaws fought in Arkansas and Missouri, most of their fighting was done inside their own territory. The Choctaws were most loyal to the Confederacy. One of the most serious battles was at Perryville in 1863, when federal troops destroyed a store containing Confederate supplies (McCullar, 1973: 464). Other battle sites were Backbone Mountain in 1863, Muddy Boggy in 1864, and Boggy Depot in 1865 (Morris and McReynolds, 1965:Map 25).

Several months after Appomattox, Chief Peter Pitchlynn finally issued a proclamation calling for peace with the U.S. government. A treaty was signed in 1866. "Amnesty for war offences was granted, slavery abolished, and provision made for freedmen" (McCullar, 1973:464, 468). Also included were plans to organize all Indian tribes into the territory of Oklahoma (Wright, 1951:108). Land was to be divided in severalty, and each tribal member "was to be given one-quarter section of land" (McCullar, 1973:469).

The Choctaw capital changed several times between the first site at Nanih Waiya and the final site at Tushkahoma (Tuskahoma).[2] In 1850 the capital was located at Doaksville, later it moved to Boggy Depot, and in 1863 Armstrong Academy was made the capital and was known officially as Chahta Tamaha. Finally, in 1883, in an area just a few miles east of old Nanih Waiya, a new capitol was built. The building was made of brick, three stories high with a mansard

[2]*Tushkahoma* means "red warrior," *tushka* meaning "warrior" and *homa* meaning "red" (Wright, 1931:30).

roof, at a cost of over $25,000. The St. Louis & San Francisco Railroad was constructed in 1887 about two miles south of Tuskahoma because the Choctaws had refused the company a monetary bonus to locate in the town. Therefore, the town was forced to move closer to the railroad station (Wright, 1931:35–36, 37, 39).

Congress passed the Dawes Act (Allotment Act) in 1887, providing for the breakup of Indian lands into individual allotments and opening up the surplus land to white settlement. Later the Dawes Commission was created to liquidate the affairs of the Choctaws and the other Civilized Tribes. At Atoka in 1897 the Choctaws made an agreement with the Dawes Commission, but the Curtis Act in 1898 provided for compulsory liquidation of the Choctaw Nation within eight years. On November 16, 1907, Oklahoma was admitted to the Union as the forty-sixth state (Fig. 18).

The Mississippi Choctaws had written their first constitution in 1826, prior to removal. At the Treaty of Dancing Rabbit Creek, they held out for the insertion of Article 14. "Although early estimates place 5,000 Indians as the number of Choctaws who remained in Mississippi, only 143 heads of families for a total of 276 persons ever received lands under ARTICLE 14." In 1842 Congress established a commission "to adjudicate the claims of the Mississippi Choctaws" (Davis, 1932:258). Problems had ensued because the Mississippi Choctaws were located primarily in an area 350 miles long and 150 miles wide, which many white settlers were claiming by squatter's right (Bounds, 1964:47–48). "Claimants who should have received land under ARTICLE 14 of the treaty of 1830 were to receive land scrip in lieu of lands." By an act approved by Congress in 1845, scrip was issued for one-half the claims at $1.25 per acre (Davis, 1932:258, 259). "The other half was retained by the government and an annual interest at the rate of five per cent was to be paid to the claimants." Thus, after fifteen years of controversy "the legal battle over the 'Choctaw Claims' in Mississippi ended." (Bounds, 1964:51).

But this period (1831–1918) for the Mississippi Choctaws was a dark one. After 1866, "surrounded as these Choctaws were by poverty, ignorance, and neglect, they lost their interest in the Western Choctaws and the Indian Territory lands." Of course,

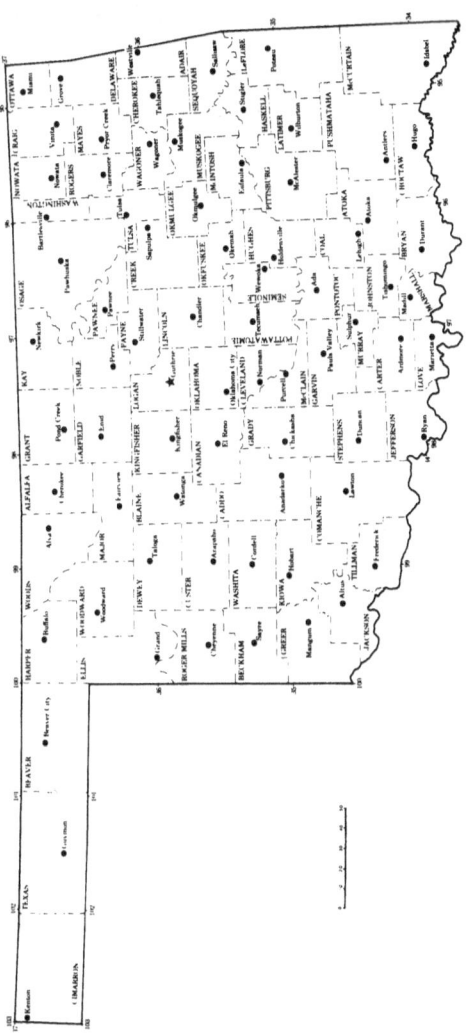

Figure 18 Oklahoma Counties, 1907. From *Historical Atlas of Oklahoma*, Second Edition, by John W. Morris, Charles R. Goins, and Edwin C. McReynolds. Copyright 1976 by the University of Oklahoma Press

when the Dawes Commission was created, it consistently held the view that Mississippi Choctaws should be removed. In 1906 tribal citizenship rolls were closed, and 1,639 Mississippi Choctaws were enrolled (Davis, 1932:260, 265). Continued migration of Mississippi Choctaws from removal to the time of Oklahoma statehood is evident by this figure, which shows a drop of more than 3,000 Choctaws from the 5,000 who originally stayed in Mississippi at the time of removal.

In summary, it is evident that many changes in the political organization of the Choctaws occurred between removal and Oklahoma statehood. However, their nation for the most part was always divided into three districts. Continued contact with the U.S. government and white immigrants caused considerable acculturation. The Choctaws kept modifying and modeling their political organization closer to that of the United States. This position is best stated by Debo: "In the background of Choctaw control of government, courts, and finance, was the supervising authority of the United States. The relationship was that of a protectorate, and was based upon the complicated system of treaties" (1961:194).

For those in Mississippi it was not a pleasant period. Land claims and continued pressure to migrate to Oklahoma persisted. Yet through all this the Mississippi Choctaws survived, and the establishment of an agency in 1918 was the dawn of a new period. But for all practical purposes their political institutions were dismantled in 1830, and they became citizens of Mississippi. Therefore, there was not much organized political activity in Mississippi during this time.

As in previous periods, the Choctaws continued to be primarily an agricultural people, both those who remained in Mississippi and those who migrated. The Oklahoma Choctaws, however, increased their ranching activities, particularly in cattle and horses. The floodplains of the Arkansas, Red, and Kiamichi rivers provided fertile land for farming. Despite lack of equipment, floods along the Arkansas River, and other problems, the Choctaws in the fall of 1833 had a surplus of 40,000 bushels of corn, which were sold to the government to aid new Choctaw immigrants. By 1836 "the Choctaw agent reported that almost all the tribesmen had well

Plate 21 Building once used as temporary council house at Nanih Waiya, near Tuskahoma. COURTESY Oklahoma Historical Society

enclosed fields of corn, potatoes, peas, beans, pumpkins and melons." The corn surplus of 50,000 bushels that year went primarily to Fort Towson. Environmental factors aided in the adoption and growing of cotton in the southern portion of the nation, particularly along the Red River. It is estimated that 500 bales of cotton were shipped down the Red in 1836. The hillier central regions of the territory were more conducive to raising cattle and sheep. But it is evident that the Choctaws had agricultural skills originally acquired in Mississippi and that they easily transferred them to the Indian Territory. "By 1840 the Nation could boast many large farms, three grist mills, three cotton gins, and an abundance of agricultural implements" (Graebner, 1945a:235, 236).

Plate 22 Remains of the site of the first Choctaw council house near Tuskahoma

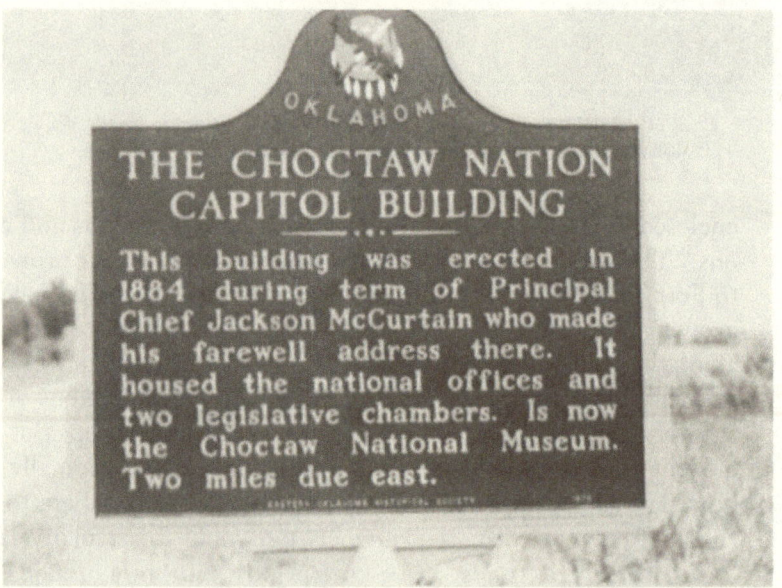

Plate 23 Choctaw capitol building historical marker

Plate 24 Sign at entrance to Choctaw capital

Plate 25 Choctaw capitol building now a museum

Plate 26 Old Town—Tuskahoma Cemetery

Plate 27 Tuskahoma Post Office

Plate 28 Choctaw Light Horsemen. COURTESY Western History Collections, University of Oklahoma Library

Plate 29 Last Choctaw Tribal Council, 1905, Tuskahoma. COURTESY of Western Oklahoma Collections, University of Oklahoma Library

In 1836 the Choctaw General Council passed resolutions concerning the position of slaves, and codes increased with the growth of slave population. Teaching of abolition was prohibited, slave children were not to be educated or to sing in public places, and slaves could not carry arms. Freed slaves, as of 1841, were expected to leave the Choctaw Nation (Bonnifield, 1973:391, 392). Population figures show that by 1839 there were 600 slaves among the Choctaws (Graebner, 1945:241). By 1860 there were 2,297 slaves and some 385 slave owners in the Choctaw Nation (Bonnifield, 1973:391). Little slavery existed in the hillier region, where farms were small and where there was little need for additional labor. As expected, slaves were abundant in the cotton-growing areas, particularly along the Red River. R. M. Jones, probably the wealthiest Choctaw, owned 227 slaves in 1860 (some authorities say that he might have had as many as 500 at one time). Jones held five plantations, the largest being 4,000 to 5,000 acres. He also had

Plate 30 Peter P. Pitchlynn, member of delegation of 1853. Painting by Charles Fenderich, 1842. COURTESY Library of Congress

trading interests in Doaksville and owned several steamboats (Graebner, 1945a:242). The average slaveholder, however, probably had six slaves (Bonnifield, 1973:391).

On the eve of the Civil War it was evident that the Choctaws, as well as the other Civilized Tribes, had made tremendous achievements in agriculture. Corn remained king, but oats, rye, wheat, cotton, peas, potatoes, pumpkins, and turnips were grown (Graebner, 1945a:248). Even pecans were exported. There were several orchards, in which pear, apple, peach, and plum trees predominated. Most farmers had domesticated stock; horses, working oxen, cattle, sheep, hogs, and domestic fowl were prevalent. Some stockmen had fine herds of horses, cattle, and sheep. Thus the Choctaws had experienced three decades of pioneer agriculture in the Indian Territory.

After the Civil War, many changes occurred; and, with increased white settlement, the Choctaws were assimilated even more into the Anglo culture. The discovery of gold in California in 1848 had increased the transient traffic via three main roads through the Choctaw Nation. Boggy Depot became prominent in this westward movement. Before the war, telegraph lines had been constructed, and in 1858 the Butterfield Overland Stage route had opened through the Choctaw Nation. "There were twelve stage stations, about six miles apart, in the Choctaw Nation" (Bonnifield, 1973:391).

An accepted practice among the Choctaws was the communal landholding system. Title to the land was considered unimportant since all land was public domain for use by Choctaw citizens. Of course, some of the best land was held by a small percentage of the people and often by those of mixed blood. Agriculture and ranching finally approached normality by 1876. Yet, judged by modern standards, the yields per acre were quite low. Statistics shortly after the war indicate that yield in cotton was slightly less than one-fifth a bale an acre, and grain averaged a "little more than 8 bushels per acre." Potatoes were introduced, and barley, beans, and hay were being reported in various statistical reports. In 1873 approximately 50,000 acres were in cultivation (Morrison, 1954:74, 75).

Barbed wire was introduced in the 1870s, but the disappearance of the open range did not occur until the late 1880s and early 1890s. Until the coming of the Missouri, Kansas, & Texas Railroad (M. K. & T., or Katy) in 1872, the economy of the Choctaw Nation was predominantly agricultural and pastoral. Few towns of any size existed. Three additional rail lines were constructed within the next twenty years. With the coming of the railroads most of the old villages became ghost towns, whose inhabitants moved to new sites along the railroad lines (Fig. 19). "Doaksville became the nearby town of Fort Towson, Skullyville disappeared into Spiro, Boggy Depot became Atoka, Perryville's inhabitants moved to McAlester" (Morrison, 1954:83). Railroads assisted in the opening of coal mines. Shortly after the M. K. & T. reached McAlester, coal mining began. The Osage Coal & Mining Company was one of the first to operate in the nation, along with the Choctaw Coal & Mining Company (Choctaw Coal & Railway Company). Names of some of the largest veins averaging two to six feet in depth were the

Choctaw Culture

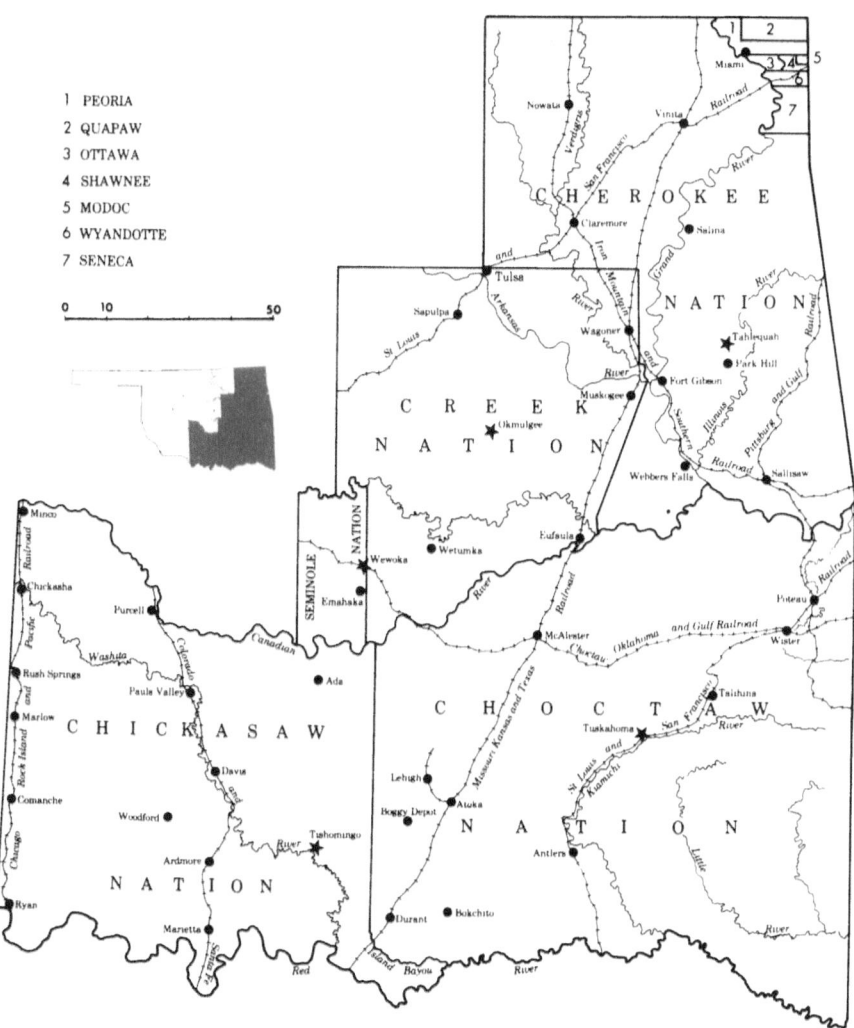

Figure 19 Indian Territory, 1889. From *Historical Atlas of Oklahoma*, Second Edition, by John W. Morris, Charles R. Goins, and Edwin C. McReynolds. Copyright 1976 by the University of Oklahoma Press

McAlester, Lower Hartshorne, and Lehigh (Morrison, 1954:84). Asphalt deposits also figured in the economy in association with coal. Mining camps sprang up, and white settlers increased. The twin cities of McAlester and Krebs and of Lehigh and Coalgate grew rapidly. According to the census of 1890, McAlester and Krebs each had 3,000 inhabitants; "Caddo, 2,170; Lehigh, 1,600; Hartshorne, 939; Coalgate, 818; and Atoka, 800" (Debo, 1934:223). Mining population in 1889 was about 2,000, "composed largely of Europeans—Czechs, Slovaks, Slovenes, Hungarians, Belgians, Germans, Frenchmen, Englishmen, Swedes and Italians" (McReynolds, 1954:268). Within five years this number had doubled, and American miners from eastern coalfields and black miners from Texas had joined the ethnic groups. By 1907, fifty mining companies were operating, and "more than 3,000,000 tons of coal were mined in that year from eleven different veins" (Morrison, 1954:84). The heyday for coal mining occurred between 1903 and 1922.

Another important natural resource that attracted a number of whites was timber. Osage orange was recognized early for its toughness and elasticity. Small sawmills existed in pre–Civil War times, but the railroads accentuated the exploitation of the Choctaw Nation's forests. With the coming of the railroad, Stringtown became an early lumber center. The number of sawmills increased to between fifteen and twenty, and they supplied telegraph poles, fence posts, staves, bridge timber, railroad ties, pickets, mining timber, and other lumber for building construction (Morrison, 1954:87, 88).

Oil and gas did not play a major role in the prestatehood years. One of the first wildcat wells, however, was drilled in 1885 near the Boggy River about twelve miles west of Atoka (Debo, 1934: 131; Morrison, 1954:86).

Back in Mississippi, the Choctaws tended to live as squatters on government land (Bounds, 1964:52). Sometimes they located in small colonies consisting of several hundred persons who inhabited huts or tents. Mostly they farmed small parcels of land, hunted, fished, and made articles, such as cane baskets, bows and arrows, and blowguns, to sell to the white settlers. The Choctaw women contributed to the family income by gathering herbs and weaving baskets (Peterson, 1970a:46). The men also produced items such as tool handles, hominy pounders, and throwing sticks to be used for barter or sale. Still another form of economic pursuit was wage labor, in which the men worked for neighboring planters as cotton pickers, firewood cutters and gatherers, and field clearers. Many Choctaws lived on the less desirable land, usually hilly or swampy. In all, it was a desperate and gloomy time economically for the Mississippi Choctaws.

Plate 31 Landscape near Atoka, Oklahoma

In summary, economic changes through this period of Choctaw history are quite evident. In Oklahoma an agricultural and pastoral economy was drastically changed by the railroads, mining was introduced, and the influx of non-Choctaws continued. In Mississippi, Choctaws experienced slower changes in their economic development, though Anglo incursion upon them in many instances was unmerciful.

Plate 32 Kiamichi landscape

Choctaws were interested in education and the elimination of illiteracy. Many Choctaws had studied at the Choctaw Academy in Scott County, Kentucky, prior to removal. This academy, which was established and operated "under the provisions of the Treaty of 1825," produced many leaders (McReynolds, 1954:170). Education and religion were often combined in the early schools and missions of the Choctaw Nation in the Indian Territory.

In 1832 Alfred Wright founded Wheelock Mission. Other early prominent schools and missions (Fig. 20) were Pine Ridge (Chuahla Female Seminary), Stockbridge, Goodwater, Spencer Academy for boys, Fort Coffee for boys, Armstrong Academy, New Hope for girls, and Goodland (Dale and Wardell, 1948:144–46). Bethabara was another early mission. Cyrus Byington, Ebenezer Hotchkin, Alfred Wright, Cyrus Kingsbury, Alexander Talley, and Isaac McCoy were important early missionaries. Most of them represented the Presbyterian, Methodist, or Baptist faith. Of course, many of these schools and missions did not really get moving until after passage of the Education Act in 1842 (McReynolds, 1954:172). Spencer Academy was probably the leading school in the Choctaw Nation in 1843. Besides boarding schools, several neighborhood schools were established. Some early ones in the Moshulatubbee District were Skullyville, Holetushi, Lupta Bok, Pine Grove, San Bois, and Stephen Holson (Parke and LeFlore, 1926:149–52).

The tribal council and the missionaries combined their efforts into a program to provide education to adult Choctaws, who received instruction in elementary arithmetic and were taught to read and write the Choctaw language (Debo, 1961:61–62). The adult Choctaws nevertheless were pleased that their children were learning the English language, so regular school classes were conducted in English.

Thus, as early as 1842, the Choctaws had created a school system controlled by the tribal council (Benson, 1860:60–62). A board of trustees was formed with a member from each district, who was responsible for the creation of a neighborhood school in his district and for the appointment of teachers. The board of trustees acted with the various missionary groups in the operation of boarding schools. In 1853 the office of superintendent of schools was initiated to preside over the board (Debo, 1961:63).

"By 1860, there were nine boarding schools plus neighborhood schools which furnished educational opportunities to approximately nine hundred students" (Bonnifield, 1973:389). Although missionary education was important, Choctaw education by the middle 1850s was beginning to move away from it somewhat. By the end of the nineteenth century some mission schools had closed or moved and new ones had been opened (Fig. 21). In 1892 the Tuskahoma Female Institute was constructed, and Peter J. Hudson was placed in charge. That same year the Jones Academy for boys was built near Hartshorne (Debo, 1932:387).

As Oklahoma statehood neared, the organization of the educational system was drastically modified. The school system passed out of tribal control, the district trustee's office was abolished, and the superintendent's position was discontinued. "Under the new regime the boarding schools became vocational schools for the training of fullbloods, and the neighborhood schools soon became a part of the public school system of the new state of Oklahoma" (Debo, 1932:391).

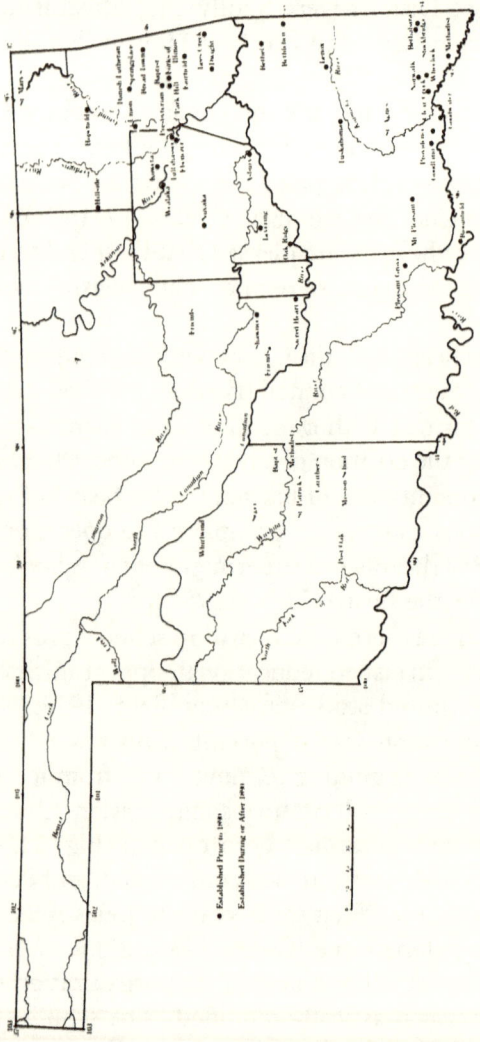

Figure 20 Missions in Oklahoma. From *Historical Atlas of Oklahoma*, Second Edition, by John W. Morris, Charles R. Goins, and Edwin C. McReynolds. Copyright 1976 by the University of Oklahoma Press

Choctaw Culture 129

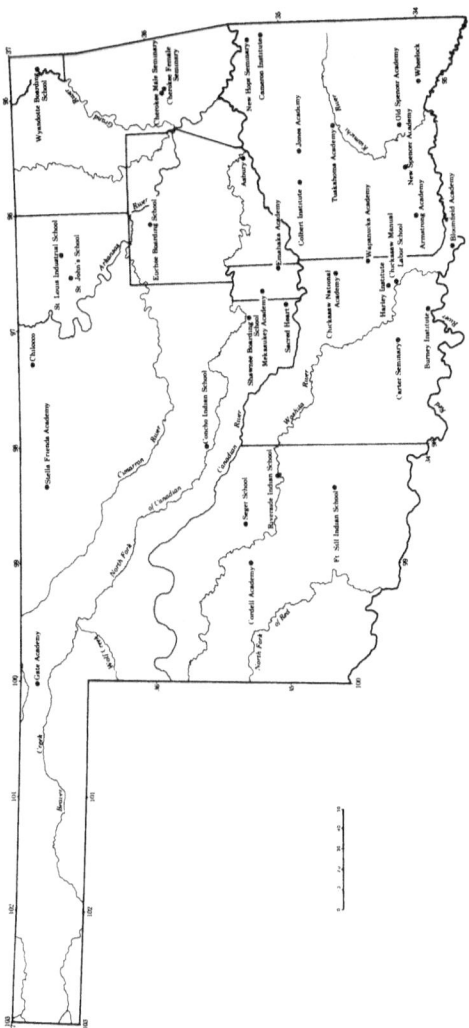

Figure 21 Oklahoma Academies. From *Historical Atlas of Oklahoma*, Second Edition, by John W. Morris, Charles R. Goins, and Edwin C. McReynolds. Copyright 1976 by the University of Oklahoma Press

Missionaries who worked among the Choctaws in Oklahoma were entitled to homesteads under the provisions of the Treaty of 1866. Because many whites soon began to take advantage of this provision by disguising themselves as missionaries, in 1876 a law was enacted providing for the expulsion of such persons. In 1881 another law was enacted, which permitted missionaries who were conducting only religious work to enter the Choctaw Nation if they possessed credentials from some board or church or from missionaries already in the territory. At any rate, the effect of the missionaries was seen in the regulations and laws passed regarding Sunday observance (Debo, 1961:229–31). In 1853 gambling on the outcome of horse races and ball games was declared illegal, and in 1873 it became unlawful to use a gun or a dog while hunting.

In Oklahoma, most Choctaws initially were Presbyterians and Methodists because of the early missionary work conducted by these denominations. But the Baptists entered the nation in 1858 and, under the Reverend J. S. Murrow, conducted successful work among the Choctaws. Then, in 1875, the first Catholic church was established at Atoka by Father Robot, with parishes at McAlester, Sacanna, Lehigh, and Krebs following soon afterward. Member-

TABLE 5 CHURCH MEMBERSHIP, 1890

	No. of Organizations	No. of Members
Southern Baptist	56	2,388
Catholic	7	735
Church of God	1	50
Congregational	4	90
Disciples of Christ	27	512
African Methodist Episcopal	6	320
Colored Methodist Episcopal	13	291
Methodist Episcopal	6	125
Methodist Episcopal South	97	2,312
Methodist Protestant	6	110
Cumberland Presbyterian	27	597
Southern Presbyterian	11	454
Northern Presbyterian	28	548
Total	289	8,532

Source: Debo, 1961

ship, totaling 8,532, of the various religious groups was reflected in the 1890 federal census (Table 5).

Increased missionary activity during this period affected the burial ceremonies. The "funeral cry" of the past was lessened to the shedding of a few tears at the time of death, and the burial occurred simply and quietly (Debo, 1961:229). On an appointed day, friends and relatives gathered at a feast, and religious services were conducted in a church or under a tree. After a eulogy, the group retired to the grave, where a "cry" took place. The other religious gatherings also were held in groves or in log churches, where the church members sang, prayed, and preached.[3]

Edwards (1932:418–19) describes the funeral ceremony of the Choctaws during the middle of the nineteenth century as follows:

> Grave-yards are coming into use; but the general practice is to bury at home. The interment takes place, as soon as the coffin and grave can be prepared. Occasionally now they wait a day.
>
> After burial they have a mourning season, during which, according to the old way, the hair is not dressed, nor the face nor clothes washed, nor do they marry. Objection has been made to friends' joining the church during that time. Every evening the bereaved go to the grave, sit or prostrate themselves by it, cover their heads, and spend a season in most bitter wailings. At other times, when friends go to the house, like Lazarus' sisters' friends, they go together to the grave to weep there.
>
> The mourning season lasts from a month to a year, according to circumstances, or to fancy. It has gradually lessened. At the end of it comes the funeral, or cry, or ai akshuchi, time of doing away, as they call it. Formerly poles were set up about the grave, which were pulled up at the cry, and the shade, which lingers till then about the grave, was driven away. This has ceased.

---

[3] As late as 1941 a modified form of the cry still existed near Boswell: Here in a modified form is still followed the old custom of holding a Funeral Cry twenty-eight days after the burial of a Choctaw. Formerly on the day of the burial, the surviving head of the family cut twenty-eight small sticks representing the duration of the lunar month, and each morning one stick was taken from the bundle and broken. When only seven sticks remained, he sent invitations to kinsmen and friends to come for the cry on the day the last stick was broken. Each family brought its own provisions of corn meal, flour, beef, and vegetables and camped near the burying ground. The Cry began with the recital by a close relative of the good qualities of the deceased, and as he proceeded the mourners, gathered around the grave with heads covered, started to cry. This ceremony sometimes lasted several days. In bad weather, it was held in the church, lighted at night by candles" (Oklahoma Writers' Project, 1941:318).

> Formerly it was a season of mirth and revelry, drinking and dancing, in connection with the cry. Now more frequently sermons are preached.
> The people generally meet the evening before and camp. A large amount of food is prepared to feed the company. Sometimes they have a sermon in the afternoon or evening. At 10 or 11 o'clock the next day, a sermon is preached, after which all go to the grave. The relatives, especially the women, sit about the grave, cover and wail, calling out the name of the relationship, as mah, svsoh mah, svsoh mah, oh my son, my son. A hymn is sung, a prayer offered, and the benediction pronounced. In a little while dinner commences. The people in successive companies sit around the table spread in the open air and then disperse.

After removal, the Mississippi Choctaws continued to be the target of conversion by the various missionary groups, but "it seems doubtful if any significant numbers of Choctaws were converted by white ministers." Although some may have been Christians and others may have been converted by white ministers, the major portion of Mississippi Choctaws were not Christians as late as 1883 (Peterson, 1970a:62). Halbert (1900:365) concurs that it was in the 1880s that Christianity began to gain a substantial hold among the Choctaws. With this adoption of Christianity the Choctaw communities again experienced major changes.

In the 1880s churches in Choctaw communities were reestablished. One such church was formed in 1884 at Tucker in Neshoba County by the Catholic Diocese of Natchez, under the direction of Father Bekker, a missionary from Holland. A Catholic school and church were maintained here with a membership of over 600 Choctaws. Thus, once again the church served as both a religious and an educational agency. In 1898 and 1899 the Methodists founded churches in Talla Chula community in Kemper County, Conehatta community in Newton County, and Phillips Chapel and Black Jack community in Neshoba County (Choctaw Agency, n.d.:4–5). But once again, as in the 1820s, a conflict arose between the Choctaws' desire to participate in their ball games and dances and the missionaries' desire for church attendance (Peterson, 1970a:70).

Plate 33 Holy Rosary Indian Mission at Tucker, Mississippi. COURTESY *Choctaw Community News*

Plate 34 Wheelock historical marker

Plate 35 Remains of Wheelock Academy

Plate 36 Wheelock Church, oldest church building in Oklahoma

Plate 37 Armstrong Academy at Bokchito, renamed Chahta Tamaha and used as capitol of Choctaw Nation, 1863–1883. COURTESY Oklahoma Historical Society

Plate 38 Remains of Armstrong Academy

Plate 39 Choctaw Female Seminary, Tuskahoma, Oklahoma. COURTESY of Western History Collections, University of Oklahoma Library

Choctaw Culture

Plate 40 Tullock-Chisk-Ko (He-who-drinks-the-juice-of-the-stone) Champion Choctaw ball player in 1834, by Catlin. COURTESY Smithsonian Institution

Plate 41 Choctaw Ball Play Dance at Skullyville by Catlin, 1834. COURTESY Smithsonian Institution

Charlie Beckett, doing fieldwork in 1946, interviewed Cemeron Wesley, chief of the more conservative Mashulaville group of Choctaws in Noxubee County, and found that many characteristics of the ancient funeral customs still persisted.

> About two days after death, the deceased is buried with a simple ceremony. One month after burial, the funeral is held. Between the time of burial and the funeral the family of the deceased return daily to the grave of the departed member to mourn. After the funeral another month is designated as the cry. During this month the relatives may go either to the home of the dead, or to the home of the chief. The big cry is at the end of the thirty days set aside for the cry. It is always in the chief's yard late in the afternoon and followed by an all-night dance. The husband or wife of the deceased may remarry after six months. The more advanced Choctaws of this area have funerals just as the White people about them. (1949:26-27)

In addition, there were some Choctaws in Kemper County who still practiced the cry "three or four weeks after burial" (Deweese, 1957:66).

During the remainder of the nineteenth century the participation of the Oklahoma Choctaws in their traditional dances and ceremonies declined. The members of the community got together with less frequency and less regularity than they had in previous periods. Even the ball game became modified, though it remained the favorite amusement. Henry Benson (1860:153–55) observed that everyone in the community continued to express much interest and enthusiasm in the ball game, particularly when the play was between communities or districts. Gambling was also associated with their stickball games. Edwards (1932:412), describing the Choctaw dances in the middle 1800s, stated that "the movement seems to be a kind of stamping trot around a circle, to the music of a violin." Men also played marbles, and "ride the bullet" was one of their popular games. Betting was frequently connected to marble games. In Mississippi, Choctaw stickball games and dances tended to persist as popular forms of recreation.

In the middle of the nineteenth century Benson (1860:50–55) recorded the individual characteristics of the Oklahoma Choctaws:

> The Choctaws were quiet and peaceful among themselves, and no less so in their bearing and intercourse with neighboring tribes. They were ordinarily temperate in their habits . . . they were a law-abiding people, rendering a cheerful and ready obedience to the authorities and laws of the country. . . .
> Men belonging to other tribes were received by the Choctaws in the spirit of friendship, and always treated with courtesy and kindness. . . .
> Jewelry and beads were universally worn by the females, but feathers were not worn in the hair, nor rings in the nose, by any of them. . . .
> Physically the Choctaws were not large and well-developed men. . . . They were below the medium height, were straight and neat in person, having small and well-formed hands and feet . . . their heads being of medium size and well-balanced; their features were smooth and the expression of the face pleasant. . . . They were rather lean in person, lithe and active, especially the males. I do not remember to have seen one full-blooded Choctaw man who was, by any means, stout and

corpulent. The females were larger, in proportion, than the males; they were less neat and not usually favored with as smooth and regular features. As they advanced in years they became stout and fleshy in person. Both males and females usually dressed after the fashion of the whites on the frontiers, except that hats and bonnets were utterly ignored . . . they were all equestrians, men, women, and children.

Edwards (1932:408–10) described the dress of the Choctaws about the same time and basically concurred with Benson, although some differences are evident:

> Many infants have no dresses regularly made. They are wrapped up in rags of quilts and the like. Children frequently run about home in the warm weather, with no other garment than nature gave them; and in winter many have but a single garment.
>
> Some of the more old-fashioned of the men wear leggings made of buckskin, dressed by themselves, drawn close around the legs and body, and fastened together with buckskin strings. But most of them now wear pantaloons. Some still wear buckskin moccasins, made of a single piece cut in proper shape and drawn up and tied over the foot, entirely without ornament. Some go barefoot; but most wear shoes. Belts are almost universal, made frequently of straps and buckles; but many are long sashes, ornamented with beadwork. This, however, is not wrought by themselves. Vests are sometimes worn. Their coat is mostly a hunting shirt, a kind of sack, of calico or homemade plaid, with several capes, every edge being adorned with plaits or fringe. In these the bright colours, pink or red, predominate.
>
> Hats are coming into use extensively; but many cling with great tenacity to a shawl of bright colours, rolled and put around the head in a circle, leaving the top of the head bare. Blankets and quilts are much worn in cold weather.
>
> The hair is now often left long; but more frequently, among people of the old style, it is cut close to the head, except a single strip over the front, or in some cases running back over the top of the head, like the crest of a helmet.
>
> They are very fond of feathers, and wear them, particularly when anything exciting is going on. It is now, however, a sign of a rowdy to wear them, and Christians avoid them. At school, when a boy puts a feather in his hat, you may begin to look out for him. They paint their faces for ornament, the prevailing colour used being red. This too, is a mark of rowdyism.

Many wear beads about their necks, the end of the string being fastened through a polished clamshell. Rings in the ears are very common, and I have seen one or two instances of a ring in the nose. The face of many in former days was ornamented with black inserted under the skin in zigzag lines from the corners of the mouth to the ears and to each side of the throat. This was done by the parents and grandparents, when the child was young. It has passed into disuse.

The main article of dress of the women in old time was simply a skirt, the cloth for which was made of the bark of trees split into threads and woven, turkey feathers being very ingeniously interwoven. This I have never seen. Shoes are sometimes worn by them, but mostly they go barefoot, or wear moccasins. Now they universally wear dresses, after the manner of white ladies, and long enough to nearly hide their bare feet and sweep the ground in grand style. In attending camp-meetings, they carry a clean dress along, and, when they wish to dress up, put it on over the other.

When they put anything on the head, it is generally a handkerchief, tied under the chin. Sun bonnets are coming somewhat into use. Seldom is a bonnet of a higher order seen there. The hair is not generally very neatly dressed. Many simply fold it and tie it behind. In this the different degrees of improvement are very manifest.

Many old women have their face tattooed as I described the men, and are elaborately decorated in the same way on the breast and arms.

Housing at this time varied from the log cabin to nice frame buildings, though glass windows were rare. "Smoking is universal, and they mix sumack with their tobacco." In medical care, bloodletting was still practiced, together with cauterizing. Steaming the body was practiced, as well as kneading. But many persons in the Choctaw Nation suffered from scrofula (Edwards, 1932:410, 415, 422).

Many of the Choctaws spoke English. But Edwards stated that the Choctaw language was rather difficult to learn. "Some missionaries learn to prepare sermons in it in 3 or 4 years; and some never learn." In the early years there were no books in Choctaw, but by the middle of the nineteenth century "the New Testament, the Old Testament to 2d Kings, a hymn book, a spelling book, reader, arithmetic, several small religious volumes and many tracts" were available in Choctaw (1932: 420,421).

Tofulla was the most important food dish for the Choctaws. It was "made of corn cracked in a wooden mortar and then boiled" (Debo, 1961:112). "Afterwards it sits in the same pot by the fire, being kept warm, till it is thoroughly soured. Then it is eaten" (Edwards, 1932:406). Other important dishes are described by Debo (1961:112): "Other native foods were *pashofa*, made of cooked meal mixed with finely cut meat and again cooked; *walusha*, of grape juice mixed with meal and sugar or cane syrup; *bahar*, of hickory nuts and walnuts beaten to a pulp to which cracked parched corn, sugar, and water were added to make a thick dough; and *abundha*, cooked corn beaten into a dough, mixed with cooked beans, wrapped in corn shucks and then boiled, and laid away in the husks until needed."

Within this historical period, changes in the kinship system were caused by the influences of missionaries and government agencies. In particular, marriage and inheritance became regulated by laws reflective of those of American society. Emphasis became placed upon patrilineal rather than matrilineal tendencies. The moiety and clan organizations ceased to exist, and the kinship system developed into a new type of organization that did not directly reflect the clan system. The effect of acculturation upon the kinship system is summarized by Eggan (1937:50):

> The patrilineal emphasis brought definite changes in the roles of males and females in the family and in the local group. The relation of a father to his children, in particular, was changed, largely at the expense of the relations between the child and the mother, and the child and the mother's brother. Specifically the relation of father and child was strengthened; the father gradually took over control of his children, became responsible for their education and training and for their behavior and marriage. Property came to be largely owned by the father and inherited by his children. Such changes must have influenced social attitudes toward relatives, as well as weakening matrilineal descent. It is this change in behavior patterns and attitudes which seems to be the medium through which the kinship patterns were modified.

During this time the Choctaw women gave birth to their children away from the house, usually under the trees, and without much ceremony (Debo, 1961:233). A few hours after giving birth, the mother carried the newborn baby into the house. The birth rate was high, but a high infant mortality rate tended to stabilize population growth.

The marriage practices of the Choctaws experienced many important changes during the Choctaw nationhood period, as the marriage laws indicate. In 1835 a law was passed in the Oklahoma Territory legalizing a brief ceremony that involved a mutual agreement of marriage performed in the presence of a preacher or captain (Debo, 1961:77). The following year, one of the most stable of all marriage restrictions was eliminated: it was declared legal to marry within the clan, or *iksa*. Benson reported that polygamy was still tolerated by the Oklahoma Choctaws in 1845, but that because of disapproval few actually followed the practice (1860:81). Then, in 1849, polygamy was officially abolished, and all those who were cohabitating were required to be married officially (Debo, 1961:77). Also in 1849, the Choctaws began to regulate intermarriage by enacting a law that required any white man living with a Choctaw woman to marry legally or to leave the nation. White men of questionable character were likewise forbidden to marry any Choctaw woman for any reason.

Another important law regulating the marriage of white men to Choctaw women was passed in 1875. It had the following provisions. "Whereas, the Choctaw Nation is being filled up with white persons of worthless character by so-called marriages to the great injury of the Choctaw people": (1) Any white man wanting to marry a Choctaw woman had to obtain a license from a circuit clerk or judge and had to swear that he had no other lawful wife. Unless the clerk or judge was satisfied that the man was telling the truth, he would not be issued a license. (2) The white man in addition had to present to the clerk or judge "a certificate of good moral character, signed by at least ten respectable Choctaw citizens by blood, who shall have been acquainted with him at least twelve months immediately preceding the signing of such certificate." (3) Before any license could be issued, the white man had to pay a $25 fee and make the following oath: "I do solemnly swear that I will honor, defend and submit to the Constitution and Laws of the Choctaw Nation, and will neither claim nor seek from the United States Government, or from the Judicial Tribunals thereof any protection, privilege or redress incompatible with the same, as guaranteed to the Choctaw Nation by the treaty stipulations entered between them, so help me God." (4) Unless the marriage contracted under the act was solemnized according to laws of the Choctaw Nation, it was invalid. (5) Any person engaged or assisting in an intermarriage that did not conform to provisions of the act would be prosecuted and fined $50. (6) The person performing the ceremony had to attach a certificate to the back of the license, which then had to be taken within thirty days to a circuit clerk to be recorded. (7) If the white spouse became a widower, he continued to be a citizen of the Choctaw Nation unless he married a white woman, in which case all rights of citizenship ceased. (8) Any white husband who abandoned his Choctaw wife would forfeit citizenship, be declared an "intruder," and be ejected from the territory (Cushman, 1899:312-14). Then, in 1887, the license fee was raised $25 to $100 (Debo, 1961:180). It should also be mentioned that names were passed through the male line and the wife took the name of the husband at the time of marriage (Benson, 1860:53).

As in the past, marriage was not a permanent bond, and divorce was permitted at the desire of either partner. Divorces were fairly common, although separations and desertions were rare (Benson, 1860:31). In instances of divorce, as early as 1852 the Choctaw laws provided that the material property be divided equally between husband and wife. It was now up to a panel of seven neutral people to decide which parent was to receive custody of the children. Later, however, divorce was placed under the jurisdiction of the circuit courts. The legal bases for divorce included impotence at the time of marriage, adultery, and cruelty. With regard to Negroes, the Choctaws never associated socially with them—their schools were separate, and their political groups were distinct—and, when intermarriage became legal, a law was passed in 1885 to make it a felony for any Choctaw to marry a freedman (Debo, 1961:232, 109).

The marriage ceremony in Mississippi in the latter part of the nineteenth century underwent some changes and began to reflect the style of the white people. Most Choctaws did get married, although a few preferred to remain unattached. According to Halbert (1882:222–24) and John Watkins (1894b:75–76), the courting consisted of the suitor approaching the young woman and either casting a pebble toward her or placing his hat or handkerchief upon her bed. If she agreed to become his wife, she simply tossed back the pebble or allowed his hat or handkerchief to remain. If she did not reciprocate, the young man went on his way. When a marriage was agreed upon, the couple decided the time and place. At the appointed time the friends and relatives of each walked toward one another and stopped about one hundred yards apart. Then the couple sat upon a blanket and presents were given, which became the property of the bride's relatives. After this, the couple became husband and wife, and a feast took place.

In summary, during the removal and Choctaw nationhood period, the Choctaws became separated into two groups—the one remaining in Mississippi, as strangers in their own land, and the other migrating to the Indian Territory, as strangers in a new land. This era involved adjustment for both groups. Debo (1961:78–79) comments:

> The Choctaws had settled a wild and remote frontier, accepted an alien religion and code of morals, established an educational system completely foreign to their aboriginal conceptions, adopted the constitutional and legal system of an unrelated racial experience, and modified their agricultural and commercial practices to conform to a complex economic system; and these innovations had been so eagerly accepted that they had become fundamental in their social, political, and economic life. Strangely enough they never showed any resentment against the Government that had driven them into exile, and they desired nothing more than autonomous development under its protection.

Of all the historical periods, the postremoval era represents the most dramatic and dynamic in Choctaw cultural and social history.

Plate 42 Choctaw Indian ballgame. COURTESY of Western History Collections, University of Oklahoma Library

5

Twentieth-Century Developments in Mississippi and Oklahoma 1907–1979

For the first half of this century, Choctaw history revolved around dissolution problems with the federal government concerning allotments and royalties from coal and other natural resources. Assimilation into the greater American and Oklahoman society was urged, but was not always successful. National legislation in the 1950s, 1960s, and 1970s affecting Indian policy also filtered down to the Choctaws, and many useful programs have been implemented. Today, particularly since the early 1970s, Choctaw self-determination and self-pride have ushered in a new era.

Historical Events

In 1918 the U.S. Senate established the Choctaw Indian Agency of the Bureau of Indian Affairs at Philadelphia, Mississippi. The conditions of the Mississippi Choctaws at this time described by Bounds (1964:55–56):

> By this time only a very few members of the tribe still owned land. The records show that 143 heads of families had received allotments, most of which had been disposed of by some means. The Choctaw people were living a seminomadic life, often in camps or small settlements. They did farm labor on a day-by-day basis. Many of them were sharecroppers.

Others camped near river bottoms where cane for basket-weaving was plentiful, and they made and sold baskets to obtain the necessities of life.

Though they lived among white people, the Choctaws spoke their native language. They still wore the brightly colored clothes that they had adopted from the early white settlers. . . .

They were not only set apart by language and dress, but they also retained many of their other tribal customs. Their doctor was still the medicine man, and he continued to use superstition and witchcraft in addition to herbs and other common remedies to cure ills. The Choctaws still held "cries" for their dead. Native dances and stick ball games remained the chief forms of recreation.

The schools had been "few and far between." Some short-term, inadequate schools operated intermittently.

In May of 1918, the federal government created a program that authorized $75,000 for the general welfare of the Choctaws (Peterson, 1970a:111–12). Three types of aid were provided for: economic, educational, and health. Of the initial funds, one-third was directed toward the purchase of farmland, one-third toward farm supplies, $5,000 toward the salaries of nonteaching staff members, and $20,000 toward education. Thus, a day school program was started in 1920, and the land-purchase program began in 1921 (Bounds, 1964:56–57).

The agency consisted of non-Choctaw leadership responsible for coordinating and directing various programs for the Choctaws. But in 1934 the Choctaw Business Committee was formed under the Indian Reorganization Act. This committee was recognized and approved by the Indian Bureau (Peterson, 1970a:139–40).

Then, in December, 1944, the secretary of the interior proclaimed that all lands held in trust by the federal government for the Mississippi Choctaws should become a reservation. He also sanctioned an election on April 20, 1945, which adopted the constitution and bylaws of the Mississippi Band of Choctaw Indians (Bounds, 1964:59). These were approved by the secretary of the interior on May 22, 1945.

The recent history of the Choctaw Indians consists primarily of a series of federal actions and programs designed to alleviate their social and economic problems, as well as to improve their over-all standard of living. The 1960s had a great impact on the Mississippi Choctaws. The Civil Rights Act of 1964, the establishment of the Office of Economic Opportunity (OEO), and the various antipoverty programs all provided the stimuli needed to improve the Choctaw quality of life. But, as Peterson (1970a:2) concludes "Throughout most of their recent history, the Choctaw have continued to live as a small isolated rural minority in an area where the dominant population is composed of Negroes and Whites. The Choctaws maintained their ethnic identity and their language by purposely not interacting with Negroes and Whites. While this separation preserved their identity as an ethnic group, it isolated them from many of the developments that were taking place in the greater society."

Several important pieces of national legislation passed in the 1970s have affected the Choctaws. Three of them are the Indian Self-Determination and Education Assistance Act, Indian Education Act, and Indian Child Welfare Act of 1978. Some of the main provisions of the latter (Public Law 95–608) are minimum federal standards for the removal of Indian children from their families, minimum federal standards for the placement of Indian children in foster homes or adoptive homes, and federal financial assistance in the operation of child and family service programs by Indian tribes and organizations; it also authorizes an Indian adult who was placed in an adoptive home as a child to petition for information on tribal affiliation and other matters. Thus, this last period represents more change to Choctaw culture and society, as well as the persistence of several of their traditional ways to which they attach primary importance.

Immediately after Oklahoma statehood, many public officials felt that private ownership of land and citizenship would encourage Choctaw assimilation into the dominant white society. But problems concerning allotment and royalties due from coal and other natural resources continued for many years.

After the Oklahoma statehood, Choctaw government was to continue under certain limitations until various tribal affairs could be resolved. In order for the tribal government to function, the president of the United States appointed a principal chief. "The offices of principal chief, national attorney, and mining trustee, with regular salaries paid out of the tribal income from coal royalties, were retained until 1948, thus continuing the tribal government in limited form, the officials serving under the supervision of the United States Office of Indian Affairs" (Wright, 1951:113). Since 1948, Oklahoma Choctaw principal chiefs have been elected.

Throughout the period of tribal affairs liquidation (1907–1948), the tribal government continued to operate in limited form. Specific meetings were held concerning certain acts and other regulations relevant to the welfare of Choctaws. One such meeting was the Albion Convention in 1922, which "unanimously adopted a special resolution to appoint a committee of five Choctaw to work out ways and means to urge and secure a settlement of all tribal affairs with the government" (Wright, 1951:113).

Beginning in the 1920s, the U.S. government began questioning its whole Indian policy. Forced acculturation and the allotment policy appeared not to be of great benefit to the American Indian. Many Indians had lost their allotted land, and reform was needed. The government launched a full-scale investigation of the social and economic conditions of the American Indians in 1928. The 872-page published report by the Institute for Government Research (the Brookings Institution) was a shocking revelation about the poverty, disease, suffering, and discontent existing among our native Americans (Debo, 1970:336).

Under John Collier's leadership in 1934, Congress passed the Indian Reorganization Act (Wheeler-Howard Act).

> This act prohibited further allotment of land still held under tribal tenure, extended the trust period on restricted allotments until further legislation by Congress, and authorized the appropriation of two million dollars a year for the acquisition of land for Indians. It permitted the organization of tribal governments with control over tribal funds and the expenditures of the Indian service and of tribal corporations for the management of communal property. It authorized a ten-million-dollar revolving loan fund for the use of tribes and individual Indians. It exempted qualified Indians from general civil service competition in appointment to positions under the Indian Bureau. (Debo, 1970:338)

Except in a few instances, most of the provisions did not apply to Oklahoma or Alaska. To fill this void in Oklahoma, in 1936 Congress passed the Oklahoma Indian Welfare Act, which applied many of the 1934 "principles to the tribeless Indians of that state." This act permitted these Indians to "organize as corporations and form co-operatives and [authorized] a special revolving loan fund of two million dollars for them" (Debo, 1970:339).

Elected Choctaw delegates met at the Goodland Indian School in 1934 to discuss tribal affairs. At this convention "resolutions were passed that included approval of the Wheeler-Howard Bill with certain amendments, organization of an advisory council of eleven Choctaw, elections by the delegates present of the principal chief recently appointed by the President, recommendation for the purchase of taxable Choctaw lands for landless members of the tribe, and suggestions that historic spots be marked and the old Council House near Tuskahoma be repaired as a monument in Choctaw history" (Wright, 1951:113). The Choctaw Advisory Council, which resulted from the Goodland Convention, met annually thereafter until 1946. But "Choctaws refused to organize under the measure" because of their dissatisfaction with the way officials of the U.S. Bureau of Indian Affairs were conducting tribal affairs (Baird, 1973:85, 86).

Since the government was extremely slow in liquidating the Choctaw estate as required by the dissolution agreements of the early 1900s, problems continued until 1951. Through the years most Choctaws sold or lost their allotted land, and today there are few who still have their original allotments. "While most Choctaws were losing their lands, the tribe as a whole nonetheless pressed the government to liquidate its common assets as provided in the dissolution agreements." By 1920, each enrolled member or his/her heirs had received $1,070 "from town lot sales and liquidation of trust funds" But slowness in the disposal of coal and asphalt lands finally resulted in the so-called Stigler Act, which enabled the U.S. government to buy the residue of the coal and asphalt lands for $8,500,000. An agreement was made in 1948, and "$350 was distributed to each of the enrolled members or their heirs in 1949" (Baird, 1973:81–83). Then, in 1951, because of annuities due to the

Oklahoma Choctaws from the U.S. government from nineteenth-century treaty negotiations, Congress paid $350,666 to the Choctaws to be distributed to the enrolled members. The money, however, was retained by the tribe for individual payment at a later date. With this payment, the liquidation period of the former Choctaw Nation came to a close.

In August of 1953, the Termination Act (House Concurrent Resolution 108) was passed by Congress. "In essence the resolution meant to free all Indians from Federal supervision by abolishing all offices of the Bureau of Indian Affairs" (Norris and McClure, 1975:8). All Indians were affected, and the act was intended "to end their status as wards of the United States, and to grant them all of the rights and privileges pertaining to American citizenship" (Debo, 1970:352). Thus, the Choctaws and other native Americans were to become "full-fledged" American citizens with no supervision or control by the federal government.

Desiring more control over remaining assets and other affairs, the Choctaws in the late 1950s proposed a plan "that would permit a measure of self-rule." The United States consented to their proposal. "Though the tribe had envisioned such a measure as a means of self-government only, the Bureau of Indian Affairs and Congress interpreted the [action] as the 'termination' of the Choctaw people as a legal entity" (Baird, 1973:86, 87). Although Chief Harry J. W. Belvin initially encouraged self-rule, he did not want to terminate the Choctaw tribal entity, which would result in the loss of funds for certain federal programs. Confusion later developed concerning his view of the Termination Act, and this was an issue in the 1975 election for principal chief of the Choctaw Nation.

According to Debo, the formation of the Oklahomans for Indian Opportunities (OIO), which was initiated in the summer of 1965 at a meeting held at the University of Oklahoma under the leadership of Mrs. LaDonna Harris, "turned out to be the most important gathering of Oklahoma Indians since the last intertribal council had met in 1888 to fight dissolution." The OIO concentrated on developing programs in community improvement, work orientation (enlisting employers to aid in training Indian workers), and youth activities (Debo, 1970:409). Since the 1964 Economic Opportunity

Act was passed, making money available for community action agencies and programs to improve the quality of life, the Choctaws and OIO have received funds to improve health care, implement Head Start programs, promote better housing, and provide job placement.

"The Civil Rights Act of 1968, with its so-called Indian Bill of Rights," has caused some Indian legal scholars to be concerned about such matters as tribal autonomy (Washburn, 1975:270). Despite some of the problems associated with the act, 1968 must be remembered as the year "the Senate finally abandoned its support of HCR 108." The abandonment of HCR 108 dealt the Termination Act its deathblow. In 1968 President Lyndon Johnson presented to Congress a special message on Indian affairs. In essence, he advocated for the Indians "an opportunity to remain in their homelands, if they choose, without surrendering their dignity; an opportunity to move to the towns and cities of America, if they choose, equipped with the skills to live in equality and dignity" (Debo, 1970:417, 411). "Johnson proposed a policy of 'maximum choice for the American Indian expressed in programs of self-help, self-development, and self-determination' " (Norris and McClure, 1975:8).

In 1975 Congress passed a new act, the Indian Self-Determination and Education Assistance Act (Public Law 93-638). The policy of self-determination provides for greater self-government and better control over tribal services. Today, Choctaw officials in Oklahoma and Mississippi frequently use the term "self-determination" to express their current administrative policies.

That same year C. David Gardner was elected principal chief. His election followed twenty-seven years of leadership under Chief Harry J. W. ("Jimmy") Belvin. Under Chief Gardner's administration, the Choctaw Nation acquired new quarters at the former Presbyterian College in Durant during the summer of 1976. Choctaw officials now have a spacious facility from which to conduct tribal affairs. Gardner was instrumental in establishing *Hello Choctaw* (a Choctaw newspaper, presently called *Bishinik*). He also helped to acquire the Community Health Representative Training

Historical Events 155

Center for Talihina, the Extended Health Care Facility for Antlers, and a community building at Idabel. Numerous other achievements were obtained by Chief Gardner before his death in January of 1978 at the age of thirty-seven.

After his death, elections were held on April 15, 1978, and Hollis Roberts was elected the new principal chief over Charles E. Brown by a margin of 339 votes—1,668 to 1,329. Robert L. Gardner is assistant chief of the Choctaw Nation. One of the problems that has taken up much of Roberts' time has been a new constitution. Chief Roberts has accomplished much during his short time in office. Recently he was able to announce that the Choctaw Nation had received a federal grant for the restoration and renovation of historic Wheelock Academy.

Plate 43 Harry J. W. Belvin, circa early fifties, principal chief of the Oklahoma Choctaw Nation from 1948 to 1975. COURTESY Chief Belvin

Plate 44 Hollis Roberts, principal chief of the Oklahoma Choctaw Nation, 1978. COURTESY Chief Hollis Roberts

Choctaw Culture

The traditional Choctaw social organization had become modified tremendously as the Choctaws separated into two distinct units, one in Mississippi and the other in Oklahoma. This division disrupted the kinship ties maintained between the two geographical areas. Consequently, "modified forms of traditional kinship organization could continue to function only in a local setting" in Mississippi. The Choctaw social organization, therefore, underwent a change from regional villages connected by matrilineal clans to singular local units consisting primarily of related nuclear family units expanding into extended kinship. Today, the local community is the most important unit of Choctaw social organization beyond the extended family (Peterson, 1970a:145, 146).

As a result of the relative isolation of the communities, social interaction among the Choctaws in Mississippi has altered. Relationships became restricted to the particular locality in which the individual lived, rather than occurring between the communities. This change reflected the lack of transportation and the distance between the communities (Peterson, 1970a:147–48). But ownership of automobiles increased among Choctaw households from 32 percent in 1962 to 66 percent in 1968, while ownership of trucks increased from 11 to 13 percent. The result was an increase in contact between communities. However, this phenomenon is too recent to detect its effect upon social organization.

The Oklahoma Choctaws became citizens of the United States in 1901. The Mississippi Choctaws had been made citizens of the state of Mississippi during the 1829–1830 session of the legislature, and the Oklahoma Choctaws became part of the state of Oklahoma in 1907, when that territory gained statehood and after the Choctaw tribal government had been abolished the preceding year. Although the Oklahoma Choctaws no longer had their national tribal government, many participated in state and local government, and some mixed bloods held county, state, and federal offices (McKee, 1971:138). The federal government stopped treating the Choctaws as a separate government within Oklahoma in 1949 and 1951.

After the Choctaw Agency was formed in Mississippi in 1918, seven Choctaw communities were established in order to provide permanent schooling and homesites. These were Pearl River, Tucker, and Bogue Chitto in Neshoba County; Red Water and Standing Pine in Leake County; Conehatta in Newton County; and Bogue Homa in Jones County (Choctaw Agency, n.d.:5).

The Mississippi Choctaws had no tribal government after the Treaty of Dancing Rabbit Creek until creation of the Choctaw Business Committee in 1934. The committee comprised seventeen members from the seven communities; after formation it received opposition from the nonsanctioned Mississippi Choctaw Indian Federation. Then, under the Reorganization Act, a council was elected to replace the committee as the governing body of the tribe. And in 1945 the Choctaw tribe became structurally organized and officially known as the Mississippi Band of Choctaw Indians, with a tribal organization known as the Tribal Council (Choctaw Agency, n.d.:6). As the constitutionally approved governing body, the council consists of sixteen members elected from the seven communities. These members may be females or males. The council possesses the authority to manage tribal finances and to decide the direction of the various economic and social programs, such as the Choctaw Action Agency, Neighborhood Youth Corps, Mainstream, Nutrition Aids, Commodity Food Program, and Choctaw Youth Rehabilitation Center (Fig. 22). The Tribal Council elects a tribal chairman to preside over the meetings. Taking the place of the chief of the past, the chairman conducts the business of the tribe and maintains an office at the Choctaw Tribal Office in the Pearl River community.

Participation by Mississippi Choctaws in the government and politics of the dominant white society has been minimal in the past. Even though they were given citizenship status in the state and the country, until recently the Choctaws were excluded from voting and jury duty because of the poll tax and literacy test requirements imposed by the state (Peterson, 1970a:223). But in recent years the Choctaw Tribal Council and especially the Community Action Program have encouraged the people to participate in political activities relevant to their own programs.

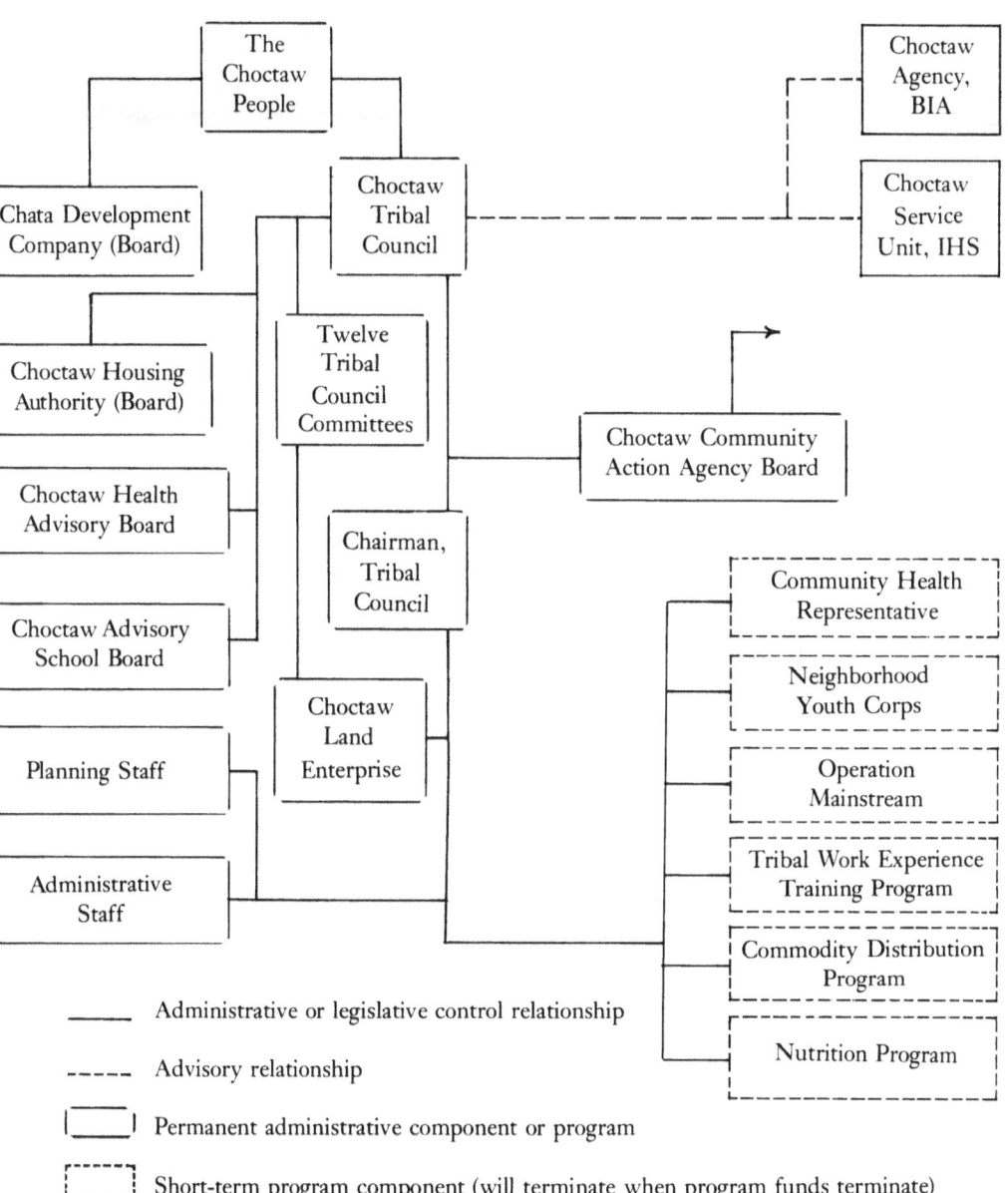

Figure 22 Mississippi Tribal Government Structure, 1971. SOURCE: Mississippi Band of Choctaw Indians. 1972

Plate 45 Phillip Martin tribal chief of the Mississippi band of Choctaws, 1979. COURTESY *Choctaw Community News*

Plate 46 Mrs. Susan Denson, of the Mississippi Choctaws, making a basket. COURTESY *Choctaw Community News*

Plate 47 Choctaw stick-ball players in Mississippi. COURTESY *Choctaw Community News*

The Choctaws have traditionally existed primarily apart from the white law enforcement officers and courts, except in instances where whites were offended or white interests were concerned (Peterson, 1970a:224). As a result, the Choctaws established their own police force and courts to which they could relate and could support with a feeling of security. Of course, the Division of Judicial Prevention and Enforcement, as it is known, operates only on reservation lands and enforces only the laws adopted by the Tribal Council. It appears that the Choctaws are increasing their participation in political activities, but the emphasis is more toward more control of their own programs.

In 1968 the tribe won a major jurisdictional battle with the state of Mississippi in *Roby Gibson* v. *E. G. Barnett, Sheriff of Neshoba County*. This case caused the recognition of the Choctaw Reservation as "Indian Country"; therefore, "criminal jurisdiction over events which transpired on the Choctaw Reservation was recognized as resting solely in the hands of the Federal or Tribal Government" (Mississippi Band of Choctaw Indians, 1972:11). This recognition was challenged in 1975 in an assault case involving two Choctaws—Smith John and his son, the late Henry Smith John. In 1978 the U.S. Supreme Court ruled that the federal government and the tribe, not the state, held jurisdiction over Indian lands in Mississippi. The ruling enabled Mississippi Choctaws to have all the rights and privileges possessed by other Indian tribes in the United States.

Tribal Chief Calvin J. Isaac has been operating a capable government since 1975. Much has been accomplished in education social programs, and economic development during his administration. But he was not chosen in his bid for reelection, and Phillip Martin was elected the new chief in June of 1979.

In Oklahoma, the Choctaw Nation was disposed of in 1906, but the office of principal chief together with some other offices were appointed by the president of the United States until 1948. In 1948, under order of the Bureau of Indian Affairs, an election was held for the office of principal chief. Finally, by order of an act passed in 1970, each of the Five Civilized Tribes was to popularly elect its own principal chief.

After Chief Belvin's election in 1948, he reestablished the advisory council. Each year Choctaws in each of the ten counties elect a county council, which consists of a chairman, vice-chairman, secretary-treasurer, and chaplain (U.S. Department of the Interior, 1973:52). "In order to be a voting member of the Choctaw Tribe, it is required that the voters be an original 1906 enrolled member or lineal descendant" (U.S. Department of the Interior, 1973:52). These councils meet quarterly with the principal chief to conduct business. Then each Labor Day weekend, a general meeting is held at the Choctaw Nation capital in Tuskahoma to inform tribal members about various matters of importance.

A breakdown of the present structure of the Oklahoma Choctaw political organization is in Figure 23. As noted, the federal government, Department of the Interior, and Bureau of Indian Affairs have jurisdiction over the Choctaws. Choctaws are also subject to the laws of the state of Oklahoma. Five Choctaws represent their people on the Intertribal Council, and five representatives are sent to the Five Civilized Tribes Foundation, Inc. In some cases, the

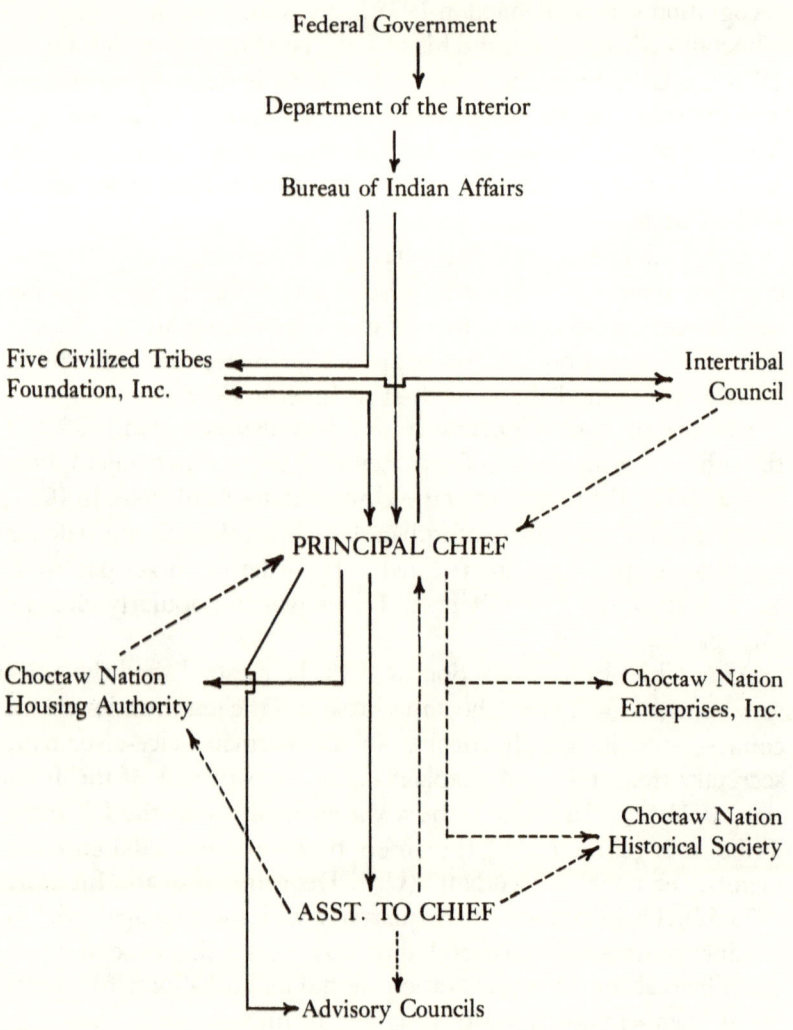

Figure 23 Oklahoma Choctaw Political Organization. SOURCE: Kiamichi Economic Development District, 1974

same members represent the Choctaws in both organizations. Currently there are three active tribal organizations: Choctaw Nation Housing Authority, Choctaw Nation Enterprises, Inc., and Choctaw Nation Historical Society. These attempt to improve Choctaw housing, provide more jobs, improve health care through a network of health clinics, improve tribal trust lands, and record and preserve Choctaw history (Kiamichi Economic Development District, 1974:7–13).

"Even though the Choctaw Nation is not officially organized by a constitution and by-laws, business entities within the tribe are authorized to conduct business as a corporate group through [a] license issued by the Oklahoma State Corporation Commission" (U.S. Department of the Interior, 1973:53). The principal chief is the chief executive of the corporative group. However, the Choctaw Nation is presently considering a new constitution.

In the 1880s the Mississippi Choctaws began to shift from being isolated squatters to being sharecroppers for white landowners. As sharecroppers, the Choctaws traded their labor in exchange for farming supplies, subsistence, and a place to live. The principal crops grown were cotton and corn. Those Choctaws living on trust land relied upon the Choctaw Agency for loans with which to obtain supplies. During the off-season Choctaw farmers usually found it necessary to work as road workers, sawmill workers, or farm workers (Peterson, 1970a:194–95).

In recent times, a few young Choctaws have left the farms to become wage earners in agriculturally related industries, such as poultry, timber, and dairying (Peterson, 1970a:200). Since the 1964 Civil Rights Act, some Choctaws have entered factory work. In spite of these developments, most of the Mississippi Choctaw families are below the poverty level. In fact, a recent study showed that an average of 31.2 percent of all Choctaw household heads were unemployed, disabled, or retired in 1969 (Harris, 1970a:3). This fact, plus limited education and occupational skills levels, accounts for the low economic status of the Choctaws.

The Bureau of Indian Affairs and the Choctaw tribal government account for about 18.5 percent of all Choctaw employment. Of the wage earners, 10.9 percent are involved in agricultural processing and 9.4 percent are employed in manufacturing. Another 24 percent of the Choctaw labor force is self-employed, principally as farm laborers, managers, or operators and service workers (Harris, 1970a:20).

Table 6 shows the skill attainment of persons in the labor force. Unfortunately, most Mississippi Choctaws are classified as semi-skilled or unskilled. Table 7 shows that, besides the unemployed, service workers, laborers (nonfarm), and operatives are the three leading occupational categories.

Table 6 SKILL ATTAINMENT OF PERSONS IN LABOR FORCE, 1974 (MISSISSIPPI)

Skill Attainment	Total Number of Persons	Employment Status Percentages		
		Employed	In Training	Unemployed
Professional/administrative	21	100.0	.0	.0
White collar	136	88.2	1.5	10.3
Skilled	59	91.5	1.7	6.8
Semi-skilled	571	64.2	9.4	26.2
Unskilled	694	58.3	8.5	33.1
Total of all persons in labor force	1481	65.3	7.8	26.9

SOURCE: Spencer, Peterson, and Kim, 1975

In an attempt to improve the occupational level of the Mississippi Choctaws, the Choctaw Agency created the Branch of Employment Assistance, which provides vocational counseling and guidance, vocational training, apprenticeship, and on-the-job training (Choctaw Agency, n.d.:7–8). This service is designed particularly to aid those from eighteen to thirty-five years old. As an origin office, the Branch of Employment Assistance forwards applicants to one of the eight Field Employment Assistance offices in Chicago, Cleveland, Dallas, Denver, Los Angeles, Oakland, San Jose, and San Francisco. Although such programs bring about increased contact with the larger American society, the expressed purpose is to improve the quality of life within the Choctaw community.

One of the duties of the Chata Development Company is to assist in the economic development of the tribe. It recently announced that General Motors would locate a plant in the Chata Industrial

Table 7 OCCUPATIONAL CLASSIFICATION OF ALL PERSONS IN THE LABOR FORCE,[a] 1974 (MISSISSIPPI)

Occupational Classification	Total		Male		Female	
	Number	Percent	Number	Percent	Number	Percent
Professional/technical	14	.9	6	.8	8	1.1
Administrative/managerial	31	2.1	23	3.1	8	1.1
New Careers program[b]	21	1.4	11	1.5	10	1.4
Clerical/misc. white collar	55	3.7	7	.9	48	6.5
Sales workers	3	.2	3	.4	0	.0
Craftsmen/foremen	46	3.1	43	5.8	3	.4
Service workers	286	19.3	107	14.4	179	24.2
Operatives	174	11.7	71	9.6	103	13.9
Transport operatives	54	3.6	52	7.0	2	.3
Laborers, non-farm	222	15.0	194	26.1	28	3.8
Farm managers/laborers	53	3.6	49	6.6	4	.5
Private household workers	8	.5	0	.0	8	1.1
Trainees	116	7.8	70	9.4	46	6.2
Unemployed	398	26.9	106	14.3	292	39.5
Totals	1481	100.0	742	100.0	739	100.0

[a]The "labor force" includes both persons who are employed and persons who are unemployed but available for work. Not included are persons who are students, disabled, retired, or otherwise not available for wage employment.

[b]New Careers trainees generally were employed on the white-collar skill level.

SOURCE: Spencer, Peterson, and Kim, 1975

Park to manufacture automobile wire harnesses. About 180 persons will eventually be employed at the plant, which began operation in April, 1979. Developments like this aid immensely in lowering unemployment and strengthening the economic viability of the tribe.

Table 8 gives the average hourly wage according to occupational classification. In a recent study, the Choctaw median family income was $3,120 (Table 9).

The Choctaw Reservation comprises seven communities totaling 17,480.92 acres (Table 10). More than 50 percent of the land owned is in the Pearl River community. In land use, more than 20 percent is timber pasture, approximately 7.5 percent is cropland, and 66 percent is timber or fallow (Table 11).

Table 8 AVERAGE HOURLY WAGES BY OCCUPATIONAL CLASSIFICATION, 1974 (MISSISSIPPI)

Occupational Classification	Average Hourly Wage	Percentage of Responded
Professional/technical	$ 4.66	93.0
Administrative/managerial	4.57	94.0
White collar/clerical/sales	2.67	91.0
Craftsmen/foremen	3.30	85.0
Service workers	2.41	94.0
Operatives	2.16	91.0
Transport operatives	2.86	83.0
Laborers	2.08	86.0
All occupations[a]	$2.48	89.9

[a]Does not include occupational groups not listed (*i.e.*, farm managers and laborers, private household workers, and trainees).

SOURCE: Spencer, Peterson, and Kim, 1975

Table 9 FAMILY INCOME, 1970 (MISSISSIPPI)

	Total Families	Percentage
Under $ 1,000	115	20.7
$ 1,000– 1,999	69	12.4
2,000– 2,999	87	15.7
3,000– 3,999	56	10.1
4,000– 4,999	55	9.9
5,000– 5,999	73	13.2
6,000– 6,999	45	8.2
7,000– 7,999	16	2.9
8,000– 8,999	11	2.0
9,000– 9,999	4	.7
10,000–11,999	21	3.7
12,000 and over	3	.5

Total families — 555
Median income — $3,120

SOURCE: U.S. Bureau of the Census, 1970; cited in Spencer 1973; proportionally adjusted from data on 547 families by Smith & Associates, 1974a

Table 10 LAND OWNED BY THE MISSISSIPPI CHOCTAW INDIANS

Community	Area (acres)	Percentage of Total
Pearl River	8,978.0	51.4
Conehatta	3,386.3	19.4
Bogue Chitto	1,848.9	10.5
Redwater	1,128.87	6.6
Tucker	1,095.0	6.3
Standing Pine	722.85	4.1
Bogue Homa	320.0	1.7
TOTAL	17,480.92	100.0

SOURCE: Smith & Associates, 1974a

Table 11 EXISTING LAND USE, 1974 (MISSISSIPPI)

Land Use Category	Pearl River	Bogue Chitto	Standing Pine	Tucker	Conehatta	Red Water	Bogue Homa	Total
Residential	165	78	39	51	72	54	20	479
Cropland	639	215	84	77	264	35	29	1,343
Open pasture	251	120	124	59	101	71	8	734
Timber pasture	2,300	243	105	59	231	110	0	3,048
Recreational	19	15	2	*	6	17	6	65
Public/federal	111	16	37	8	11	20	30	233
Commercial	1	0	0	0	0	0	0	1
Timber or fallow	5,542	1,178	362	848	2,712	842	257	11,741
Industrial	30	0	0	0	0	0	0	30
TOTAL	9,058	1,865	753	1,102	3,397	1,149	350	17,674

SOURCE: Smith & Associates, 1974a
*Recreational land is on property of Catholic church, section 22.

Table 12 CHOCTAW LAND STATUS IN ACRES IN OKLAHOMA

County	Individually Owned	TRIBAL				Gov't. Administrative	Totals
		Unallotted	Purchased	USA in Trust	Total Tribal		
Atoka	13,147	649.10	0	0	649.10	0	13,796.
Bryan	7,614	47.35	0	0	47.35	0	7,661.
Choctaw	15,649	133.63	0	0	133.63	0	15,782.
Coal	3,328	0	0	0	0	0	3,328.
Haskell	8,162	71.15	0	25.00	96.15	0	8,258.
Hughes	3,588	0	0	0	0	0	3,588.
Latimer	10,090	1,849.62	0	797.97	2,647.59	121.97	12,859.
LeFlore	11,713	207.62	0	0	207.62	0	11,920.
McCurtain	35,640	1,542.68	1.63	0	1,544.31	4.84	37,189.
Pittsburg	11,150	2,714.02	0	0	2,714.02	540.00	14,404.
Pushmataha	12,596	70.00	2,637.00	0	2,707.00	0	15,303.
Total	132,677	7,285.17	2,638.63	822.97	10,746.77	666.81	144,090.

SOURCE: U.S. Department of the Interior, 1973

Prior to Oklahoma statehood, much Choctaw land was held in common by the tribe. But through the years much has been sold. Of the present total of 144,090.58 acres in the Choctaw Nation, 92 percent is individually owned and almost 7.5 percent is owned by the tribe (Table 12). During the past thirty years, the emphasis has changed from cotton and corn to cattle, improved pastureland, soybeans, and peanuts. Choctaws have made the shift from farming to manufacturing jobs. Some of the best Choctaw farmland has been sold to non-Indians, and much of the present Choctaw tribal holdings are post oak and blackjack land. Yet many Choctaws still live on their allotted land. The question arises of what to do with their present land and how to improve the economic livelihood of the Choctaws.

Before Oklahoma statehood and for several years into this century, the Choctaw economy focused on agriculture, forestry, and mineral production. Within the last thirty years emphasis has shifted to manufacturing. Today the Choctaw Nation still identifies with these four basic industries. However, other occupations have been added. A large number of Choctaws and other Indians in the ten-county Choctaw Nation are employed in wholesale and retail trade, hospitals and health services, public administration, construction, and services. These five occupational categories, together with manufacturing, account for 78.6 percent of all Indians (Choctaws and others) employed (Table 13).

Adaptation to change, and in this instance change from agricultural to nonagricultural jobs, has been a trait of Choctaw culture. Some rural Choctaws have had difficulty adapting to industrial punctuality, particularly when they "consider it impolite to pass a friend or relative without engaging in conversation. The term 'Indian time' has often been used to explain tardiness" (Kiamichi Economic Development District, 1974:34). But many Choctaws have adjusted.

Table 13 DISTRIBUTION OF EMPLOYED TEN-COUNTY CIVILIAN LABOR FORCE 16 YEARS OF AGE AND OLDER BY INDUSTRY, 1970 (OKLAHOMA)

	Ten-County Indian Percentage	Ten-County Indian	Ten-County Total Percentage
Agriculture, forestry, and fishing	4.3	106	7.2
Mining	.9	22	1.5
Construction	8.5	210	9.8
Manufacturing	24.6	607	18.9
Transportation, communication, and utilities	4.8	118	5.9
Wholesale and retail trade	13.3	328	19.2
Banking, insurance, and real estate	1.5	37	2.2
Services	8.0	197	7.8
Hospitals and health services	13.0	321	6.0
Education	4.7	116	8.9
Welfare, religious, and nonprofit	3.2	79	2.0
Legal, engineering, and miscellaneous professional services	2.0	49	1.3
Public administration	11.2	276	9.3
Total number of employed civilian labor force	100.0	2,466	54,463

SOURCE: Kiamichi Economic Development District, 1974

Since agriculture, forestry, mining, and manufacturing have been identified as sources of income to the Choctaw Nation, each of these will be commented on separately. The number of farms has been declining, but the size has been increasing. "The major crops grown in the ten-county area in 1971 in order of acreage are: hay, soybeans, peanuts, cotton, sorghum, wheat, oats, corn, and barley" (U.S. Department of the Interior, 1973:75). Few Choctaws, however, are gainfully employed in agriculture. Livestock trends since 1967 show an increase in cattle and calves, a decline in milk cows, and a slight decline in hogs; Le Flore and McCurtain counties are the only ones with poultry of any significance. In some economic plans designed to improve tribal livestock, it has been suggested that the tribe utilize some of its 10,000-plus tribal acres for the production of breeding stock using one of the exotic breeds such as Charolais, Limousin, Maine-Anjou, Brown Swiss, Simmental, and South Devon.

Forestry and commercial lumbering were started in the Choctaw Nation prior to statehood. The use of wood for railroad ties and for making equipment needed for coal mining was significant. Today a large paper mill is operated by Weyerhauser near Valliant, and Weyerhauser also has a lumber products plant at Wright City. Some Indians are employed at these two sites. Establishment of charcoal production and briquetting operations has been considered by economic planners for the Choctaw Nation.

Located in the Choctaw Nation are such minerals as oil and natural gas, coal, limestone, sand and gravel, quartz crystals, and volcanic ash, as well as smaller deposits of zinc, lead, and copper. However, as of 1973, "only one producing oil well exists on tribal land and it is located in the middle of Lake Eufaula" (U.S. Department of the Interior, 1973:135). Although "several coal deposits and mines exist on tribal allotted land," it should be remembered that the tribe "sold all their tribal coal and asphalt rights in 1948" (U.S. Department of the Interior, 1973:135).

In 1950, 40 percent of all persons employed in the ten-county area of the Choctaw Nation were in agriculture, forestry, fisheries, and mining. As of 1970, the figure was down to 8.6 percent (Kiamichi Economic Development District, 1974:41). Occupa-

Choctaw Culture

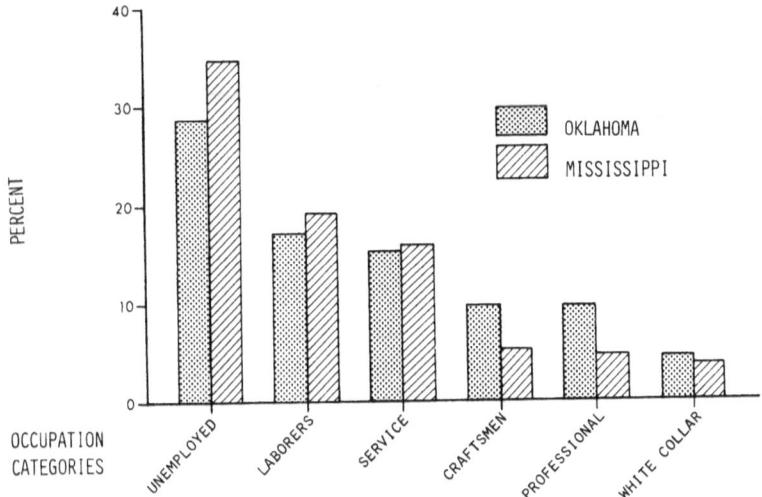

Figure 24 Occupational classifications of Oklahoma and Mississippi Choctaw. SOURCE: McKee and Norris, 1976b

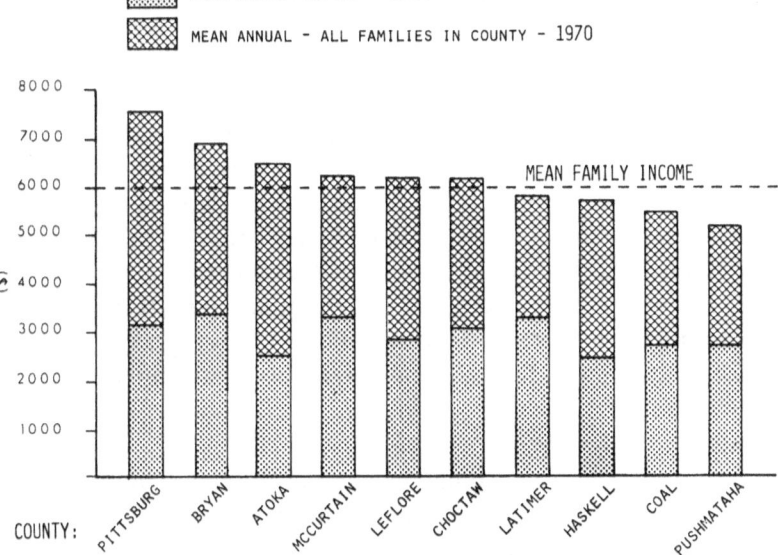

Figure 25 Choctaw income v. overall income for Oklahoma counties in Choctaw nation. SOURCE: McKee and Norris, 1976b

tional shifts among the Choctaws have therefore occurred, with employment in agriculture being reduced and jobs in nonagricultural sectors being increased. In 1970 unemployment in the Choctaw Nation was 5.6 percent, whereas for all Indians it was slightly higher at 8.7 percent (U.S. Department of the Interior, 1973:110). As of 1974, 10,447 persons were employed in manufacturing in the Choctaw Nation. Of that total, 607 (5.8 percent) were Indian. Since the Choctaw Nation is only 5.6 percent Indian, Indians appear to be getting a relative percentage of the employment (Kiamichi Economic Development District, 1974:56).

More than one-third of all persons employed in manufacturing are working in McAlester. However, some communities have higher Indian populations than others. It is hoped that, where industrial jobs are available and where Indian population concentrations are higher, increases will also be reflected in the percentage of Indian employment in that area.

Most of the industry in the Choctaw Nation is grouped around apparel, wood products, and food and kindred products. Most of these industries are labor intensive. There are some who feel that the ten-county area should begin to push for more technology and capital-intensive industries.

A recent census revealed the following information about Choctaw occupational classification and income in the ten-county Choctaw Nation (Norris, Hagle, and Harries, 1975). Nearly 60 percent of the employable Oklahoma Choctaws are laborers or service workers or are unemployed (Table 14). Less than 14 percent of the Oklahoma Choctaws hold professional and white-collar jobs. Figure 24 compares occupational classifications for Oklahoma and Mississippi Choctaws. The mean Choctaw family income in 1975 was $2,928 (Table 15, Fig. 25), whereas the mean family income of the ten-county area was $6,200. Many Oklahoma Choctaws are living in poverty.

In religion the Mississippi Choctaws are predominantly Baptist. The Baptist church began establishing churches in each of the permanent Indian communities at the beginning of the twentieth century; as of 1970 there were thirteen churches with a membership of over one thousand (Choctaw Agency, n.d.:4–5). By creating a line of churches throughout the communities, the Baptists helped to bring together Choctaws from the various communities. This togetherness was produced especially through the activities offered by the New Choctaw Baptist Association. The Baptist churches have also acted as a training area for developing local leaders. This is particularly true since Choctaws have complete control of their own Baptist churches, which are separated from those of the whites and blacks. The Choctaw Baptist churches likewise have served as important locations for community activities, especially for elderly Choctaws (Peterson, 1970a: 190, 192).

Table 14 OCCUPATIONAL CLASSIFICATION OF EMPLOYED[a] CHOCTAWS, 1975 (OKLAHOMA)

Occupation	Number	Percentage
Professional	340	9.5
White collar	148	4.1
Craftsmen	337	9.4
Operatives	270	7.6
Service	502	14.0
Laborers	604	16.9
Farm workers	131	3.7
Unemployed	1,001	28.0
No information	242	6.8
Total	3,575[b]	100.0[c]

[a]Data are for all persons 21 years old and older, only.

[b]Oklahoma total does not include clerical (209), sales (117), private household workers (40), because corresponding Mississippi data were not available.

[c]Percentages based only on data used.

SOURCE: McKee and Norris, 1976b

The Roman Catholic church ranks second among the Mississippi Choctaws, with three churches and a membership of about three hundred. It has influenced individual Choctaw families, but its overall effect has been primarily in one community; unlike the Baptist church the Catholic church has not brought different communities together. Control of the Choctaw Catholic church has remained principally with the mission workers (Peterson, 1970a: 165, 190).

Table 15 CHOCTAW INCOME, 1975 (OKLAHOMA)

County	Mean Family Income, 1970 Entire County	Mean Choctaw Family Income, 1975	Difference
Atoka	$6,592	$2,570	$4,022
Bryan	6,875	3,290	3,585
Choctaw	6,103	3,081	3,022
Coal	5,658	2,777	2,881
Haskell	5,722	2,436	3,286
Latimer	5,870	3,235	2,635
LeFlore	6,146	2,905	3,241
McCurtain	6,232	3,113	3,119
Pittsburg	7,615	3,149	4,466
Pushmataha	5,188	2,723	2,465
Average	$6,200	$2,928	$3,272

SOURCE: McKee and Norris, 1976b

The third largest religious body among the Mississippi Choctaws today is the Methodist church, which maintains two churches and has a membership of approximately 150. Other active denominations among the Choctaws are the Pentecostal church and the Mennonite church, which established a mission at Mashulaville in 1958 and a church near Nanih Waiya in 1960 (Choctaw Agency, n.d.:5).

Most Oklahoma Choctaws are Protestant, principally Presbyterian, Baptist, and Methodist. "The Methodist Episcopal church probably has the largest membership" (Wright, 1951:117).

Prior to the establishment of the Choctaw Agency, the Choctaws in Mississippi lacked adequate educational facilities, although the various religious agencies among them had provided mission schools from time to time. In fact, the poor educational condition was a major reason for formation of the Choctaw Agency. A federal day school program commenced in 1920 with the opening of schools at Pearl River, Tucker, and Standing Pine communities (Bounds, 1964:56-57). Each school was supplied one teacher, who also assisted in supervising the farm and welfare programs. Then, in 1923, a farm agent was added to the staff as a specialist.

Other day schools were opened on land provided by a government land-purchase program begun in 1921. These one-teacher schools were the Bogue Homa School opened in 1922, the Red Water School opened in 1925, the Conehatta School begun in 1928, and the Bogue Chitto School founded in 1930. But not until 1964 was a high school, Choctaw Central High School at Pearl River, made available to the Choctaw students (Choctaw Agency, n.d.:6–7). Before that year, those students wanting to attend high school had to go to Oklahoma or Kansas or to public non-Choctaw high schools. Consequently, few Choctaws completed high school before 1964.

For over a decade the Choctaw schools have increasingly improved. The Bureau of Indian Affairs presently operates four day schools and three boarding schools, with a total enrollment of about 1,250 students. All of the Choctaw schools are fully accredited by the state and are staffed by certified teachers. Besides the basic academic subjects, Choctaw students also receive instruction in home economics and vocational and technical subjects. The Choctaw Agency also provides a kindergarten summer program, which allows preschool Choctaw children the opportunity to learn English and other basic skills needed to succeed in school.

Recently, the federal Office of Education approved a grant of over $50,000 to the Choctaw Agency for a career education program. The funds are designed to support demonstration projects, educational enrichment programs, and the training of teachers, teacher aides, and social workers. Along with an adult education program operated by the Tribal Council, the direction of Choctaw education is toward providing Choctaws with the preparation necessary to compete with non-Choctaws for jobs. Education is viewed as the foundation to future advancements by the Choctaw people. But Choctaw leaders want more community control of their educational programs, rather than leaving it in the hands of the Bureau of Indian Affairs.

Statistically, it is evident that the Choctaws have had an uphill struggle with regard to education. Less than 5 percent of the Choctaws in 1969 had a high school diploma, and less than one-fifth had completed more than eight years of formal schooling. Almost 49 percent had no more than a third grade education. Also, over one-third (34.1 percent) of the Choctaws either had no formal schooling at all or had completed less than one year (Harris, 1970a:3, 20). In addition, the literacy rate of the Choctaws is much lower than the Mississippi state average, which itself is low with respect to the national average. The low educational attainment of the Choctaws is largely responsible for their low economic level.

Results from a recent Choctaw census in Mississippi show that, for those aged sixty-five and above, none have gone to college and nearly 90 percent have not gone beyond the third grade (Spencer, Peterson, Kim, 1975:18). Of the total population, 77.9 percent have not graduated from high school, less than 7 percent have gone to college, and the median grade completed was eighth (Table 16). Nationally, the median grade completed for Native Americans was 9.8 in 1970.

Table 16 EDUCATIONAL ATTAINMENT OF PERSONS 16 YEARS OF AGE AND OLDER AND MEDIAN GRADE COMPLETED, 1974 (MISSISSIPPI)

Highest Grade Completed	Total	Percentages by Age					
		16–19	20–24	25–34	35–44	45–64	65+
0–3 yrs.	26.7	2.3	4.7	13.6	32.1	56.3	88.1
4–7 yrs.	20.9	9.9	12.5	20.9	33.4	30.5	6.7
8–11 yrs.	30.3	72.1	34.9	31.8	21.9	5.5	3.0
12 yrs.	13.6	12.7	30.8	19.9	6.0	3.8	.7
13–15 yrs.	5.9	1.1	15.3	10.3	3.3	1.0	.0
16+	1.0	.0	.6	2.5	1.1	.7	.0
Not reported	1.7	2.0	1.2	1.0	2.2	2.2	1.5
Total number of persons	2118[a]	355	321	513	365	416	133
Median grade completed	8	9	11	9	6	3	0

[a]Fifteen persons whose age was not reported were included in the total figures but were necessarily excluded from the age breakdown percentages.
SOURCE: Spencer, Peterson and Kim, 1975

In Oklahoma, most Choctaw students attend the public schools. Some reside at the Jones Academy dormitory and attend public schools in Hartshorne four miles to the west. Some reside in dormitories outside the Choctaw Nation, such as Carter Seminary at Ardmore and the Eufaula Dormitory at Eufaula but, like at Jones, attend public schools. In addition, some Choctaws attend the two Bureau of Indian Affairs boarding schools at Wyandotte (elementary) and Tahlequah (high school). Choctaws also go to the Goodland School near Hugo. Many Choctaws attend Southeastern Oklahoma State University in Durant, Eastern Oklahoma State College in Wilburton, and the University of Oklahoma. Except for Jones Academy, not many of the old academies, such as Wheelock, Old and New Spencer, Armstrong, Tuskahoma, Cameron Institute, New Hope Seminary, and Colbert Institute, remain.

The median school year completed for Indians living in the Choctaw Nation in about 1972 was 8.9 years (Kiamichi Economic Development District, 1974:185). A census conducted in 1975 and directed by Robert Norris showed that less than 10 percent of the Choctaws had achieved less than a third grade education and that the mean school year completed was 10. More than 15 percent had some college training. Table 17 shows educational attainment by grade completed and age. Progress in education over the past four decades has certainly been achieved when one considers the study made of 100 Choctaw families in 1932, which showed that 45.2 percent of the men, 41.3 percent of the women, and 9 percent of the children were illiterate (Merrill, 1940:92).

Figures 26 and 27 compare Oklahoma and Mississippi educational attainment. Evidence suggests that the Oklahoma Choctaws have a slight edge over their Mississippi counterparts in education.

Table 17 EDUCATIONAL ATTAINMENT OF PERSONS 16 YEARS OF AGE AND OLDER AND MEAN GRADE COMPLETED, 1975 (OKLAHOMA)

Highest Grade Completed	Total	Percentages by Age					
		16–19	20–24	25–34	35–44	45–64	65 +
0–3 yrs.	9.2	2.8	2.4	2.4	4.2	13.5	21.6
4–7 yrs.	12.8	1.2	1.2	3.4	9.2	20.6	27.7
8–11 yrs.	35.5	58.8	24.9	27.3	35.0	32.7	34.4
12 yrs.	27.2	30.2	43.4	42.0	32.9	20.5	8.3
13–15 yrs.	10.6	6.9	23.0	16.1	11.6	8.1	4.9
16 +	4.7	.2	5.0	8.7	7.1	4.7	3.2
Total persons	9016	1336	916	1463	1190	2460	1651
Mean grade completed	10	11	12	12	11	9	8

SOURCE: McKee and Norris, 1976

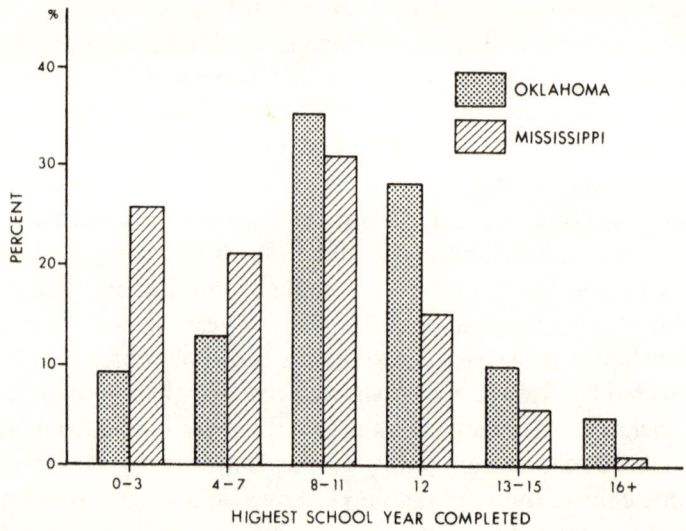

Figure 26 Educational attainment of Oklahoma and Mississippi Choctaw. SOURCE: McKee and Norris, 1976b

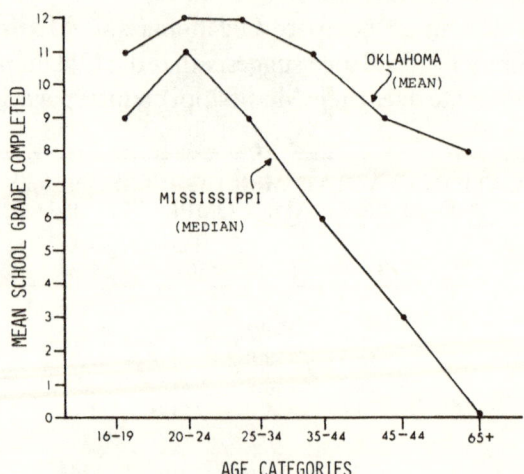

Figure 27 Choctaw educational attainment by age categories and mean/median grade completed. SOURCE: McKee and Norris, 1976b

In recreation, the traditional Choctaw stickball games have almost been replaced by participation in modern sports, and the traditional dances have given way to modern dances. But both activities continue to be learned and played principally for exhibition purposes.

One of the major opportunities to present exhibitions of these traditional activities is the annual Mississippi Choctaw Fair, which was organized in 1950. The fair affords the Choctaws a chance to show young Choctaws and non-Choctaws the many colorful aspects of their past and present life. At the fair there are daily performances of the ceremonial dances of the past, stickball games between different communities, blowgun contests, and other demonstrations and traditional customs (Choctaw Agency, n.d.:10). Plans to improve tourism in the Choctaw areas also have been made.

In Oklahoma, Choctaws participate in modern sports. Stickball is still played, but softball is a major sport. In the Choctaw Nation recreational and tourism facilities are plentiful. Such places as Indian Mounds at Spiro, Lake Wister State Park, Robert S. Kerr Dam, Ouachita National Forest and its Skyline Drive, Robbers Cave State Park, the Choctaw Capitol, Wheelock Mission Church, Broken Bow Reservoir and Beaver Bend State Park, Lake Eufaula and Fountainhead and Arrowhead state parks, Boggy Depot, Raymond Gary Recreation Area, and Lake Texoma State Park are some of the major recreation and tourist sites in the Choctaw Nation. However, most of them are predominantly attended by the white population. Choctaws have been instrumental in establishing Tuskahoma as a visitors' center. A rise in the sale of arts and crafts items has added some income to the Choctaw people. In addition, income is derived from the resale of other Indian-produced items such as turquoise and silver from the American Southwest.

Two of the three major reasons for organizing the Choctaw Agency in Mississippi have been dealt with, namely, the poor economic and educational conditions of the Choctaws. The third reason was inadequate health care.

Plate 48 Choctaw health center at the Pearl River Community, Mississippi. COURTESY *Choctaw Community News*

At the time the agency was formed, the health problem was so severe that the first two directors were doctors (Bounds, 1964:56). Since 1926 a twenty-eight-bed hospital has been maintained by the federal government for the Choctaws (Choctaw Agency, n.d.:9). In 1955 the health program was placed under the Public Health Service of the Indian Health, Education, and Welfare Agency. Since then the hospital has been remodeled, and the health services have been expanded. Approximately one hundred babies are delivered at the hospital each year, and the diagnostic and therapeutic facilities are available to all who need them. Various preventive medicine programs also have been established. As a result of these efforts, Choctaw morbidity and mortality rates have declined in recent years, but much remains to be done before the Choctaws can enjoy an optimum standard of health.

In April, 1976, a new Choctaw health center was dedicated (*Choctaw Community News*, March 26, 1976:1–18). It has three wards—general medical, pediatrics, and obstetrics and gynecology. The center has a total of forty rooms and twenty beds.

A program initiated in 1965, with the purpose of alleviating the poor housing and lack of sanitary facilities prevalent in the Choctaw communities, is the Choctaw Housing Authority (Harris, 1970a:41). Through this program, 205 low-rent housing units had been constructed as of 1974. Sixty-one were under construction throughout the seven Choctaw communities (Smith & Associates, 1974a:97). More units are planned to meet the housing needs of the Choctaw people, and the ultimate objective is to provide every Choctaw family with standard housing.

Two other health-related programs for the Mississippi Choctaws are the construction of a nursing home and the planning of an elderly housing center. The purpose of the Choctaw Nursing Home is to provide adequate care for elderly Choctaws who do not have a satisfactory residence and/or who might be a burden on the family (Mississippi Band of Choctaw Indians, 1973:1). The nursing home has facilities for ten people, and plans are being made to expand the facilities into an elderly housing center. Besides an expanded sixteen-bed center for the elderly, eight one-bedroom homes are planned. Areas for dining, recreation, and other services are also to be provided.

In Oklahoma, the major hospital is the Indian Health Service Hospital at Talihina. An Indian Health Service Center is located at Broken Bow, and two Indian Health Service health stations are located at Antlers and Hugo. However, plans are to phase out the health station at Antlers, to make the station at Hugo a center, and to establish a health center at McAlester. A health center is also planned for Eufaula.

Adequate housing has been a problem for Oklahoma Choctaws, and in 1966 the Indian Housing Authority was organized. The five members of this board were appointed by Chief Belvin. As of March 6, 1973, 885 mutual-help houses were occupied and 331 were under construction in the Choctaw Nation (U.S. Department of the Interior, 1973:50). A housing improvement program also is available to Choctaws.

In 1950, according to the U.S. census, Choctaw population in a nine-county area in east Mississippi numbered 2,260. In 1968 the Choctaw population totaled 3,127 persons. In 1974 (the most recent count), Mississippi Choctaws numbered 3,779 (Spencer, Peterson, and Kim, 1975:4). Of the seven communities, Pearl River is the most populated (Fig. 28, Table 18). Population projections for the Choctaw Reservation and Choctaw Agency service area for the years 1980–2000 are in Table 19.

Table 18 MISSISSIPPI CHOCTAW POPULATION CHANGE, 1968–1974

Community	Population 1968	Population 1974	Change Since 1968	Change Per Year
Bogue Chitto	738	830	+ 92	15.3
Bogue Homa	72	130	+ 58	9.7
Conehatta	544	591	+ 47	7.8
Pearl River	883	1,183	+300	50.0
Redwater	381	418	+ 37	6.2
Standing Pine	234	278	+ 44	7.3
Tucker	275	130	+ 74	12.3
	3,127	3,779	+652	108.6

SOURCE: Smith & Associates, 1974a

Table 19 RESERVATION AND CHOCTAW AGENCY SERVICE AREA POPULATION FORECASTS (MISSISSIPPI)

	1980	1985	1990	1995	2000
Pearl River					
On reservation	1,148	1,269	1,390	1,512	1,633
Community total	1,191	1,317	1,443	1,569	1,695
Bogue Chitto					
On reservation	449	487	525	564	602
Community total	939	1,019	1,099	1,179	1,259
Conehatta					
On reservation	348	372	396	420	445
Community total	676	723	770	817	864
Redwater					
On reservation	282	315	348	381	414
Community total	472	527	582	637	692
Standing Pine					
On reservation	201	211	221	231	241
Community total	280	294	308	322	336
Tucker					
On reservation	184	173	163	152	142
Community total	260	245	230	215	200
Bogue Homa					
On reservation	82	83	85	88	92
Community total	82	87	92	97	102
Reservation total	2,694	2,910	3,128	3,348	3,569
Choctaw Agency Service Area Total	3,900	4,212	4,524	4,836	5,148

SOURCE: Smith & Associates, 1974a

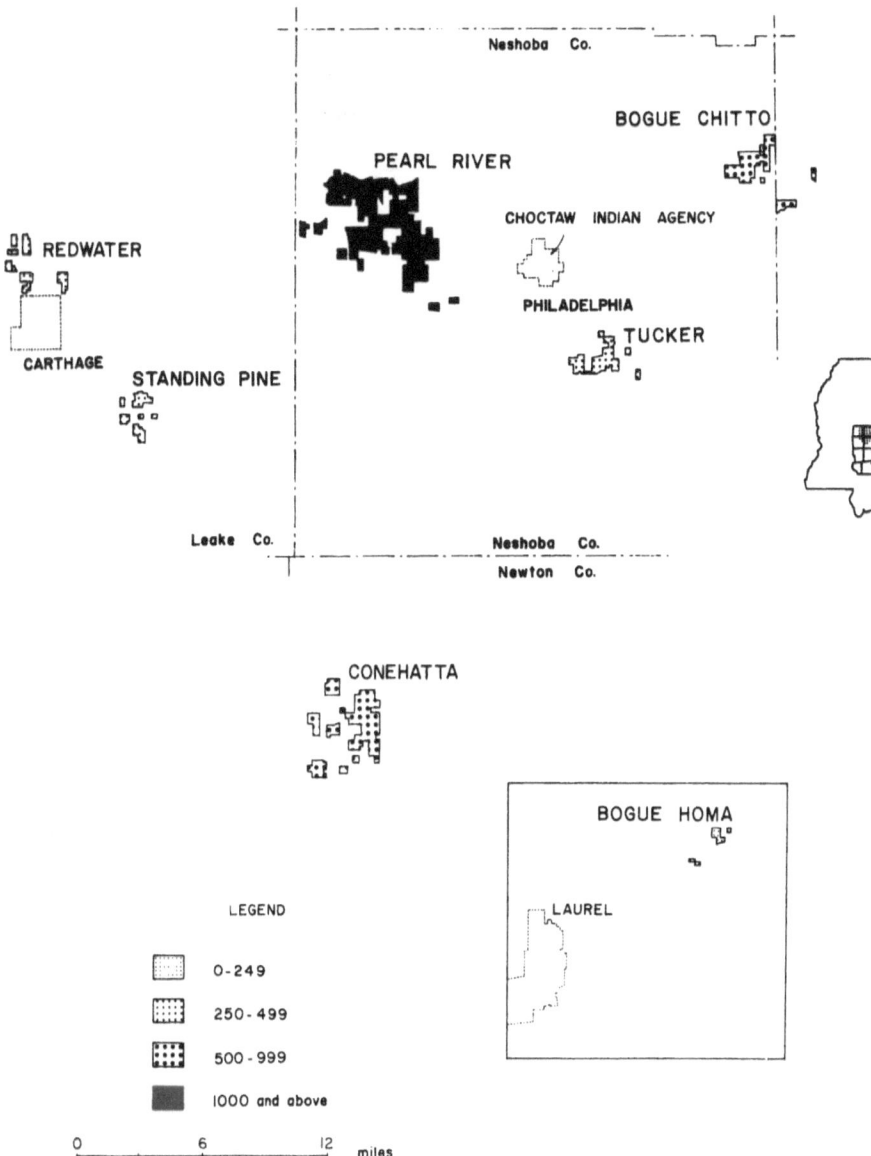

Figure 28 Choctaw population, 1974. SOURCE: McKee, 1976

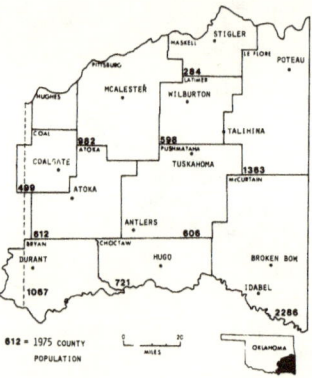

Figure 29   The Choctaw Nation, 1975. SOURCE: McKee and Norris, 1976a

Table 20   OKLAHOMA CHOCTAW POPULATION CHANGE, 1950–1975

County	Population 1950	Population 1975	Change Since 1950	Change Per Year
Atoka	292	612	+320	12.8
Bryan	404	1,067	+663	26.5
Choctaw	337	721	+384	15.4
Coal	183	499	+316	12.6
Haskell	236	284	+ 48	1.9
Latimer	487	598	+111	4.4
LeFlore	575	1,363	+788	31.5
McCurtain	1,540	2,286	+746	29.8
Pittsburg	434	982	+548	21.9
Pushmataha	349	606	+257	10.3
	4,837	9,018	+4,181	167.2

SOURCE: McKee and Norris, 1976a

In 1950, 43 years after Oklahoma statehood, the Choctaw population in the former Choctaw Nation was 4,837 (this U.S. census total is considered to be low). In a census conducted in 1975, which was based upon Choctaw self-identification, Choctaw population totaled 9,018 persons (Norris, Hagle, and Harries, 1975:25–34). However, according to blood quanta, only 2,930 persons were half or more than half Choctaw. Distribution of these Choctaws is shown in Figure 29 and Table 20. The highest concentration is in McCurtain County; the lowest is in Haskell County. There appears to be a lessening of population density the farther away from McCurtain and Le Flore counties. This location factor seems to have existed since the time Choctaws were first removed to Oklahoma. Oklahoma Choctaws between 1950 and 1975 increased their population approximately 170 persons per year. If this trend continues, Choctaw population by the year 2000 should number between 13,000 and 14,000 persons.

There are two important features of the age and sex structures of the sample population of Choctaws (Table 21, Fig. 30). They are the comparatively large number of young people in the population and the change in the sex ratios from young to old. Of 12,801 Choctaws in Mississippi and Oklahoma, 7,291 (57 percent) are under the age of twenty-five and 8,678 (68 percent) are under the age of thirty-five. The youthfulness is more pronounced in the Mississippi Choctaws. By comparison, most counties in the United States have between 35 and 45 percent of the population under 25 years.

Besides the Mississippi-Oklahoma differences in the number of young Choctaws, the difference between the percentages of those over sixty-five also should be noted. Eleven percent of the Oklahoma Choctaws are over sixty-five, but only 3.5 percent of the Mississippians are over that age. That are more female Choctaws than male in Oklahoma. In Mississippi, the sexes are nearly equally divided. The difference is accounted for in the older population. It can be seen from Table 21 and Figure 30 that, in both Mississippi and Oklahoma, males outnumber females only in the youngest age category.

Table 21 MISSISSIPPI AND OKLAHOMA CHOCTAW POPULATION BY AGE AND SEX

OKLAHOMA, 1975

Age	Total	Male	Female	Percentage		
				Total	Male	Female
Under 25	4,950	2,533	2,417	54.9	28.1	26.8
25–34 years	874	395	479	9.7	4.4	5.3
35–44 years	692	286	406	7.7	3.2	4.5
45–64 years	1,509	629	880	16.7	7.0	10.0
65 and over	993	389	604	11.0	4.3	6.7
Total	9,018	4,232	4,786	100.0	47.0	53.0

MISSISSIPPI, 1974

Age	Total	Male	Female	Percentage		
				Total	Male	Female
Under 25	2,341	1,186	1,155	61.9	31.4	30.5
25–34 years	513	238	275	13.6	6.3	7.3
35–44 years	365	160	205	9.6	4.2	5.4
45–64 years	416	212	204	11.0	5.6	5.4
65 and over	133	59	74	3.5	1.6	2.0
Age unknown	15	7	8	.4	.2	.2
Total	3,783[a]	1,862	1,921	100.0	49.2	50.8

[a]Note that four additional persons are added to the total given in Table 18.
SOURCE: McKee and Norris, 1976a; Spencer, Peterson, and Kim, 1975

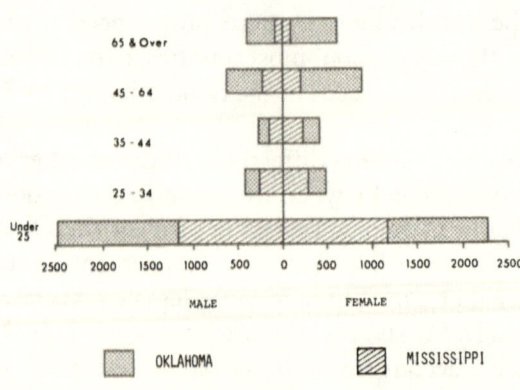

Figure 30 Age and sex structure of Choctaw population. SOURCE: McKee and Norris, 1976b

Mississippi Choctaws have become increasingly aware of the Choctaws living in western Tennessee. In 1974, 140 Choctaws were living in 31 households, 40 in Memphis and the remaining 100 in small rural communities within a 50-mile range of Memphis. Table 22 summarizes their population structure.

Table 22 POPULATION OF WESTERN TENNESSEE COMMUNITY BY AGE AND SEX, 1974

Age	Total		Male		Female	
	Number	Percent	Number	Percent	Number	Percent
Under 5 years	19	13.6	9	6.4	10	7.1
5–9 years	22	15.7	10	7.1	12	8.6
10–14 years	21	15.0	8	5.7	13	9.3
15–19 years	18	12.9	3	2.1	15	10.7
20–24 years	9	6.4	4	2.9	5	3.6
25–29 years	17	12.1	7	5.0	10	7.1
30–34 years	10	7.1	5	3.6	5	3.6
35–39 years	6	4.3	4	2.9	2	1.4
40–44 years	7	5.0	4	2.9	3	2.1
45–49 years	2	1.4	2	1.4	0	.0
50–54 years	7	5.0	3	2.1	4	2.9
55–59 years	2	1.4	1	.7	1	.7
Total	140	100.0	60	42.8	80	57.1
Median age: 16.5						

SOURCE: Spencer, Peterson, and Kim, 1975

The traditional native dress of the Mississippi and Oklahoma Choctaws has been replaced by the styles of the dominant American culture. Some of the older Mississippi Choctaw women still wear brightly colored, ankle-length, full-skirted dresses and continue to allow their long hair to flow loosely down their backs. But usually this is done more as a recognition of their identity than as a regular dress habit. The men seldom wear the traditional costume, except at the Choctaw Fair. In Oklahoma most Choctaws dress in modern American style with a touch of Indian identity.

The major kinship system in Mississippi Choctaw society during the twentieth century consists of locality groupings of nuclear families held together through extended kinship. Thus, the Choctaws in a certain locale are related to one another and belong to a specific group, which is basically congruent with the clan. The clan thus holds the local group together, rather than tying together different communities as it did in the past. The twentieth-century Choctaw is more likely to choose a marriage partner from the same community or at least from an adjacent community. In fact, in 1968, almost 64 percent of all Choctaw couples comprised partners from the same community. Even when individuals from different communities married, they tended to reside in the home community of one of the partners (Peterson, 1970a:147, 149). In sum, then, the local Mississippi Choctaw community has become a kinship unit. The kinship system has basically broken down in Oklahoma.

The Mississippi Choctaw family has changed in its activities and functions, but it has, at the same time, maintained the separateness of the Choctaw society from the dominant American society.

Women are beginning to give birth to their children in hospitals, the Choctaw Agency is providing care for the elderly, various sources outside the family are providing adequate housing and health care, and the educational, political, and religious activities are sought outside the family. In spite of these changes, there has been relatively little intermarriage between Choctaws and non-Choctaws, thus keeping the Choctaws distinct and isolated from the larger society (Peterson, 1970a:162–63).

The Mississippi Choctaws have large families. In 1969, 8.6 percent of the households had five children, over 14 percent had six or more, and the median number of children per family was two. Many Choctaw households tend to have more than two adults. A little over half the families (53.6 percent) had only two adults, but over 46 percent had more than two. Another finding indicated that almost one out of every five Choctaw households had a female as its head. Choctaw family units are also relatively intact. Only 8.2 percent of the household heads were divorced or separated, and less than 15 percent were widowed (Harris, 1970a:3, 19). Thus, the Choctaw family typically has a large number of children and several adult relatives living in one dwelling. Choctaw is still the language spoken most often in the home. Table 23 summarizes language spoken according to community.

With respect to the problems the twentieth-century families experience, low wages or not enough money was the one most often cited in Mississippi. Inadequate housing was the second most frequent response. The fact that the lack of education was not stated as a family problem could show that the Choctaws may not fully realize that education might be the way to eradicate the other two problems. It is noteworthy that the three major problems existing before creation of the Choctaw Agency are still with some Choctaw families today. With the new programs of the agency, the future of the Mississippi Choctaw family appears to be much brighter than the past has been.

Table 23 LANGUAGE SPOKEN MOST OFTEN IN HOUSEHOLD BY COMMUNITY, 1974 (MISSISSIPPI)

Community	Choctaw	English	Both[a]	Not Reported
		Percentages		
Bogue Chitto	90.7	4.3	4.3	.6
Bogue Homa	63.0	7.4	29.6	.0
Conehatta	86.8	3.9	9.3	.0
Pearl River	71.0	10.7	17.9	.4
Redwater	81.6	6.9	11.5	.0
Standing Pine	90.7	1.9	7.4	.0
Tucker	72.8	11.1	16.0	.0
Total	80.3	7.1	12.3	.3

[a]Approximately equal use of Choctaw and English.
SOURCE: Spencer, Peterson, and Kim, 1975

In Oklahoma, the Choctaw family has much pride and dignity. Parents have a deep concern to provide their children with a good education. One example of this effort is the success of the Title IV Indian Education Program in the Idabel schools. Emphasis also has been placed upon better housing, quality health care, and more job opportunities.

Religion is still an important part of Choctaw life in Oklahoma. The monthly church singing is an integral part of the social calendar of many Choctaw families.

In a 1975 census of Oklahoma Choctaws, 5,298 households were interviewed. Total population in the households amounted to 16,998 persons, of whom 13,822 were Indian (Norris, 1977:1). Only 18.7 percent of the population was non-Indian due largely to intermarriages. Furthermore, only 9,018 of 13,822 persons who were Indians were Choctaw. The majority of the remaining Indian population, 3,397 persons, was Cherokee (Norris, 1975:36). The number of persons per household averaged 3.21 (Norris, 1977:1). However, the average number of "persons per household increases as the percentage of non-Indians per household decreases" (Norris, 1975:10). McCurtain County had the largest number of persons (3.88) per household, whereas Haskell County averaged 2.9 persons per household (Norris, 1977:1).

6

Epilogue

Throughout much of their history the Choctaws have been primarily a sedentary agricultural group, living in small villages. In Mississippi and Oklahoma their land basically has been divided into three districts. Their population usually has ranged between 12,000 and 20,000 persons for the past three hundred years. To be sure, the Choctaws are intelligent, friendly, and law-abiding. They generally have tried to be friends with the United States government. In short, they have been the "good guys," or they are as Swanton described them, "just folks." Sometimes the good guys do not receive the notoriety that the more vociferous tribes achieve; such has been the case of the Choctaws. Choctaw history, to some extent, is quiet and orderly compared with that of some of the Plains tribes. Thus Choctaws have not received the attention that they deserve.

Throughout most of their history, the Choctaws have been receptive to material, technological, and governmental changes. This is not to say, however, that these changes occurred without resistance. The Choctaws were usually amenable to a "just" solution, and in most cases approached specific problems with the U.S. government in a spirit of cooperation. It is evident that, from the time of removal until Oklahoma statehood, the Choctaws adopted many of the political, religious, social, economic, and technological traits of American society as a whole. The Oklahoma Choctaws are somewhat more assimilated into the greater society than are the Mississippi Choctaws. Nevertheless, both groups appear to be trying to preserve important tribal traits while adopting some of the better traits of the predominant surrounding Anglo culture.

There have been many dark moments in Choctaw history, particularly the treatment of the Mississippi Choctaws from 1834 to 1918 and the ending of the Choctaw Nation in 1906 in Oklahoma. But by-and-large, Choctaw history is one of quiet change. It is a history of a group resistant to violence as a way to solve problems.

It should be noted that not all of the Choctaws today are living in the Choctaw Nation in southeast Oklahoma or on the reservation in Mississippi. These two areas account for only 12,801 Choctaws. According to the 1970 U.S. census, the Choctaw tribe and its counterpart the Houma (primarily located in Louisiana) numbered 23,562, making this group the seventh largest native American tribe in the United States behind the Navajo (96,743), Cherokee (66,150), Sioux (47,825), Chippewa (41,946), Pueblo (30,971), and Lumbee (27,520).

Numerous Choctaws in this century have migrated from Oklahoma and Mississippi to various locations, including Dallas, Los Angeles, and Chicago. Their population has become slightly dispersed and displays varying degrees of assimilation.

Despite the cultural changes the Choctaws have experienced, they remain today a distinct ethnic group with their own language and unique traditions. Their culture, showing no signs of extinction, is viable and dynamic. In Mississippi as well as in Oklahoma, Choctaws today are closer to establishing greater control over their own affairs since removal and dissolution of their nation. Bilingual programs, various job-training programs, housing and health development projects, and spirited leadership in furthering the "self-determination" policy all combine to enhance the quality of life for the Choctaws.

APPENDIX

APPENDIX

1
Treaty of Dancing Rabbit Creek

A treaty of perpetual friendship, cession and limits, entered into by John H. Eaton and John Coffee for and in behalf of the Government of the United States, and the Mingoes, Chiefs, Captains, and Warriors of the Choctaw Nation, begun and held at Dancing Rabbit Creek on the 15th of September in the year 1830.

WHEREAS the General Assembly of the State of Mississippi has extended the laws of said state to persons and property within the chartered limits of the same, and the President of the United States has said that he cannot protect the Choctaw people from the operation of those laws. Now, therefore, that the Choctaws may live under their own laws in peace with the United States, and the State of Mississippi, and have, accordingly agreed to the following articles of treaty.

ARTICLE 1. Perpetual peace and friendship is pledged and agreed upon, by and between the United States, and the Mingoes, Chiefs and warriors of the Choctaw Nation of Red people, and that this may be considered the treaty existing between the parties, all other treaties heretofore existing and inconsistent with the provisions of this are hereby declared null and void.

ARTICLE 2. The United States, under a grant specially to be made by the President of the United States, shall cause to be conveyed to the Choctaw nation, a tract of country West of the Mississippi river in fee simple, to them and their descendants, to insure to them while they shall exist as a nation, and live on it, beginning near Fort Smith, where the Arkansas boundary crosses the Arkansas river, running thence to the source of the Canadian Fork if in the limits of the United States, or to those limits; thence due South to Red river, and down Red river to the West boundary of the territory of Arkansas, thence North along that line to the beginning. The boundary of the same to be agreeable to the treaty made and concluded at Washington City in the year 1825. The grant to be executed, so soon as the present treaty shall be ratified.

ARTICLE 3. In consideration of the provisions contained in the several articles of this treaty, the Choctaw nation of Indians consent, and hereby cede to the United States the entire country they own and possess East of the Mississippi river, and they agree to remove beyond the Mississippi river, early as practicable, and will so arrange their removal, that as many as possible of their people not exceeding one half of the whole number shall depart during the falls of 1831 and 1832 the residue to follow during the succeeding fall of 1833. A better opportunity, in this manner, will be afforded the government to extend to them the facilities and comforts which it is desirable should be extended in encouraging them to their new homes.

ARTICLE 4. The government and people of the United States, are hereby obliged to secure to the said Choctaw nation of red people the jurisdiction and government of all the persons and property that may be within their limits West, so that no state or territory shall ever have a right to pass laws for the government of the Choctaw nation of red people and their descendents: and that no part of the land granted them shall ever be embraced in any territory or state, but the United States shall forever secure said Choctaw nation from and against all laws, except such as from time to time, may be enacted in their national councils, not inconsistent with the constitution, treaties and laws of the United States; and except as may and which have been enacted by Congress to the extent that Congress under the constitution are required to exercise a legislation over Indian affairs. But the Choctaws, should this treaty be ratified, express a wish that Congress may grant to the Choctaws the rights of punishing by their own laws, any white man who shall come into their nation, and infringe any of their national regulations.

ARTICLE 5. The United States are obliged to protect the Choctaws from domestic strife, and from foreign enemies, on the same principles that citizens of the United States are protected; so that whatever would be a legal demand upon the United States for defence or for wrongs committed by an enemy of a citizen of the United States, shall be equally binding in favor of the Choctaws, and in all cases where the Choctaws shall be called upon, by a legally authorized officer of the

United States, to fight an enemy, such Choctaw shall receive the pay and other benefits, which citizens of the United States receive in such cases: provided, no war shall be undertaken or prosecuted by said Choctaw nation, but by declaration made in full council, and to be approved by the United States, unless it be in self defence against an open rebellion, or against an enemy marching into their country; in which cases they shall defend until the United States are advised thereof.

ARTICLE 6. Should a Choctaw, or any party of Choctaws, commence acts of violence upon the person or property of a citizen of the United States or join any war party against any neighboring tribe of Indians, without the authority in the preceding article and except to oppose an actual or threatened invasion, or rebellion, such person so offending shall be delivered up to an officer of the United States, if in the power of the Choctaw nation that such offender may be punished, as may be provided in such cases by the laws of the United States; but if such offender is not within the control of the Choctaw nation, then said Choctaw nation shall not be held responsible for the injury done by said offender.

ARTICLE 7. All acts of violence committed upon persons and property of the people of the Choctaw nation, either by citizens of the United States, or neighboring tribes of red people, shall be referred to some authorized agent by him to be referred to the President of the United States, who shall examine into such cases, and see that every possible degree of justice is done to said Indian party of the Choctaw nation.

ARTICLE 8. Offenders against the laws of the United States, or any individual state, shall be apprehended and delivered to any duly authorized person where such offender may be found in the Choctaw country, having fled from any part of the United States, but in all such cases application must be made to the agent or the chiefs and the expense of his apprehension and delivery, provided for, and paid by the United States.

ARTICLE 9. Any citizen of the United States, who may be ordered from the nation by the agent and constituted authorities of the nation, and refused to obey, or return to the nation, without the consent of the aforesaid persons, shall be subject to such pains and penalties as may be provided by the laws of the United States, in such cases. Citizens of the United States travelling peaceably under the authority of the laws of the United States, shall be under the care and protection of the nation.

ARTICLE 10. No person shall expose goods, or other articles for sale, as a trader, without permission from the constituted authorities of the nation, or authority of the laws of the Congress of the United States, under penalty of forfeiting the articles; and the constituted authorities of said nation shall grant no license, except to such persons as reside in the nation and are answerable to the laws of the nation. The United States shall be particularly obliged to assist to prevent ardent spirits from being introduced into the nation.

ARTICLE 11. Navigable streams shall be free to the Choctaws who shall pay no higher toll or duty than citizens of the United States. It is agreed further that the United States shall establish one or more post offices in said nation and may establish such military post roads, and posts, as they may consider necessary.

ARTICLE 12. All intruders shall be removed from the Choctaw nation and kept without it. Private property to be always respected, and on no occasion taken for public purposes without just compensation being made therefor to the rightful owners. If an Indian unlawfully steals any property from a white man, a citizen of the United States, the offender shall be punished, and if a white man unlawfully takes anything from an Indian, the property shall be restored, and the offender punished. It is further agreed that when a Choctaw shall be given up to be tried, for any offense against the laws of the United States, if unable to employ council to defend him, the United States will do it, that his trial may be fair and impartial.

ARTICLE 13. It is consented that a qualified agent shall be appointed, for the Choctaws, every four years unless sooner removed, by the President, and he shall be removed on petition of the constituted authorities of the nation the President being satisfied there is sufficient cause shown. The agent shall fix his residence convenient to the great body of the people, and in the selection of an agent, immediately after the ratification of this treaty, the wishes of the Choctaw nation on the subject, shall be entitled to great respect.

ARTICLE 14. Each Choctaw head of a family, being desirous to remain, and become a citizen of the States, shall be permitted to do so, by signifying his intention to the agent within six months from the ratification of this treaty, and he or she shall thereupon be entitled to a reservation of one section of six hundred and forty acres of land, to be bounded by sectional lines of survey; in like manner, shall be entitled to one half that quantity, for each unmarried child which is living with him, over ten years of age, and a quarter section to such child as may be under ten years of age to adjoin the location of the parent. If they reside upon said lands intending to become citizens of the States, for five years after the ratification of this treaty, in that case, a grant of land in fee simple shall be issued: said reservation shall include the present improvement of the head of the family, or a portion of it. Persons who claim under this article shall not lose the privileges of a Choctaw citizen, but if they ever remove are not to be entitled to any portion of the Choctaw annuity.

ARTICLE 15. To each of the Chiefs in the Choctaw nation (to wit), Greenwood LeFlore, Nutackachie and Mushulatubbee, there is granted a reservation of four sections of land two of which shall include and adjoin their present improvements and the other two located where they please but on unoccupied, unimproved lands; such sections shall be bounded by sectional lines, and with the consent of the President, they may sell the same. Also, to the three principal chiefs, and to their successors in office, there shall be paid two hundred and fifty dollars, annually while they shall continue in their respective offices; except to Mushulatubbee, who, as he has an annuity of one hundred and fifty dollars, for life, under a former treaty, shall receive only the additional sum of one hundred dollars, while he shall continue in office, as chief. And if in addition to this the nation shall think proper to elect an additional principal chief of the whole to superintend and govern, upon republican principles, he shall receive annually, for his services, five hundred dollars, which allowance to the chiefs, and their successors in office, shall continue for twenty years. At any time when in military service, and while in service by authority of the United States, the district chiefs, under, and by selection of the President, shall be entitled to the pay of Majors; and the other chief, under the same circumstances, shall have the pay of a Lieutenant Colonel. The speakers of the three districts, shall receive twenty five dollars a year, for four years: and the three secretaries, one to each of the chiefs, fifty dollars each, for four years. Each Captain of the nation, the number not to exceed ninety-nine, thirty-three from each district, shall be furnished, upon removing to the West, with each a good suit of clothes, and a broad sword, as an outfit, and for four years, commencing with the first of their removal shall each receive fifty dollars a year, for the trouble of keeping their people at order in settling: and whenever they shall be in military service, by authority of the United States, shall receive the pay of a captain.

ARTICLE 16. In wagons, and with steamboats, as may be found necessary, the United States agree to remove the Indians to their new homes, at their expense, and under the care of discreet and careful persons, who will be kind and brotherly to them. They agree to furnish them with ample corn and beef, or pork for themselves and families, for twelve months, after reaching their new homes. It is agreed further, that the United States will take all their cattle, at the valuation of some discreet person to be appointed by the President, and the same shall be paid for in money after their arrival at their new homes, or other cattle, such as may be desired, shall be furnished them; notice being given, through their agent of their wishes upon this subject of their removal, that time to supply the demand may be afforded.

ARTICLE 17. The several annuities and sums secured under former treaties, to the Choctaw nation and people, shall continue, as though this treaty had never been made. And it is further agreed, that the United States, in addition, will pay the sum of twenty thousand dollars for twenty years, commencing after their removal to the West, of which in the first year after their removal, ten thousand dollars shall be divided and arranged, to such as may not receive reservations under this treaty.

ARTICLE 18. The United States shall cause the lands hereby added, to be surveyed: and surveyors may enter the Choctaw country for that purpose; conducting themselves properly, and disturbing or interrupting none of the Choctaw people. But no person is to be permitted to settle within the nation, or the lands to be sold, before the Choctaws shall remove. And for the payment of the several amounts secured in this treaty. The lands hereby ceded, are to remain in a fund pledged to that purpose, until the debt shall be provided for and arranged. And further it is agreed, that in the construction of this treaty, wherever well founded doubts shall arise, it shall be construed most favourably towards the Choctaws.

ARTICLE 19. The following reservations of land are hereby admitted. To Col. David Folsom, four sections of which two shall include his present improvement, and two may be located elsewhere, on unoccupied, unimproved land.

To J. Garland, Col. Robert Cole, Tuppanahomer, John Pitchlynn, John Charles Juzan, Johokebetubbe, Eraychahobea, Ofehoma, two sections each, to include their improvements, and to be bounded by sectional lines; and the same may be disposed of and sold, with the consent of the President, and that others, not provided for, may be provided for, there shall be reserved as follows:

First, one section to each head of a family, not exceeding forty in number, who, during the present year, may have had in actual cultivation with a dwelling house thereon, fifty acres or more. Secondly, three quarter sections after the manner aforesaid, to each head of a family, not exceeding four hundred and sixty, as shall have cultivated thirty acres or less than fifty, to be bounded by quarter section lines of survey, and to be contiguous and adjoining. Third, one half section as aforesaid, to those who shall have cultivated from twenty to thirty acres; the number not to exceed four hundred: Fourth, a quarter section as aforesaid, to such as shall have cultivated from two to twelve acres: the number also, not to exceed three hundred and fifty persons. Each of said classes of cases, shall be subject to the limitations contained in the first class and shall be so located as to include that part of the improvement, which contains the dwelling house. If a greater number shall be found to be entitled to reservations, under the several classes of this article, than it is stipulated for under the limitation prescribed; then, and in that case the chiefs, separately and together, shall determine the persons who shall be excluded in the respective districts. Fifth, any captain, the number not exceeding ninety persons, who, under the provisions of this article shall receive less than a section, he shall be entitled to an additional quantity of half a section, adjoining to his other reservation. The several reservations secured under this article, may be sold, with the consent of the President of the United States; but should any prefer it, or omit to take a reservation for the quantity he may be entitled to, the United States will, on his removing, pay fifty cents an acre, after reaching their new homes; provided, that before the first of January next, they shall provide to the agent, or some other authorized person, to be appointed, proof of his claim to the quantity of it. Sixth. Likewise children of the Choctaw nation, residing in the nation, who have neither father nor mother, a list of which, with satisfactory proof of parentage, and orphanage, being filed with agent in six months, to be forwarded to the War Department, shall be entitled to a quarter section of land, to be located under the direction of the President, and with his consent, the same may be sold, and the proceeds applied to some beneficial purpose for the benefit of said orphans.

ARTICLE 20. The United States agree and stipulate as follows, that for the benefit and advantage of the Choctaw people, and to improve their condition, there shall be educated under the direction of the President, and at the expense of the United States, forty Choctaw youths, for twenty years. This number shall be kept at school; and as they finish their education, others, so supply their places, shall be received, for the period stated. The United States agree also, to erect a council house, at some convenient, central point, after their people shall be settled, and a house for each chief; also, a church, for each of the three districts, to be used as school houses, until the nation may conclude to build others: and for these purposes, ten thousand dollars shall be appropriated. Also fifty thousand dollars (viz.) twenty-five hundred dollars annually, shall be given for the support of three teachers of schools, for twenty years. Likewise, there shall be furnished the following articles; twenty one hundred blankets; to each warrior who emigrated, a rifle, moulds, wipers and ammunition: one thousand axes, ploughs, hoes, wheels, and cards, each, and four hundred looms. There shall also be furnished one ton of iron, and two hundred weight of steel annually to each district, for sixteen years.

ARTICLE 21. A few Choctaw warriors yet survive, who marched and fought in the army of General Wayne; the whole number stated not to exceed twenty. These, it is agreed, shall hereafter while they live, receive twenty-five dollars a year; a list of them to be early as practicable, and within six months, made out and presented to the agent, to be forwarded to the War Department.

ARTICLE 22. The chiefs of the Choctaws have suggested, that their people are in a state of rapid advancement, in education and refinement and have expressed a solicitude that they might have the privilege of a delegate on the floor of the House of Representatives extended to them. The commissioners do not feel that they can, under a treaty stipulation, accede to the request: but at their desire, present it in the treaty, that Congress may consider of and decide the application.

Done and signed and executed by the commissioners of the United States, and the Chiefs, Captains, and headmen of the Choctaw nation, at Dancing Rabbit Creek, this 27th day of September, eighteen hundred and thirty.

[Signed by 172 Choctaw leaders and the two American commissioners, John Eaton and John Coffee.]

(De Rosier, 1970:174-182).

2
Chiefs of the Choctaws

District Chiefs in Mississippi

Southern District Chiefs

Pushmataha 1803–1824
General Hummingbird 1824–1826
Sam Garland 1826–1830

Western District Chiefs

Apukshunnubbee. 1802–1824
Robert Cole 1824–1826
Greenwood Le Flore 1826–1830

Eastern District Chiefs

Moshulatubbee. 1809–1826
David Folsom. 1826–1830

District Chiefs During Removal, 1830–1834

Moshulatubbee District . . . . .Moshulatubbee
Apukshunnubbee District . . . . .Greenwood Le Flore
Pushmataha District . . . . .Nitukechi

District Chiefs in Indian Territory

Moshulatubbee District

Moshulatubbee	1834–1836
Joseph Kincaid	1836–1838
John McKinney	1838–1842
Nathaniel Folsom	1842–1846
Peter Folsom	1846–1850
Cornelius McCurtain	1850–1854
David McCoy	1854–1857

Apukshunnubbee District

Thomas Le Flore	1834–1838
James Fletcher	1838–1842
Thomas Le Flore	1842–1850
George W. Harkins	1850–1857

Pushmataha District

Nitukechi	1834–1838
Pierre Juzan	1838–1841
Isaac Folsom	1841–1846
Nitukechi	(died)
Silas D. Fisher	1846–1850
George Folsom	1850–1854
David McCoy	1854–1857

Principal Chiefs or Governors of the Choctaw Nation

Alfred Wade	1857–1858
Tandy Walker	1858–1859
Brazil Le Flore	1859–1860
George Hudson	1860–1862
Sam Garland	1862–1864
Peter Pitchlynn	1864–1866
Allen Wright	1866–1870
William J. Bryant	1870–1874
Coleman Cole	1874–1878
Isaac Garvin	1878–1880
Jack McCurtain	1880–1884
Edmund McCurtain	1884–1886
Thompson McKinney	1886–1888
Ben Smallwood	1888–1890
Wilson N. Jones	1890–1894

Jefferson Gardner 1894–1896
Green McCurtain 1896–1900
Gilbert W. Dukes 1900–1902
Green McCurtain 1902–1910
Victor M. Locke, Jr.* 1911–1918
William F. Semple*..1918–1922
William H. Harrison* 1922–1929
Ben Dwight* 1930–1937
William A. Durant* 1937–1948
Harry J. W. Belvin 1948–1975
Clark David Gardner 1975–1978
Hollis Roberts 1978–

There is no written record of a complete list of past tribal chiefs in Mississippi after removal to the present.
*appointed by the president of the United States
Source: Compiled by I. C. Gunning, n.d. $_a$:69–70

Bibliography

Books

Baird, W. Daniel 1972 *Peter Pitchlynn: Chief of the Choctaws.* Norman: University of Oklahoma Press.
———1973 *The Choctaw People.* Phoenix: Indian Tribal Series.
Benson, Henry C. 1860 *Life Among the Choctaw Indians and Sketches of the South-West.* Cincinnati: L. Swormstedt & A. Poe.
Bettersworth, John K. 1959 *Mississippi: A History.* Austin: Steck Company.
Bounds, Thelma V. 1961 *An Indian Tribe of Mississippi: Meet Our Choctaw Friends.* New York: Exposition Press.
———1964 *Children of Nanih Waiya.* San Antonio: Naylor Company.
Claiborne, J. F. H. 1880 *Mississippi as a Province, Territory, and State.* Jackson, Miss.: Power & Barksdale.
Conklin, Paul 1975 *Choctaw Boy.* New York: Dodd, Mead, & Company.
Cotterill, Robert S. 1954 *The Southern Indians: The Story of the Civilized Tribes Before Removal.* Norman: University of Oklahoma Press.
Cushman, Horatio B. 1899 *History of the Choctaw, Chickasaw, and Natchez Indians.* Greenville, Tex.: Highlight Printing House.
———1962 *History of the Choctaw, Chickasaw, and Natchez Indians.* Norman: University of Oklahoma Press.
Dale, Edward Everett, and Morris L. Wardell 1948 *History of Oklahoma.* Englewood Cliffs: Prentice-Hall, Inc.
Debo, Angie 1934 *The Rise and Fall of the Choctaw Republic.* Norman: University of Oklahoma Press.
———1940 *And Still the Waters Run.* Princeton: Princeton University Press.
———1949 *Oklahoma: Foot-Loose and Fancy-Free.* Norman: University of Oklahoma Press.
———1961 *The Rise and Fall of the Choctaw Republic.* 2nd ed. Norman: University of Oklahoma Press.

———1970 *A History of the Indians of the United States.* Norman: University of Oklahoma Press.
Densmore, Frances 1972 *Choctaw Music.* New York: DaCapo Press.
DeRosier, Arthur H., Jr. 1970 *The Removal of the Choctaw Indians.* Knoxville: University of Tennessee.
DeVorsey, Louis, Jr. 1966 in *The Indian Boundary in the Southern Colonies, 1763-1775.* Chapel Hill: University of North Carolina Press. Press.
Ethridge, George H., and Walter Nesbit Taylor 1938 *Mississippi: A History.* Vol. II. Jackson, Miss.: Historical Record Association.
Foreman Grant 1934 *The Five Civilized Tribes.* Norman: University of Oklahoma Press.
———1953 *Indian Removal: The Emigration of the Five Civilized Tribes of Indians.* Norman: University of Oklahoma Press.
Fundaburk, Emma Lila 1958 *Southeastern Indians: Life Portraits.* Luverne, Ala.: Emma Lila Fundaburk.
Gaines, George Strother 1928 *Dancing Rabbit Creek Treaty.* Birmingham: Birmingham Printing Company.
Gibson, Arrell M. 1960 *A Guide to Regional Manuscript Collections.* Norman: University of Oklahoma Press.
———1965 *Oklahoma: A History of Five Centuries.* Norman: Harlow Publishing Company.
Goode, Charles N. 1933 *Oklahoma Place Names.* Norman: University of Oklahoma Press.
Guyton, Pearl Vivian 1952 *Our Mississippi.* Austin: Steck Company.
Hardee, Robert L. 1972 *Drums of the Toli.* Mabelvale, Ark.: Foreman-Payne, Publishers.
Hastain, E. 1908 *Index to Choctaw-Chickasaw Deeds and Allotments.* Muskogee, Okla.: E. Hastain.
Hodge, Frederick Webb 1907 *Choctaw.* Handbook of American Indians North of Mexico. Washington, D.C.: Government Printing Office.
Hudson, Charles M. 1975 *Four Centuries of Southern Indians.* Athens: University of Georgia Press.
Kappler, Charles 1929 *Indian Affairs, Laws, and Treaties.* 4 vols. Washington, D.C.: Government Printing Office.
Lafarge, Oliver 1956 *A Pictorial History of the American Indian.* New York: Crown Publishers, Inc.
Lewis, Anna 1959 *Chief Pushmataha, American Patriot.* New York: Exposition Press.
Maxwell, Amos D. 1953 *The Sequoyah Constitution Convention.* Boston: Meador Publishing Company.
McCracken, Harold 1959 *George Catlin and the Old Frontier.* New York: Bonanza Books.
McReynolds, Edwin C. 1954 *Oklahoma: A History of the Sooner State.* Norman: University of Oklahoma Press.
Milligan, Dorothy 1977 *The Indian Way: Choctaws.* Wichita Falls: Nortex Press.
Morris, John W., Charles R. Goins, and Edwin C. McReynolds 1976 *Historical Atlas of Oklahoma.* Norman: University of Oklahoma Press.

Morris, John W., and Edwin C. McReynolds 1965 *Historical Atlas of Oklahoma.* Norman: University of Oklahoma Press.
Morrison, Olin Dee 1965ₐ *North America in Antique Maps, 1520–1865.* Athens, Ohio: E. M. Morrison.
——1965ᵦ *The American South.* Historical Atlas III, Pt. 2, Mississippi–West Virginia. Athens, Ohio: E. M. Morrison.
Murdock, George P. 1960 *Ethnographic Bibliography of North America.* New Haven: Human Relations Area Files.
Oklahoma City Council of Choctaws 1976 *English Choctaw Dictionary.* 6th ed. Reprint of Cyrus Byington, *Dictionary of the Choctaw Language.* Oklahoma City: Oklahoma City Council of Choctaws, Inc.
Oklahoma Writers' Project 1941 *Oklahoma.* Norman: University of Oklahoma Press.
Ruth, Kent 1957 *Oklahoma: A Guide to the Sooner State.* Norman: University of Oklahoma Press.
Shirk, George H. 1965 *Oklahoma Place Names.* Norman: University of Oklahoma Press.
Smith, Allene DeShazo 1951 *Greenwood LeFlore and the Choctaw Indians of the Mississippi Valley.* Memphis: C. A. Davis Printing Company, Inc.
Spicer, Edward H. 1961 *Perspectives in American Indian Culture Change.* Chicago: University of Chicago Press.
Swanton, John R. 1931 *Source Material for the Social and Ceremonial Life of the Choctaw Indians.* Bulletin No. 103. Washington, D.C.: Government Printing Office.
Tubbee, Okah 1848 *A Sketch of the Life of Okah Tubbee, Alias William Chubbee, Son of the Head Chief, Mosholeh Tubbee, of the Choctaw Nation of Indians.* Springfield, Mass.: H. S. Taylor.
Washburn, Wilcomb E. 1975 *The American Indian.* New York: Harper & Row Publishers, Inc.
Williams, Samuel Cole n.d. *Adair's History of the American Indians.* Originally published by Promontory Press in New York, 1930. New York: Arno Press.
Wright, Muriel H. 1951 *A Guide to the Indian Tribes of Oklahoma.* Norman: University of Oklahoma Press.
Young, Mary Elizabeth 1961 *Redskins, Ruffleshirts, and Rednecks.* Norman: University of Oklahoma Press.

Articles

Abbot, Martin 1952 "Indian Policy and Management in Mississippi Territory, 1798–1817." *Journal of Mississippi History,* 14 (July): 153–69.
Alex, Bradley, and Annie Williams 1973 "Choctaw Social Dancing." *Nanih Waiya,* 1 (Fall):30–33.
Andrews, T. F. 1965 "Freedmen in Indian Territory: A Post–Civil War Dilemma." *Journal of the West,* 4 (July):367–76.
Bacon, Willard Keith 1973 "Legends of Nanih Waiya." *Nanih Waiya,* 1 (Fall):2–3.
Benson, Henry C. 1926 "Life Among the Choctaw Indians." *Chronicles of Oklahoma,* 9 (June):156–61.

Bonnifield, Paul 1973 "Choctaw Nation on the Eve of the Civil War." *Journal of the West,* 12 (July):386–402.

Brinegar, Bonnie 1977 "Choctaw Place—Names in Mississippi." *Mississippi Folklore Register,* 11 (Fall):142–50.

Brown, Loren N. 1938 "The Choctaw-Chickasaw Court Citizens." *Chronicles of Oklahoma,* 16 (Dec.):425–43.

———1944 "The Appraisal of the Lands of the Choctaws and Chickasaws by the Dawes Commission." *Chronicles of Oklahoma,* 22 (Summer):177–91.

Brown, Maurice 1970 "A Sociolinguistic Study of Choctaw." *Southern Quarterly,* 9 (Oct.):41–49.

Bryce, J. Y. 1928 "About Some of Our First Schools in Choctaw Nation." *Chronicles of Oklahoma,* 6 (Sept.):354–94.

Buckner, H. F. 1879 "Burial Among the Choctaws." *American Antiquarian and Oriental Journal,* 2:55–58.

Bushnell, David I. 1909 "The Choctaw of Bayou Lacomb, St. Tammany Parish, Louisiana." *Bulletin of Bureau of American Ethnology,* 48:1–37.

———1910 "Myths of the Louisiana Choctaw." *American Anthropologist,* 12:526–35.

———1917 "The Choctaw of St. Tammany." *Louisiana Historical Quarterly,* 1:11–20.

Byington, C. 1915 "A Dictionary of the Choctaw Language." *Bulletin of Bureau of American Ethnology,* 46:1–611.

Cabaniss, A. 1975 "Ackia: Battle in the Wilderness, 1736." *History Today,* 25 (Dec.): 810–17.

Campbell, T. N. 1951 "Medicinal Plants Used by the Choctaw, Chickasaw, and Creek Indians." *Journal of the Washington Academy of Science,* 41:285–90.

———1959$_a$ "Choctaw Subsistence." *Florida Anthropologist,* 12:9–24.

———1959$_b$ "The Choctaw Afterworld." *Journal of American Folklore,* 72:146–54.

Collins, Henry Bascon, Jr. 1925 "Anthropometric Observations of the Choctaw." *Journal of Physical Anthropology,* 8 (Oct.-Dec.), 425–36.

———1927 "Archeology Potsherds from Choctaw Village Sites in Mississippi." *Journal of the Washington Academy of Science,* 17 (May), 260–63.

———1928 "Additional Anthropometric Observations on the Choctaw." *Journal of Physical Anthropology,* 11:353–55.

Coker, William Sidney 1965 "Pat Harrison's Efforts to Reopen the Choctaw Citizenship Rolls." *Southern Quarterly,* 3 (Oct.): 36–61.

Conlan, Czarina C. 1926 "David Folsom." *Chronicles of Oklahoma,* 4 (Dec.): 340–55.

———1928 "Necrology, Peter P. Pitchlynn." *Chronicles of Oklahoma,* 6 (June):215–24.

———1929 "Site of Dancing Rabbit Creek Treaty Preserved." *Chronicles of Oklahoma,* 7 (Sept.): 323–38.

Culbertson, James 1927 "The Fort Towson Road." *Chronicles of Oklahoma,* 5 (Dec.):414–21.

Davis, Edward 1932 "The Mississippi Choctaws." *Chronicles of Oklahoma,* 10 (June):257–67.

Debo, Angie 1932 "Education in the Choctaw Country After the Civil War." *Chronicles of Oklahoma,* 10 (Sept.):385–91.

DeRosier, A. H., Jr. 1958 "John C. Calhoun and the Removal of the Choctaw

Indians." *South Carolina Historical Association Proceedings*, 33–45.
———1959 "Pioneers with Conflicting Ideals: Christianity and Slavery in the Choctaw Nation." *Journal of Mississippi History*, 21 (July):174–89.
———1960 "Negotiations for the Removal of the Choctaw: U.S. Policies of 1820 and 1830." *Chronicles of Oklahoma*, 38 (Spring):85–100.
———1962 "Thomas Jefferson and the Removal of the Choctaw Indians." *Southern Quarterly*, 1 (Oct.): 52–62.
———1967$_a$ "Andrew Jackson and Negotiations for the Removal of the Choctaw Indians." *Historian*, 29 (May):343–62.
———1967$_b$ "Choctaw Removal of 1831: A Civilian Effort." *Journal of the West*, 6 (April):237–47.
Dillard, Anthony Winston 1899 "The Treaty of Dancing Rabbit Creek Between the United States and the Choctaw Indians in 1830." *Alabama Historical Society Transactions, 1898–1899*, 3:99–106.
Doran, Michael R. 1975–76 "Population Statistics of Nineteenth Century Indian Territory.", *Chronicles of Oklahoma*, 53 (Winter):492–515.
———1976 "Antebellum Cattle Herding in the Indian Territory" *Geographical Review*, 66 (Jan.):48–58.
Edwards, John 1932 "The Choctaw Indians in the Middle of the Nineteenth Century." *Chronicles of Oklahoma*, 10 (Sept.):392–425.
Edwards, T. A. 1949 "Early Developments in the C and A." *Chronicles of Oklahoma*, 27 (Summer):148–61.
Eggan, Fred 1937 "Historical Changes in the Choctaw Kinship System." *American Anthropologist*, 39:34–52.
Ford, J. A. 1936 "Analysis of Indian Village Site Collections from Louisiana and Mississippi." *Louisiana Department of Conservation Anthropological Studies*, 2:1–285.
Foreman, Carolyn Thomas 1928 "The Choctaw Academy." *Chronicles of Oklahoma*, 6 (Dec.):452–80.
——— 1932 "The Choctaw Academy." *Chronicles of Oklahoma*, 10 (March):76–114.
Foreman, Grant 1928 "Early Past Offices of Oklahoma." *Chronicles of Oklahoma*, 6 (March):1–25.
Fortune, Porter L., Jr. 1973 "The Formation Period." In Richard Aubrey McLemore, ed. *A History of Mississippi*. Hattiesburg: University and College Press of Mississippi.
Gaines, George Strother 1928 "Dancing Rabbit Creek Treaty." *Historical and Patriotic Series of Alabama State Department of Archives and History*, 10:1–31.
Gibson, A. M. 1965 "The Choctaws." *Sooner Magazine*, (July):1–6.
——— 1973 "The Indians of Mississippi." In Richard Aubrey McLemore, ed. *A History of Mississippi*. Hattiesburg: University and College Press of Mississippi.
Graebner, N. A. 1945$_a$ "Pioneer Indian Agriculture in Oklahoma." *Chronicles of Oklahoma*, 23 (Autumn):232–48.
———1945$_b$ "The Public Land Policy of the Five Civilized Tribes." *Chronicles of Oklahoma*, 23 (Summer):107–18.
———1945–46 "Provincial Indian Society in Eastern Oklahoma." *Chronicles of Oklahoma*, 23 (Autumn):323–37.
Haag, W. G. 1953 "Choctaw Archeology." *Newsletter of the Southeastern Archeological Conference*, 3:25–28.
Halbert, Henry S. 1882 "Courtship and Marriage Among the Choctaws." *Ameri-

can Naturalist, 16:222–24.

———1893 "Oklahoma Hannali; or, the Six Towns District of the Choctaws." *American Antiquarian and Oriental Journal*, 15:146–49.

———1894 "A Choctaw Migration Legend." *American Antiquarian and Oriental Journal*, 16:215–16.

———1895 "The Choctaw Robin Goodfellow." *American Antiquarian and Oriental Journal*, 17:157.

———1899 "Nanih Waiya, the Sacred Mound of the Choctaws." *Publications of the Mississippi Historical Society*, 2:223–34.

———1900 "Funeral Customs of the Mississippi Choctaws." *Publications of the Mississippi Historical Society*, 3:353–66.

———1900$_a$ "District Divisions of the Choctaw Nation." *Publications of the Alabama Historical Society, Miscellaneous Collections*, 1:375–85.

———1901$_b$ "The Choctaw Creation Legend." *Publications of the Mississippi Historical Society*, 4:267–70.

———1902$_a$ "Story of the Treaty of Dancing Rabbit." *Publications of the Mississippi Historical Society*, 6:373–402.

———1902$_b$ "The Last Indian Council on Noxubee River." *Publications of the Mississippi Historical Society*, 4:271–80.

Hiemstra, William L. 1948–49 "Presbyterian Missions and Mission Churches Among the Choctaw and Chickasaw Indians, 1832–1865." *Chronicles of Oklahoma*, 26 (Winter):459–67.

Holmes, Jack D. L. 1968 "The Choctaws in 1795: A Choctaw Census of 1795, District of Six Villages." *Alabama Historical Quarterly*, 30 (Spring):33–49.

———1973 "A Spanish Province, 1779–1798." In Richard Aubrey McLemore, ed. *A History of Mississippi*. Hattiesburg: University and College Press of Mississippi.

Hudson, Peter James 1939 "A Story of Choctaw Chiefs." *Chronicles of Oklahoma*, 17 (March):7–16.

Jordan, H. Glenn 1976 "Choctaw Colonization in Oklahoma." *Chronicles of Oklahoma*, 54 (Spring):16–33.

Kelley, Arthell 1973 "The Geography." In Richard Aubrey McLemore, ed. *A History of Mississippi*. Hattiesburg: University and College Press of Mississippi.

Knight, Oliver 1953 "Fifty Years of Choctaw Law." *Chronicles of Oklahoma*, 31 (Spring):76–95.

Langlen, Mrs. Lee J. 1927 "Malmaison, a Place in a Wilderness: Home of General LeFlore." *Chronicles of Oklahoma*, 5 (Dec.):371–81.

Lanman, Charles 1870 "Peter Pitchlynn, Chief of the Choctaws." *Atlantic Monthly*, 25 (April):486–99.

Lincecum, Gideon 1904 "Choctaw Traditions About Their Settlement in Mississippi and the Origin of Their Mound." *Publications of the Mississippi Historical Society*, 8:521–42.

———1905–06 "Life of Apushimataha." *Publications of the Mississippi Historical Society*, 9:415–85.

Love, William A. 1911 "The Mayhew Mission to the Choctaws." *Publications of the Mississippi Historical Society*, 11:363–402.

Lucas, Aubrey K. 1973 "Education in Mississippi from Statehood to the Civil War." In Richard Aubrey McLemore, ed. *A History of Mississippi*. Hattiesburg: University and College Press of Mississippi.

Meserve, John Bartlett 1936 "The Indian Removal Message of President Jackson." *Chronicles of Oklahoma*, 14 (March):63–67.
McCullar, Marion Ray 1973 "Choctaw-Chickasaw Reconstruction Treaty of 1866." *Journal of the West*, 12 (July):462–70.
McKee, Jesse O. 1971 "The Choctaw Indians: A Geographical Study in Cultural Change." *Southern Quarterly*, 9 (Jan.):107–41.
McLoughlin, W. G. 1974 "Choctaw Slave Burning: A Crisis in Mission Work Among the Indians." *Journal of the West*, 13 (Jan.):113–27.
Miner, Craig 1969 "The Struggle for an East-West Railway into Indian Territory, 1870–1882." *Chronicles of Oklahoma*, 47 (Spring):560–81.
Morrison, James D. 1949 "News for the Choctaws." *Chronicles of Oklahoma*, 27 (Summer):207–22.
——— 1954 "Problems in the Industrial Progress and Development of the Choctaw Nation." *Chronicles of Oklahoma*, 32 (Spring):70–91.
Morrison, William B. 1925 "Diary of Rev. Cyrus Kingsbury." *Chronicles of Oklahoma*, 3 (June):152–57.
——— 1938 "The Saga of Skullyville." *Chronicles of Oklahoma*, 16 (June): 234–40.
Muldrow, O. F. 1927 "Choctaw." *Chronicles of Oklahoma* 5 (Dec.):406.
Murdock, George Peter 1957 "World Ethnographic Sample." *American Anthropologist*, 59:664–87.
Ogden, Florence [Sillers] 1946 "A Famous Indian Lawsuit" *Journal of Mississippi History*, 8 (July):121–28.
Parke, Frank E., and J. W. Le Flore 1926 "Some of Our Choctaw Neighborhood Schools." *Chronicles of Oklahoma*, 4 (June):149–52.
Penman, John T. 1978 "Historic Choctaw Towns of the Southern Division." *Journal of Mississippi History*, 40 (May):133–41.
Peterson, John H., Jr. 1972 "Assimilation, Separation, and Out-Migration in an American Indian Group." *American Anthropologist*, 74 (Oct.):1286–95.
——— 1974 "Commentary." *Human Organization*, 33 (Fall):311–18.
——— 1975 "Mississippi Choctaw Identity: Genesis and Change." In John W. Bennett, ed. *New Ethnicity*. Minneapolis: West Publishing Company.
——— 1976 "The Choctaws in Mississippi." In William C. Sturtevant, ed. *The Southeast*. Vol. XII of *Handbook of North American Indian*. Washington, D.C.: Smithsonian Institution.
Phelps, Dawson A. 1952 "The Choctaw Mission: An Experiment in Civilization." *Journal of Mississippi History*, 14 (Jan.): 35–62.
Plaisance, Aloysius 1954 "The Choctaw Trading House, 1803–1822." *Alabama Historical Quarterly*, 16 (Fall and Winter): 393–423.
Riley, Franklin L. 1904 "Choctaw Land Claims." *Publications of the Mississippi Historical Society*, 8:345–95.
Schlenker, Jon A. 1975 "An Historical Analysis of the Family of Choctaw Indians." *Southern Quarterly*, 13 (July): 323–34.
Spalding, Armita Scott 1967 "From the Natchez Trace to Oklahoma: Development of Christian Civilization Among the Choctaws, 1800–1860." *Chronicles of Oklahoma*, 44 (Spring):2–24.
Spence, Lewis 1955 "Choctaws." *Encyclopedia of Religion and Ethics*, 3:567–69.
Spencer, Barbara G., Gerald O. Windham, and John H. Peterson, Jr. 1975 "Occupational Orientations of an American Indian Group." In J. S. Picou and R. E. Campbell (eds.), *Career Behavior of Special Groups*. Columbus, Ohio:

Charles E. Merrill Publishing Company.

Spoehr, Alexander 1947 "Changing Kinship Systems." *Field Museum of Natural History*, 33:153–235.

Swanton, John R. 1918 "An Early Account of the Choctaw Indians." *Memoirs of the Anthropological Association*, 5 (No. 2):51–72.

Synderfaard, Rex 1974 "The Final Move of the Choctaws." *Chronicles of Oklahoma*, 52 (Summer):207–19.

Todd, T. L. 1975 "Clause Versus Sentence in Choctaw." *Linguistics*, 161 (Oct.):39–67.

Tubby, Austin, and Annie Williams 1973 "Chata Siya Hoka: I Am a Choctaw." *Nanih Waiya*, 1 (Fall):10–11.

Wade, John Williams 1904 "The Removal of the Mississippi Choctaws." *Publications of the Mississippi Historical Society*, 8:397–426.

Watkins, John A. 1894$_a$ "A Contribution to Choctaw History." *American Antiquarian and Oriental Journal*, 16:257–65.

——1894$_b$ "The Choctaws in Mississippi." *American Antiquarian and Oriental Journal*, 16:69–77.

West, R. T. 1959 "Pushmataha's Travels." *Chronicles of Oklahoma*, 37 (Summer):162–74.

Wilson, T. Paul 1975 "Delegates of the Five Civilized Tribes to the Confederate Congress." *Chronicles of Oklahoma*, 53 (Fall):353–66.

Winsor, H. M. 1973 "Chickasaw-Choctaw Removal Relations with the United States, 1830–1880." *Journal of the West*, 12 (July):356–71.

Wright, A. 1828 "Choctaws." *Missionary Herald*, 25:178–83.

Wright, J. B. 1959 "Ranching in the Choctaw and Chickasaw Nations." *Chronicles of Oklahoma*. 37 (Fall):294–300.

Wright, Muriel H. 1927 "Old Boggy Depot." *Chronicles of Oklahoma*, 5 (March):5–17.

——1928 "The Removal of the Choctaws to the Indian Territory, 1830–1833." *Chronicles of Oklahoma*, 6 (June):103–28.

——1929 "Brief Outline of the Choctaw and the Chickasaw Nations in the Indian Territory." *Chronicles of Oklahoma*, 7 (Dec.):388–413.

——1930 "Early Navigation and Commerce Along the Arkansas and Red Rivers in Oklahoma." *Chronicles of Oklahoma*, 8 (March):66–88.

——1931 "Historic Spots in the Vicinity of Tuskahoma." *Chronicles of Oklahoma*, 9 (March):27–42.

——1958 "American Indian Corn Dishes." *Chronicles of Oklahoma*, 36 (Summer):155–66.

——1962 "Seals of the Five Civilized Tribes." *Chronicles of Oklahoma*, 40 (Autumn):214–18.

Wright, Muriel H., and George H. Shirk 1953 "Artist Mollhausen in Oklahoma, 1853." *Chronicles of Oklahoma*, 31 (Winter):392–441.

Young, F. B. 1830 "Notices of the Choctaw and Choktah Tribe." *Edinburgh Journal of Natural and Geographical Science*, 2:13–17.

Theses and Dissertations

Baird, W. David 1965 "Spencer Academy: The Choctaw 'Harvard,' 1842–1900." Master's thesis, University of Oklahoma.
Baum, Laura Edna 1940 "Agriculture Among the Five Civilized Tribes, 1865–1906." Master's thesis, University of Oklahoma.
Beckett, Charlie Mitchell 1949 "Choctaw Indians Since 1830." Master's thesis, Oklahoma A. & M.
Brown, Loren Nunn 1937 "The Work of the Dawes Commission Among the Choctaw and Chickasaw Indians." Ph.D. dissertation, University of Oklahoma.
Cantwell, Emmett Howell 1965 "A History of the Choctaw Trading House, 1802–1822." Master's thesis, Louisiana State University.
Coe, Pamelia 1960 "Lost in the Hills of Home: Outline of Mississippi Choctaw Social Organization." Master's thesis, Columbia University.
Denison, Natalie Morrison 1938 "Presbyterian Missions and Missionaries Among the Choctaw to 1907." Master's thesis, University of Oklahoma.
DeRosier, Arthur H., Jr. 1959 "The Removal of the Choctaw Indians from Mississippi." Ph.D. dissertation, University of South Carolina.
Deweese, Orval H. 1957 "The Mississippi Choctaws." Master's thesis, Mississippi State College.
Drain, Myrtle 1928 "A History of the Education of the Choctaw and Chickasaw Indians." Master's thesis, University of Oklahoma.
Farr, Eugene Ijams 1948 "Religious Assimilation, a Case Study: The Adoption of Christianity by the Choctaw Indians of Mississippi." Th.D. dissertation, New Orleans Baptist Theological Seminary.
Jacobson, Daniel 1954 "Koasati Culture Changes." Ph.D. dissertation, Louisiana State University.
Kenaston, Monte Ray 1972 "Sharecropping, Solidarity, and Social Cleavage: The Genesis of a Choctaw Sub-Community in Tennessee." Ph.D. dissertation, Southern Illinois University.
Langford, Etha M. 1953 "A Study of the Educational Development of the Choctaw Indians in Mississippi." Master's thesis, University of Southern Mississippi.
Lea, Emma Lan 1934 "The Choctaw and Chickasaw Indians: A Geographic Study." Master's thesis, George Peabody College for Teachers.
Merrill, Pierce Kelton 1940 "The Social and Economic Status of the Choctaw Indians." Master's thesis, University of Oklahoma.
Morrison, James Davidson 1951 "Social History of the Choctaw, 1865–1907." Ph.D. dissertation, University of Oklahoma.
Peterson, John H., Jr. 1970a "The Mississippi Band of Choctaw Indians: Their Recent History and Current Relations." Ph.D. dissertation, University of Georgia.

Ridley, Betty C. 1965 "Relationship Between Family Characteristics and Level of Living of Three Ethnic Groups, with Special Emphasis on the Choctaw Indians." Master's thesis, University of Georgia.

Schlenker, Jon A. 1974 "An Historical Analysis of the Social and Cultural Life of the Choctaw Indians with Emphasis upon the Family Life." Master's thesis, University of Southern Mississippi.

Spalding, Armita S. 1974 "Cyrus Kingsbury, Missionary to the Choctaws." Master's thesis, University of Oklahoma.

Spencer, Barbara G. 1973 "Occupational Orientations of Choctaw Indian High School Students in Mississippi." Master's thesis, Mississippi State University.

Tolbert, Charles M. 1958 "A Sociological Study of the Choctaws in Mississippi." Ph.D. dissertation, Louisiana State University.

Toler, Vera Alice 1936 "Greenwood LeFlore, Choctaw Chieftain and Mississippi Planter." Master's thesis, Louisiana State University.

Underwood, William Henry 1931 "A History of Atoka County." Master's thesis, University of Oklahoma.

Miscellaneous

Choctaw Agency n.d. *The Mississippi Band of Choctaw Indians*. Philadelphia, Miss.: Bureau of Indian Affairs.

Choctaw Nation of Oklahoma 1977 *Directory of Services in the Choctaw Nation*. Durant, Okla.: Office of the Choctaw Nation.

Design Collective 1975$_a$ *Landscape Manual: Mississippi Band of Choctaw Indians*. Jackson, Miss.: Design Collective.

———1975$_b$ *Master Development Plans: Mississippi Band of Choctaw Indians*. Jackson, Miss.: Design Collective.

———1975$_c$ *Zoning: Mississippi Band of Choctaw Indians*. Jackson, Miss.: Design Collective.

Economic Development and Planning Office 1977 *Mississippi Band of Choctaw Indians Overall Economic Development Program, 1978–1982*. Philadelphia, Miss.: Economic Development and Planning Office.

Eric Hill Associates, Inc. 1975 *Environmental Impact Statement: Edinburg Dam and Lake Pearl River, Mississippi*. 2 vol. and abstract.

Gunning, I. C. n.d.$_a$ *A Royal Family of Choctaws or the Choctaw Story*. Wilburton, Okla.: Eastern Oklahoma Historical Society.

———n.d.$_b$ *Prehistoric People of Oklahoma and Their Culture*. Wilburton, Okla.: Eastern Oklahoma Historical Society.

———n.d.$_c$ *The Butterfield Overland Mail Through Eastern Oklahoma*. Wilburton, Okla.: Eastern Oklahoma Historical Society.

———n.d.$_d$ *The Edwards Store or Old Red Oak*. Wilburton, Okla.: Eastern Oklahoma Historical Society.

———1975 *When Coal Was King: Coal Mining Industry in the Choctaw Nation*. Wilburton, Okla.: Eastern Oklahoma Historical Society.

Harris, Nick 1970$_a$ *Initial Housing Element, Choctaw Indian Reservation Areas*. Jackson: Mississippi Research and Development Center.

———1970$_b$ *Pearl River Community Comprehensive Development Plan*. Jackson: Mississippi Research and Development Center.

———1970$_c$ *Planning Goals and Objectives for Choctaw Indian Reservation Areas*. Jackson: Mississippi Research and Development Center.

Hill, Bill H., and Paul L. Parker 1975 *Preliminary Health Plan for the Choctaw Nation*. Wilburton, Okla.: Kiamichi Economic Development District.

Kiamichi Economic Development District 1974 *Overall Economic Development Program for the Choctaw Nation*. Wilburton, Okla.: Kiamichi Economic Development District.

McKee, Jesse O., and Robert E. Norris 1976$_a$ "A Geographical Analysis of Demographic and Economic Characteristics of the Choctaw Indian in Oklahoma and Mississippi." *Geographical Perspectives on Native American Topics and Resources*, 1:89–102.

Mississippi Band of Choctaw Indians 1966 "Overall Economic Development Program: Mississippi Band of Choctaw Indians." Mimeograph.

———1972, 1973, 1974 *Accelerated Progress Through Self Determination*. 1st, 2nd, and 3rd annual reports Pearl River: Mississippi Band of Choctaw Indians.

———1973 *An Evaluation of the Current Status of the Choctaw Nursing Home*. Philadelphia, Miss.: Mississippi Band of Choctaw Indians.

———1975 "Revised Constitution and Bylaws." Mimeograph.

———1976 *Community Services Directory*. Pearl River: Mississippi Band of Choctaw Indians.

Noblin Research 1968 *Economic Feasibility Study for Proposed Recreational-Tourism Development for Mississippi Choctaw Indians*. Jackson, Miss.: Noblin Research.

Norris, Robert E., Paul Hagle, and Keith Harries 1975 *Choctaw Census, 1975*. Stillwater: Geography Extension, Oklahoma State University.

Norris, Robert E. 1977 *Choctaw Census, 1975*. Vol. II. Stillwater: Geography Extension, Oklahoma State University.

Parker, Paul L., and Kenneth G. Thompson 1975$_a$ *Preliminary Health Plan for the Choctaw Nation*. Wilburton, Okla.: Kiamichi Economic Development District.

———1975$_b$ *Preliminary Housing Plan for the Choctaw Nation*. Wilburton, Okla.: Kiamichi Economic Development District.

Parker, Paul L. 1974 *Programming and Management Strategy and Communications System for the Development of the Choctaw Nation Comprehensive Plan*. Wilburton, Okla.: Kiamichi Economic Development District.

Pearmain, John 1935 *Indian Office Handbook of Information, Mississippi Choctaws*. Philadelphia, Miss.: Choctaw Agency.

Peithman, Irvin M. 1961 *The Choctaw Indians of Mississippi*. Carbondale: Southern Illinois University.

Peterson, John H., Jr. 1970$_b$ *Socio-economic Characteristics of the Mississippi Choctaw Indians*. Report 34. Starkville: Mississippi State University Social Science Research Center.

Peterson, John H., Jr., and James R. Richburg 1971 *The Mississippi Choctaws and Their Educational Program*. Ser. I, Community Studies, Study 21. Ed. Robert Havighurst. Educational Resources Information Center, U.S. Department of Health, Education, and Welfare.

Raisz, Erwin 1957 *Landforms of the United States*. Cambridge, Mass: Erwin Raisz.

Research and Development Center 1968 *Tourist Development Potentials of the Missis-*

sippi Choctaw Indian Reservation. Jackson: Mississippi Research and Development Center.

Roark, Michael O. 1976 *Nineteenth Century Population Distributions of the Five Civilized Tribes in Indian Territory, Oklahoma*. Syracuse University Discussion Paper, No. 15. Syracuse, N.Y.: Syracuse University.

Rouquette, Dominique n.d. "The Choctaws". Manuscript. Louisiana State University Library, New Orleans.

Spencer, Barbara G., John H. Peterson, Jr., and Choong S. Kim 1975 *Choctaw Manpower and Demographic Survey, 1974*. Philadelphia, Miss.: Mississippi Band of Choctaw Indians.

Smith, Wilbur, & Associates 1974$_a$ *Comprehensive Plan, Mississippi Band of Choctaw Indians*. Columbia, S. C.: Wilbur Smith & Associates.

────── 1974$_b$ *Indian Village Feasibility, Mississippi Band of Choctaw Indians*. Columbia, S. C.: Wilbur Smith & Associates.

U.S. Bureau of the Census 1970 *Census of Population, Subject Reports, American Indians*.

U.S. Department of the Interior 1973 *The Choctaw Nation: Its Resources and Development Potential*. Report No. 213. Billings, Mont.: Department of the Interior, Bureau of Indian Affairs.

────── 1974 *Report of Program Activities, Fiscal Year 1974*. Muskogee, Okla.: Department of the Interior, Bureau of Indian Affairs.

Willcoxon, E. H., Jr. 1973 *Choctaw Recreation Development, Edinburg Reservoir*. Starkville: Mississippi State University.

Unpublished Papers

Bailey, Wilfrid C. 1963 "Factors Associated with Changes in Land Operations of the Mississippi Band of Choctaw Indians." Social Science Research Institute, University of Georgia. Mimeograph.

Ferguson, Bob 1962 "A Choctaw Chronology." Tennessee Archaeological Society. Mimeograph.

Harris, Keith D., Robert E. Norris, and Paul Hagle 1976 "Spatial Variations in Selected Socioeconomic Characteristics of the Choctaw Indian Nation in Oklahoma." Paper presented to Southwestern and Rocky Mountain Division, American Association for the Advancement of Science, Tucson, Ariz.

Isaac, Calvin J. 1976 "Second State of the Tribe." Mississippi Band of Choctaw Indians. Mimeograph.

McKee, Jesse O., and Robert E. Norris 1976$_b$ "A Historical Demographic and Economic Analysis of the Choctaw Indian in Mississippi and Oklahoma." Paper presented to the Southern Regional Demographic Group, New Orleans. Mimeograph.

McKee, Jesse O. 1976 "The Past 200 Years: The Choctaw Indians and the United States Government." Paper presented to the Southeastern Division, Association of American Geographers, Fredericksburg, Va.

Norris, Robert E., and Robert W. McClure 1975 "The Geography of the 1975 Vote for Principal Chief of the Choctaw Nation of Oklahoma." Paper presented to the Oklahoma Academy of Sciences, Tulsa. Mimeograph.

Peterson, John H., Jr. 1975$_a$ "Reservation, Reservoir, and Self Determination: A Case Study of Reservoir Planning as It Affects an Indian Reservation." Mississippi State University. Mimeograph.

———1975$_b$ "The Third Time Around: An Interpretation of Choctaw History." Mississippi State University. Mimeograph.

———1971 "What Bushnell Ignored: Louisiana Choctaw Life at the End of the Nineteenth Century." Paper presented to American Society for Ethnohistory, Athens, Ga.

Salkin, Marcia Huddleton, Robert E. Norris and Paul Hagle 1974 "A Regional Health Status Indicator for the Choctaw Nation." Paper presented to Oklahoma Academy of Sciences, Tulsa. Mimeograph.

Newspapers

Bishinik. Published by the Choctaw Nation of Oklahoma, Durant; Okla.
Choctaw Community News. Published by the Mississippi Band of Choctaw Indians, Philadelphia, Miss.

Manuscript Collections

Baton Rouge, La. Louisiana Room, Louisiana State University Library
Hattiesburg, Miss. Mississippi Room, University of Southern Mississippi Library
Jackson, Miss. Mississippi Department of Archives and History
Norman, Okla. University of Oklahoma Library
   Western History Collection
   Phillips Collection
Oklahoma City, Okla. Oklahoma Historical Society, Indian Archives
   Grant Foreman Collection
   Indian-Pioneer Papers
Tulsa, Okla. Gilcrease Institute of American History and Art
Washington, D.C.
   Library of Congress
   National Archives
      Records of the Department of Interior
      Records of the Office of Indian Affairs
      Records of the House of Representatives
      Records of the U.S. Senate

Index

Agriculture; *see* Economic development
Albion Convention: 151
Allotted land: 152
Allotment Act: 93; *see also* Dawes Act
Ancestors: *see* Creation legends, Migration legends
Antlers, Okla.: 155, 183
Apukshunnubbee: 53
Apukshunnubbee, District of: 99, 107
Ardmore, Okla.: 177
Arkansas Post, Ark.: 77
Arkansas River: 77, 81, 99, 114
Armstrong Academy: 90, 111, 126, 179
Armstrong, Francis W.: 78
Armstrong, William: 77, 78
Atoka, Okla.: 122, 124, 130
Atoka Agreement: 95, 112

Ball play: 23–25; *see also* Recreational activities
Baptist Association, New Choctaw: 175
Baptist: 130, 174, 175; *see also* Religious organization
Barnett, E. G.: 162
Bekker, Father: 132
Belvin, Harry J. W.: 153, 154, 163, 183
Bethabara, Okla.: 126
Bethel, Miss.: 56
Bienville, Jean Baptise LeMoyne de: 32, 34
Black Jack, Miss.: 132
Body, characteristics of: 26; *see also* Individual characteristics
Boggy Depot, Okla.: 84, 90, 111, 122, 181
Bogue Chitto, Miss.: 158, 177
Bogue Homa, Miss.: 158, 177
Bone-pickers: 22, 74; *see also* Religious organization and Funeral ceremony
Branch of Employment Assistance: 166
Broken Bow, Okla.: 183
Brown, Charles E.: 155
Bullen, Joseph: 54, 69

Bureau of Indian Affairs: 152, 153, 163, 165, 177
Burial practices: 22, 45; *see also* Religious organization
Byington, Cyrus: 56, 72, 126

Cabins: 19; *see also* Housing
Calhoun, John C.: 57, 71
Cameron Institute: 179
Carter Seminary: 178
Cass, Lewis: 77
Catholic church: 130; *see also* Religious organization
Census, population: (1831), 77; (1860), 90; (1867), 90; (1885), 91, 93; (1906), 95, 96; (1910), 98; *see also* Population
Chata Development Company: 166, 167
Chahta Tamaha: 90, 111
Chahtah: 6
Cherokee: 192
Chickasaws: migration legends, 6–9; creation legends, 10–12; wars with French, 32, 33, 34; District in 1837, 84; Treaty of 1855, 87; 107, 109
Chikasah: 6
Choctaws: in western Tennessee, 189
Choctaw Academy: 72, 126
Choctaw Agency: 100, 158
Choctaw Business Committee: 149, 158
Choctaw Coal and Mining Co.: 122
Choctaw Fair, Miss.: 181
Choctaw Housing Authority: 182
Choctaw Indian Agency: establishment of in Philadelphia, Miss., 148
Choctaw Indians: economic development, 17–21, 40, 43–44, 68–69, 114–15, 120–22, 124–25, 165–67, 170–72, 174; educational activities, 71–73, 126–27, 176–78, 178–79; family cycle, 28–31, 47–49, 73–74, 142–45, 190–92; history of, 5, 6–8, 10–15, 32–38, 50–51, 53–64, 75–78,

223

Choctaw Indians (cont.)
  81, 84, 87, 90–91, 93, 95–98, 148–155; individual characteristics, 26–27, 46, 139–42, 189; political organization, 16–17, 40, 66–68, 107–12, 114, 157–58, 162–63, 165; recreational activities, 22–26, 45–46, 72–73, 139, 181; religious organization, 21–23, 44–45, 69–70, 126, 127, 130–31, 132, 138–39, 174–76; removal of, 77–78, 81, 84; social organizations, 16, 38–40, 65–66, 100, 106, 157
Choctaw Nation: disposal of, 163
Choctaw Nation Enterprises, Inc.: 165
Choctaw Nation Historical Society: 165
Choctaw Nation Housing Authority: 165
Citizenship U.S.: pertaining to Choctaws, 157
Civil Rights Act: 150, 154, 165
Clans: 16, 40, 65, 66; *see also* Social organization
Clark, J. B.: 77
Climate: 5
Coalgate, Okla.: 124
Coffee, John: 61, 63
Colbert Institute: 179
Cole, Robert: 58
Collier, John: 151
Conehatta, Miss.: 132, 158, 177
Confederacy: 90, 111
Courtship: 29, 30; *see also* Family cycle
Creation legends: 6, 10–12
Crops: *see* Economic development
Cross, L. T.: 78
Curtis Act: 95, 112

Dairying: *see* Economic development
Dances: 26; *see also* Recreational activities
Dancing Rabbit Creek: 61, 62, 63, 64, 75, 76, 84, 96, 107, 112, 158
Dawes Act: 93, 112; *see also* Allotment Act
Dawes Commission: 93, 97, 98, 112, 114
DeSoto, Hernando: 12
Divorce: *see* Family cycle
Doaks Stand, Treaty of: 57, 58, 84
Doaksville, Okla.: 84, 90, 100, 110, 111, 121, 122
Dress: 27, 140–141; *see also* Individual characteristics
Dupuy Stark: 69
Durant, Okla.: 154, 179

Eagletown, Okla.: 84, 100
Eastern Oklahoma State University: 179

Eaton, John H.: 61, 63, 76–77
Economic Opportunity Act: 153–154
Economic development: in indigenous period, 17–21; in European-American period, 40, 43–44; in land cessions and acquisitions period, 68–69; in Indian Territory (1831–1906), 114–15, 120–122; in Mississippi from (1831–1917), 124–25; in Mississippi (1918–1979), 165–67; in Oklahoma (1907–1979) 170–72, 174
Ecore a' Fabre, Ark.: 78
Educational activities: in land cessions and acquisitions period, 71–73; in Indian Territory (1831-1906), 126–27; in Mississippi (1918–1979), 176–78; in Oklahoma (1907–1979), 178–79
Eliot Mission: 71
Employment: *see* Economic development
English: contact with Choctaws, 14, 15; intrusion into Choctaw country, 35, 36
Eufaula Dormitory: 178
Eufaula, Lake: 172
Eufaula, Okla.: 183

Family cycle: in indigenous period, 28–31; in European-American period, 47–49; in land cessions and acquisitions period, 73–74; between (1831–1917), 142–45; between (1918-1979), 190–92
Ficklin, John A.: 69
Folsom, David: 61, 67, 71
Folsom, Peter: 97
Food: 19–20, 142
Forestry: *see* Economic development
Fort Adams, Treaty of: 50, 51
Fort Coffee: 100; school for boys, 126
Fort Confederation: 37
Fort Confederation, Treaty of: 51
Fort Nogales: 37
Fort Rosalie: 33
Fort Smith: 81
Fort Towson: 78, 81, 90, 97, 100, 122
Fishing: early techniques, 18
Freedmen: 91
French: contact with Choctaws, 15; wars of, 32–35
Funeral ceremony, 131–32; *see also* Bonepickers; Religious organization

Gaines, George S.: 61, 77, 78
Games played: 46, 139; *see also* Ball-play, Stickball, Recreational activities
Gardner, David C.: 154–155

Index

Gardner, Robert L.: 155
Gibson, George: 77
Gibson, Roby: 162
Goodland: school, 126, 179; convention, 152
Goodwater, Okla.: 126
Government: *see* Political organization
Grandpré, Treaty of: 35

Hair styles: 46; *see also* Individual characteristics
Harris, LaDonna: 153
Hartshorne, Okla.: 127, 178
Haskell County: 187
Health: in Mississippi, 181–82; in Oklahoma, 183
Hinds, Thomas: 57, 58
Hoe Buckintoopa, Treaty of: 51
Homa, Shulush: 34, 35
Hopewell, Treaty of: 37, 50
Horse Prairie, Okla.: 78
Hospitals: *see* Health
Hotchkin, Ebenezer: 126
Housing: 19, 141, 182–83
Hudson, Peter J.: 127
Hugo, Okla.: 179, 183
Hunting: 18; *see also* Economic development

Iberville, Pierre LeMoyne, d': 15
Idabel, Okla.: 155, 191
Indian Agency, Choctaw: at Philadelphia, Miss., 98
Indian Child Welfare Act: 150
Indian Education Act: 150
Indian Reorganization Act: 149, 151, 152; *see also* Wheeler Howard Act
Indian Self-Determination and Education Assistance Act: 150, 154
Indian Territory: 76, 77, 78, 81, 84, 87, 96, 97
Individual characteristics: 26–27, 46, 139–42, 189
Issac, Calvin J.: 163

Jackson, Andrew: 54, 57, 58, 59, 60, 61
Johnstone, George: 36
John, Henry Smith: 163
John, Smith: 163
Johnson, Lyndon: 154
Jones Academy: 127, 178, 179
Jones County: 98, 158
Jones, R.M.: 120

Judicial Prevention and Enforcement, Division of: 162

Kemper County: 97, 132
Kiamichi River: 99, 114
Kincaid, Joseph: 107
Kingsbury, Cyrus: 56, 126
Kinship: in indigenous period, 27–28; in European-American period, 46–47; from (1831–1917), 142; in twentieth-century, 189–190; *see* 73, 100; *see also* Social organization
Krebs, Okla.: 124, 130

Lafourche Parish: 98
Language: 16, 72; *see also* Individual characteristics
Land: 17, for land use and ownership; *see also* Economic development
Lauderdale County: 97
Leake County: 97, 98, 158
Leased land: 110
LeFlore County: 172, 187
LeFlore, Greenwood: 61, 67, 71, 99
LeFlore, Thomas: 107
Legends: *see* Creation and Migration
Lehigh, Okla.: 90, 124, 130
Little Rock, Ark.: 77, 81, 84
Livestock: *see* Economic development
Louisiana: Choctaws in, 98
Lower Hartshorne, Okla.: 124

McAlester, Okla.: 90, 122, 123, 130, 183
McCoy, Issac: 126
McCurtain County: 172, 187, 192
McKee, John: 38
Manufacturing: *see* Economic development
Marriage customs: 30–31, 143–45; *see also* Family cycle
Martin, Phillip: 163
Mashulaville, Miss.: 138, 176
Mayhew, Miss.: 56, 71, 72
Medical: 141, *see also* Health
Memphis, Tenn.: 77, 81, 84, 189
Mennonite Church: 176
Methodist churches: in Mississippi, 176; *see also* Religious organization
Migration legends: 6–9
Minerals: *see* Economic development
Mingo: 16, 17
Mining: *see* Economic development
Missions: 56, 69–70, 126–27; *see also* Religious organization and Educational activities

Missionaries: 54–57, 69–70; *see also* Religious organization
Mississippi: admitted to union, 54
Mississippi Band of Choctaw Indians: formation of, 158
Mississippi River: 77, 81, 84
Missouri, Kansas and Texas Railroad: 90
Mitchell, Samuel: 38
Mobila (Mobile): 13, 14
Moieties: 16, 39, 40; *see also* Social organization
Moshulatubbee: 57, 58, 61
Moshulatubbee, District of: 99, 107, 127
Mountain Fork, Okla.: 78
Mount Dexter, Treaty of: 53, 54
Murrow, J. S.: 130

Nanih Waiya: description of mound, 6; meaning of in creation and migration legends, 6–12; early capital in Indian territory, 90, 107, 111; in Mississippi, 176
Natchez: 33
Negroes: 144, 150
Neshoba County: 97, 98, 132, 158, 162
Newell Station, Miss.: 56, 72
New Hope Seminary: 126, 179
Newton County: 97, 98, 132, 158
Nitakechi: 61, 99, 107
Noxubee County: 97, 138

Occupations: *see* Economic development
Office of Economic Opportunity: 150
Oklafalaya (Red River), District of: 99
Oklahoma: 98
Oklahomans for Indian Opportunity: 153, 154
Oklahoma Indian Welfare Act: 152
Oklahoma, University of: 179
Old Miller Courthouse, Okla.: 78, 100
Osage Coal and Mining Co.: 122
Ouachita River: 78

Pearl River: 158, 167, 176, 177, 183
Pentecostal Church: 176
Perryville, Okla.: 84, 111, 122
Personality: 27; *see also* Individual characteristics
Philadelphia, Miss.: 98, 148
Phillips Chapel: 132
Pine Ridge: 126
Pitchlynn, John: 53
Pitchlynn, Peter: 111
Poindexter, George: 57

Political organization: in indigenous period, 16–17; in European-American period, 40; during land cessions and acquisitions period, 66–68; in Choctaw Nation (1831–1906), 107–12; in Mississippi (1831–1917), 112, 114; in twentieth-century, 157–158, 162–63, 165
Population: during 1700s, 39; count prior to and at completion of removal, 76; in (1860), 90; in (1867), 90; in (1885), 91, 93; in (1906), 95–96; of Choctaws in Mississippi (1950), (1968), (1974), 183; of Choctaws in Oklahoma (1950), (1975), 187; *see also* Census
Presbyterians: 130; *see also* Religious organization
Presbyterian College: 154
Proclamation of 1763: *see* Treaty of Paris
Providence, Lake, La.: 78
Puckshenubbee: 58
Pushmataha: 54, 57, 58–59
Pushmataha, District of: 99, 107

Queen Anne's War: 32

Railroads: 90, 112, 122; *see also* Economic development
Ranching: *see* Economic development
Recreational activities: in indigenous period, 22–26; in European-American period, 45–46; in land cessions and acquisitions, 72–73; in Choctaw Nation (1831–1906), 139; twentieth century in Mississippi and Oklahoma, 181
Red River: 114, 115, 120
Red River (Oklafalaya), District of: 99
Red Water, Miss.: 158, 177
Religious organization: in indigenous period 21–23; in European-American period, 44–45; in land cessions and acquisitions period, 69–70; in Choctaw Nation (1831–1906), 126–27, 130–31; in Mississippi (1831–1917), 132, 138–39; twentieth century in Mississippi and Oklahoma, 174–76
Removal: Choctaw, 77–78, 81, 84
Reorganization Act: 158
Reservation: formation of in Mississippi, 149
Revolution, American: 36
Robot, Father: 130
Roberts, Hollis: 155

Index

Rockroe, Ark.: 81, 84
Roman Catholic: churches in Mississippi, 174; *see also* Religious organization and Educational activities

Sacanna, Okla.: 130
St. Louis and San Francisco Railroad: 112
St. Stephens, Treaty of: 54
Sawmills: *see* Economic development
Schools: *see* Educational activities, Missions, Religious organization
Scott County: 97, 98
Scrip: 87, 96
Skullyville: 84, 90, 110, 111, 122, 127
Skullyville, Constitution of: 110
Slaves: among Choctaws during 1700s, 39; 110, 120, 121
Social organization: in indigenous period, 16; in European-American period, 38–40; in land cessions and acquisitions period, 65–66; in Choctaw Nation (1831–1906); in Mississippi (1831–1917), 100, 106; in twentieth century, 157
Southeastern Oklahoma State University: 179
Spanish: contact with Choctaws, 12–14; early colonial activities, 36–38
Spencer Academy: 100, 126, 179
Spiro, Okla.: 122
Standing Pine, Miss.: 158, 176
Stephenson, J. R.: 76
Stickball: 139, 181; *see also* Ball play and Recreational activities
Stigler Act: 152
Stockbridge, Okla.: 126

Tahlequah, Okla.: 179
Talihina, Okla.: 155, 183
Talla Chula, Miss.: 132
Talley, Alexander: 70, 126
Tecumseh: 54
Termination Act: 153, 154
Terrebonne Parish: 98
Timber: *see* Economic development
Trade: early types in indigenous period, 21; *see also* Economic development
Treaty of Doaksville: 84, 107
Treaty of Paris: 35
Treaty of 1825: 59
Treaty of 1855: 87
Treaty of 1866: 90, 91, 111, 130
Tucker, Miss.: 132, 158, 176
Tuscaloosa: 13, 14
Tuskahoma, Okla.: 90, 107, 112, 127, 163, 179, 181

Valliant, Okla.: 172
Vicksburg, Miss.: 77, 78, 81

War of 1812: 54
Ward, William: 76, 96
Washington, Ark.: 77
Wesley, Cemeron: 138
Wheeler Howard Act: 149, 151, 152; *see also* Indian Reorganization Act
Wheelock Academy: 155
Wheelock Mission: 126, 181
Wheelock, Okla.: 100, 179
White River: 81, 84
Wilburton, Okla.: 179
Wilkinson, General: 51
Williams, L. C.: 56
Winston County: 6, 97, 98
Wright, Alfred: 126
Wright City, Okla.: 172
Wyandotte, Okla.: 179

www.ingramcontent.com/pod-product-compliance
Lightning Source LLC
Chambersburg PA
CBHW022057160426
43198CB00008B/257